Oracle JDeveloper 10g: Empowering J2EE Development

HARSHAD OAK

Oracle JDeveloper 10g: Empowering J2EE Development
Copyright ©2004 by Harshad Oak
Originally published by Apress 2004

ISBN 978-1-59059-142-0   ISBN 978-1-4302-0706-1 (eBook)
DOI 10.1007/978-1-4302-0706-1

Trademarked names may appear in this book. Rather than use a trademark symbol with every occurrence of a trademarked name, we use the names only in an editorial fashion and to the benefit of the trademark owner, with no intention of infringement of the trademark.

Technical Reviewer: Kenneth Cooper Jr.

Editorial Board: Steve Anglin, Dan Appleman, Gary Cornell, James Cox, Tony Davis, John Franklin, Chris Mills, Steven Rycroft, Dominic Shakeshaft, Julian Skinner, Martin Streicher, Jim Sumser, Karen Watterson, Gavin Wray, John Zukowski

Assistant Publisher: Grace Wong

Project Manager: Tracy Brown Collins

Copy Editor: Kim Wimpsett, Brian MacDonald

Production Manager: Kari Brooks

Production Editor: Janet Vail

Proofreaders: Elizabeth Barry and Patrick Vincent

Compositor: Kinetic Publishing Services, LLC

Indexer: Valerie Perry

Cover Designer: Kurt Krames

Manufacturing Manager: Tom Debolski

To my wonderful parents, Aai and Baba

Contents at a Glance

Contents

Foreword

JAVA HAS COME A LONG WAY since its birth in the mid-1990s and, as you will discover in this book, so have Java development tools.

With the growth of the Java language comes an ever-increasing complexity of the platform. You need the power of an Integrated Development Environment (IDE) when you are dealing with vast amounts of technologies, Application Programming Interfaces (APIs), code, and metadata.

Modern Java IDEs cover the entire development life cycle from design to deployment, including coding, debugging, tuning, testing, and controlling source. There is no longer a need to buy several different tools from several different vendors to get the job done. This will save you time and money because you don't have to set up and maintain different environments or deal with multiple vendors when you have an issue.

So, what's next for Java development tools? There are two major requirements that the tools need to address going forward. First, because you are dealing with so much code, the tools need to automate more of the programming work. This area of guided coding techniques includes features such as quick fix error detection and correction, refactoring, code formatting, and other coding assistance features.

Second, the overall complexity of developing in Java is still very high, making the language accessible mainly to expert programmers. This is where development frameworks come to the rescue by providing a more visual and declarative development environment, shielding you from the underlying complexities of the platform. This is similar to how Windows development became accessible to the masses after the introduction of frameworks such as Visual Basic, PowerBuilder, and Oracle Forms.

Oracle is marching forward on both fronts with JDeveloper 10*g*. The first installment of 10*g* introduces the Oracle Application Development Framework (ADF), and the second will address programmer productivity.

With this book, Harshad Oak has found the "sweet spot" for people planning to use Oracle JDeveloper. Whether you are evaluating JDeveloper or have recently decided to start developing with it, this book gives you everything you need to get up and running with the tool and explore the wide range of capabilities it offers.

Over the course of the book, you will become familiar with the JDeveloper IDE and learn about Java technologies such as Servlets, Java Server Pages, Enterprise JavaBeans, and Web Services. Harshad also introduces Oracle ADF. For more information about the framework and other features of the product, you can turn to the Oracle Technology Network at http://otn.oracle.com/products/jdev.

I am convinced you will enjoy reading this book, and I hope you will get a chance to try out JDeveloper.

Roel Stalman
Senior Director of Product Management, Application Development Tools
Oracle Corporation

About the Author

 **Harshad Oak** has a master's degree in computer management from Symbiosis, India, and is a Sun Certified Java Programmer and a Sun Certified Web Component Developer. He is the founder of Rightrix Solutions (http://www.rightrix.com), which is primarily involved in software development and content management services. Harshad has been part of several J2EE projects at i-flex Solutions and Cognizant Technology Solutions. Furthermore, he has written several articles about Java/J2EE for CNET Builder.com (http://www.builder.com). Harshad also coauthored the book *Java 2 Enterprise Edition 1.4 Bible* (Wiley & Sons, 2003) and is currently working on a book about Jakarta Commons for Apress.

Harshad is passionate about all kinds of writing and has published articles on a wide array of subjects ranging from terrorism to wildlife. He is an avid nature lover and enjoys reading nonfiction books. He hopes to retire as soon as possible to any sparsely populated place that provides just the basic necessities of life. A cutting-edge PC and a lightning fast Internet connection do, however, fall into the "basic necessities of life" category.

Feel free to send all comments and suggestions to harshad@rightrix.com.

About the Technical Reviewer

Kenneth Cooper Jr., is a senior principal instructor with a major IT company in Silicon Valley. He has worked in the Java arena for more than five years specializing in the J2EE areas of Java technology and has worked with all versions of JDeveloper since its inception, as AppBuilder 1.0, approximately five years ago.

Prior to working in industry he was in academia where he taught computer science for 25 years. His areas of specialization were language theory, database systems, and operating systems.

He currently lives in the Bluegrass region of central Kentucky. He would like to dedicate his efforts to his wife, Patricia, for her support.

Acknowledgments

THIS BOOK HAS BEEN a remarkable journey where so many people across continents have played a part. Thanks for all the effort, time, and interest you all have put into this book. My thanks go out to Tracy for managing the project as a whole, to Doris for the marketing and book promotion, and to Steve for ensuring that the book stayed on course. Ken did a great job of the tech review, and John and Craig were responsible for giving initial direction to the book. Kim and Brian had the tough task of ironing out the language and structure of each chapter.

Thanks to Laura and Stacey at Studio B for being an important part of all my book assignments and always keeping author interests the top priority. Thanks to Roel for helping me with the book's content and for writing a foreword for the book.

You all are very, very special to me. Thanks a lot.

My family and friends have of course played a huge part in this book becoming a reality. Thank you to Baba, Charu, Subodh, and Chinmay. Sangeeta had the not so enjoyable task of having to read rough drafts of chapters and suggest changes. Thanks a lot.

I also want to thank all the people through the ages who have worked toward spreading peace on the planet. These apostles of peace have ensured that human society does not crumble into anarchy. While the world keeps shrinking, we still seem to work so hard to hate and hurt fellow beings. We distinguish on religion, race, caste, creed, color, and whatnot. Are these things really so important? None of us chose our religion, caste, creed, color, or where and to whom we would be born. We all are essentially good people capable of caring and loving. Please give this a thought. We all need to exterminate this virus of hate that is rapidly spreading across all human systems.

CHAPTER 1

Emergence of the IDE

JUST A FEW YEARS AFTER it emerged, Java established itself as one of the hottest technologies around. Remarkably enough, Java still enjoys that status; Java today is alive and kicking. Backed with good standards support and a healthy open-source culture to boast of, Java is comfortably placed. Over the years, Java has grown at a rapid pace; however, Java tools have never managed to keep pace with Java.

My first experience with Java was at about the same time as I was also getting familiar with Visual Basic. Although most Visual Basic books quickly got me generating useful applications, Java books tended to meander—explaining how amazing applets were and how they were going to transform the Internet. By the time you were done with a beginner's book on Java, more often than not, all you could create were some stupid and perfectly useless applets.

The problem, as I figured out after wasting quite a lot of time trying to make myself believe that Java was really amazing, was that I was trying to compare a tool with a language. It was not Visual Basic the language that I found fascinating, but it was the remarkably easy-to-use tool that Microsoft had wrapped around it. For my money, Java was saved by the gradual shift it made toward the server side. Considering the quality of Java graphical user interface (GUI) tools that existed until a few years back, Java applets never had it in them to truly transform the Internet. It was only a matter of time before people gave up on Java applets. The time and system requirements to get applets running on the client side were a big contributor to the applet downfall.

Things have changed. With the emergence of great server-side technologies from the Java stable, Java is now a major force to reckon with for enterprise application development. What has been particularly delightful is the quality of Java development tools that have emerged in the recent past—tools often referred to as *integrated development environments* (IDEs). As scary as the phrase may sound, an IDE is just a one-stop shop for all your development requirements for a certain language. So if you are using a Java IDE and still have to write javac on the command prompt, either you are not using the thing well or the tool cannot really be called an IDE. Most of the big-name companies have a good Java development tool to boast of: Sun Java Studio, Borland JBuilder, IBM WebSphere Studio Application Developer (WSAD), and of course Oracle JDeveloper.

Most of these IDEs are well integrated with another tool from the same vendor. For example, WSAD makes working with WebSphere Application Server a lot easier, and JDeveloper simplifies working with the Oracle application or database server.

In this book, I will take you through Java and Java 2 Enterprise Edition (J2EE) while keeping the focus firmly on JDeveloper. I will dwell on some of the fundamentals of each topic involved. However, the emphasis is really on getting you working with JDeveloper—using it to tackle any task in the Java and J2EE domain that you want to accomplish. Well, considering how complex J2EE has become and the pace at which it is evolving, *any task* is a rather adventurous phrase to use. To rephrase, you can use it to tackle *almost any task* in the Java and J2EE domain that you want to accomplish.

From Notepad to JDeveloper

For the Java developer, the transition from using Notepad and the command prompt for all development to using sophisticated tools such as JDeveloper has been an interesting one. Notepad is a Windows-specific product, but I am using it here to represent basic text editors across operating systems.

Notepad was the tool everybody had; just start the thing, save the file as a .java file, and use the command prompt to compile and run it. Simplicity is really the key to why this form of Java development has lasted so long and is still very much with us. Using a basic editor makes perfect sense when you are not using any third-party libraries, when the code is fewer than, say, 100 lines, and when one file is an independent entity.

During the 1990s when Java was still in its early days, Notepad served Java well. It kept the focus firmly on the language and did not overwhelm the user with a million features. This has been one of the primary reasons why the Java language blossomed, and developers soon got very good using the Java language, and not just a tool.

This era of Notepad lasted for quite some time. Notepad was followed by compact yet feature-rich editors such as EditPlus, TextPad, and so on. These have the capability to make development a lot easier, with powerful search capability, color-coding, and so on. These editors will always have a solid following. They are not resource hungry, and even an ancient 486 machine will suffice.

After Java mellowed and grew into a wide gamut of areas, the Java IDEs of today emerged. The first thing that is obvious with most of these Java IDEs is that they eat up system resources. So anybody who does not have a fast machine (*fast* being a term relative to when you are reading this book) should think twice before using these IDEs. However, things are not all bad. Considering the range of features that these tools boast of, you soon will be able to forgive them for taking ages to start up or do some basic stuff.

The emergence of Servlets, Java Server Pages (JSPs), Enterprise JavaBeans (EJBs), and now Web Services is what made powerful Java IDEs relevant to Java development. EJBs and application servers have played a particularly important part in making Java IDEs widely acceptable. The entire process of creating different kinds of EJBs and then deploying them to various application servers was just too complicated for most developers like myself. This led to the need for tools that can simplify the entire process and automate as much of it as possible.

The new-age Java IDEs do exactly that and a lot more.

The IDE Alternatives

The key to the success of J2EE has been the community process that is very much part of its growth. Although Sun Microsystems is still the primary company involved in the growth of Java, it alone is not steering the ship. Many companies are contributing, and even giants such as IBM, Oracle, and so on have chipped in to make J2EE the robust and powerful platform that it is.

Until recently, development tools have not been taken that seriously. No community process was in place to control the path these tools took. With Java, all players involved in the community process knew that to compete with Microsoft, the only real option was to stick together. If IBM, Oracle, and others had come up with their own blends and flavors of Java, Java would have certainly been dead by now.

The Java IDE market, however, does not seem to have benefited from this cooperation that exists with Java. Most of the big players have come up with their proprietary Java development tool. Most, if not all, of these tools are handy but do not have much in common that would serve the larger interest of the growth of all Java development tools.

Attempts at achieving cooperation in the domain of IDE development have been made, with the creation of IDE platforms. IDE platforms are an attempt to provide a common set of components that are required for the creation of any desktop application, more specifically for the creation of an IDE. Once a tool vendor has the platform and the set of components built into the platform, it can focus on creating proprietary components that build on the platform and handle a particular requirement not already handled by the platform. Because the basic requirements for creating the application are taken care of by the platform, creating feature-rich and complex applications becomes a lot easier. The applications being developed are also more robust because the platform code being used underneath is solid and well tested.

Two of the most promising IDE platforms around are NetBeans and Eclipse. You will now take a closer look at what these platforms have to offer.

NetBeans

NetBeans is an open-source platform over which the NetBeans IDE has been built. Sun Microsystems has built Sun Java Studio around the NetBeans platform. The platform takes care of most features that a desktop application would require. NetBeans provides window management, toolbar management, wizard frameworks, automatic updates, and other features to the application being developed.

Although NetBeans was perhaps the first real attempt to come up with a common IDE platform, it has not received enough support from other vendors to make it the platform of choice. Figure 1-1 shows the NetBeans IDE, which is free for commercial as well as noncommercial use.

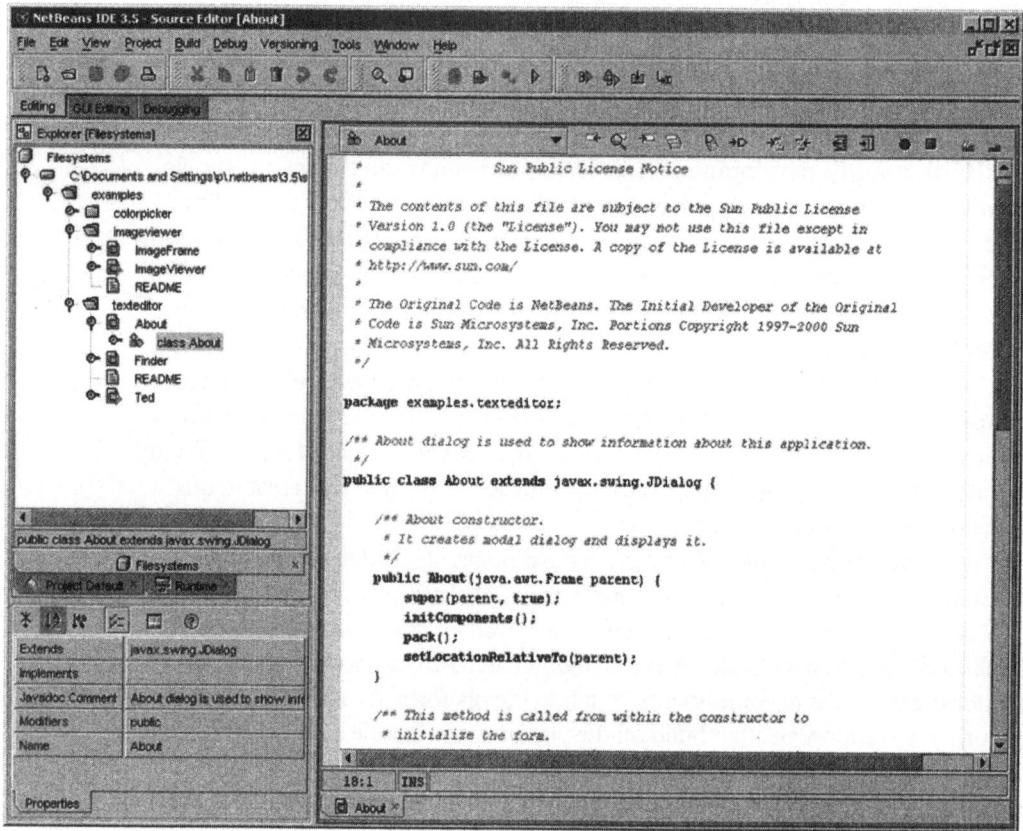

Figure 1-1. The NetBeans IDE

Eclipse

Eclipse is IBM's foray into creating an IDE platform. It is open source and highly extensible. Terming it as a *Java IDE* would be rather unfair because the Eclipse platform itself is said to be operating system and language neutral. Although Eclipse currently is known primarily for Java development, support for many other languages such as COBOL, Python, and so on is well under way. With companies such as Oracle, SAP, and Hewlett-Packard also agreeing to join the Eclipse project, Eclipse is certainly gaining momentum. Furthermore, IBM has certainly put its muscle behind the Eclipse platform, and newer IBM tools such as WSAD 5 are based on the Eclipse platform.

As shown in Figure 1-2, Eclipse has an organized feel about it—something that not all IDEs can boast of.

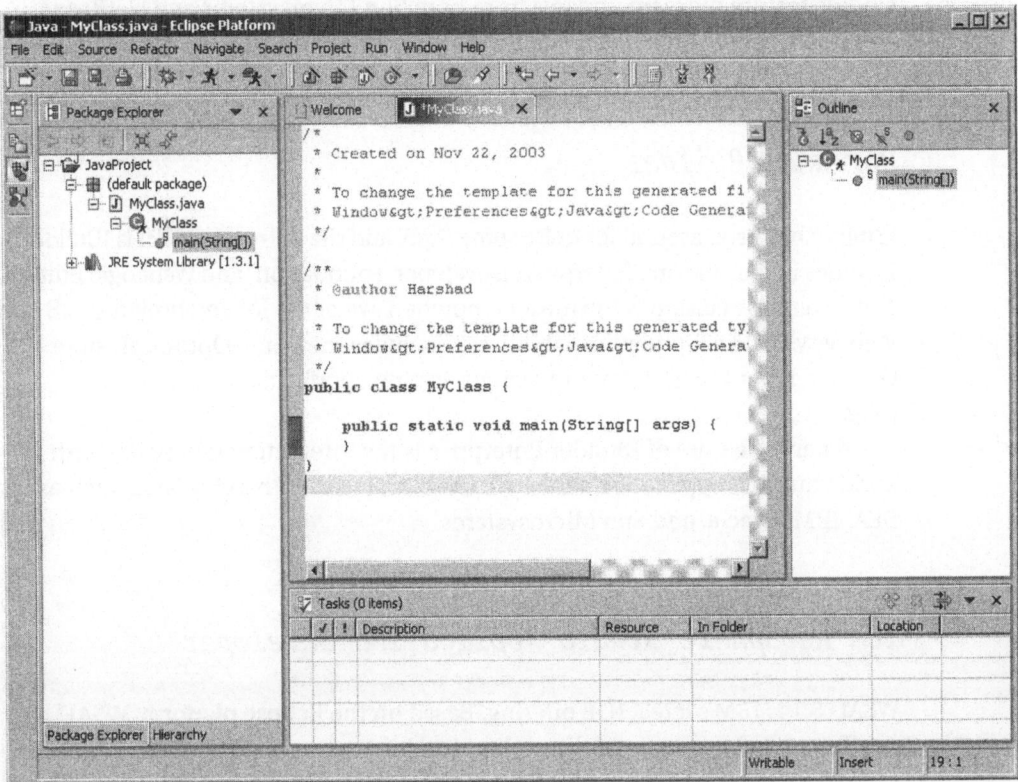

Figure 1-2. The Eclipse platform

Other Commonly Used IDEs

There is definitely no dearth of Java development tools, as is apparent from the Java tools listed on any of the popular Java Web sites. I will now present a quick roundup of some Java IDEs that are arguably the ones used most widely by developers.

Sun Java Studio

Sun Java Studio is based on the open-source NetBeans platform and has undergone a number of confusing name changes over the past year or so. What was earlier Forte for Java became Sun ONE Studio and has now become Sun Java

Studio Standard 5 update 1. Sun ONE Studio Mobile Edition is a specialized tool for developing and testing applications for handheld devices.

This version offers a number of enterprise application development capabilities and a Model View Controller (MVC)–based application framework. Being based on the NetBeans platform, this IDE is evolving quite rapidly. The Auto Update feature picks up updates from both Sun Microsystems and NetBeans, so the IDE seems to keep getting better while you use it.

Borland JBuilder

JBuilder has been around for quite some time, and the current version is JBuilder X. It comes in four flavors: Enterprise, Developer, Foundation, and WebLogic Edition. The Enterprise edition is the most comprehensive of the lot and provides EJB and Web Service development capabilities. It includes the entire OptimizeIt suite. OptimizeIt is a tool to monitor your application's performance and resource usage.

A handy feature of JBuilder Enterprise is the integration it provides with a wide range of application servers from vendors other than Borland, such as BEA, IBM, Oracle, and Sun Microsystems.

IBM WebSphere Studio Application Developer

WSAD 5.1 is IBM's latest IDE offering. Based on the Eclipse platform, WSAD has a different feel from any of the earlier development tools from IBM. WSAD is primarily meant for development targeted at the WebSphere Application Server. WSAD 5.1 supports both WebSphere Application Server 4 and 5. It is also quite competent at abstracting the developer from many of the complexities of J2EE development.

However, WSAD is not kind to machines at the lower end of configurations. It demands a minimum of 512 megabytes (MB) of random access memory (RAM) with 768MB being the recommended option. So although I did enjoy fiddling with WSAD, my machine certainly did not.

Oracle JDeveloper

Isn't this entire book about JDeveloper? A little patience, and you will soon know all you need to know.

The Rise of JDeveloper

Until a few years ago, Oracle was not much of a player in the Java market. However, Oracle has since come up with a J2EE application server and a good Java tool with JDeveloper. It has now pretty much created a niche for itself in the Java marketplace.

Oracle is an active member of the J2EE community. It is participating in many Java specification requests (JSRs) and quite vociferously supports the need for the creation of standards and adherence to them. It also is one of the few companies that can boast of a top-notch product in both the J2EE application server and the IDE market.

As adoption of J2EE grows, the need for quality J2EE tools that hide the inherent complexity of J2EE from the developer has grown. Oracle with JDeveloper 10*g* has made a significant effort in this direction. JDeveloper versions prior to 9*i* did not make much of an impact. JDeveloper 9*i* adopted some of the good things that existed in earlier versions, and JDeveloper 10*g* takes things even further. Although JDeveloper 9*i* was quite a radical leap for JDeveloper, JDeveloper 10*g* makes it an even more mature and refined offering.

Oracle's competitive pricing, JDeveloper's great set of features, and its easy availability at the Oracle Technology Network (OTN) make it seem that Oracle certainly has a winner in the making with JDeveloper 10*g*.

Summary

In this chapter, you received a bird's-eye view of where Java and J2EE development—and more specifically, where Java IDEs—are at currently. In the following chapter, you will zoom in and get a little closer to the core topic of JDeveloper and where it stands in this battle for the Java IDE space. Considering how passionate most Java developers are about the language and the tools they use, it is certainly not an easy task to make a Java developer use a certain tool.

You will take JDeveloper for a spin in the chapters to follow, and I will try to show you why it is a winner all the way.

Getting Started with JDeveloper

IN CHAPTER 1, I talked a bit about where the integrated development environment (IDE) market stands today and some of the many IDE offerings on the market. This chapter will give you a quick overview of JDeveloper's features and then dwell on getting JDeveloper up and running on your machine.

 NOTE *This book is based on JDeveloper 10g Preview version. Because 10g was actually meant to be version 9.0.5, the About dialog box still says Version 9.0.5.0.0 Preview (Build 1375); this might not be the case with the final release.*

Downloading JDeveloper

The first thing you have to do is download a copy of JDeveloper from the Oracle Technology Network (OTN).

 NOTE *OTN is the primary source of knowledge and information about all things Oracle. I recommend you explore this resource at http://otn.oracle.com.*

JDeveloper is available as a free download, and the copy available is a fully functional one, so it will do well for the purpose of this book. To download JDeveloper, you have to register at the OTN; registration is free. Once registered, browse to the "JDeveloper" section and pick up JDeveloper version 10g.

 TIP *If you have a fast Internet connection, you should choose the complete JDeveloper package. This download includes the Java software development kit (JSDK) and JDeveloper documentation. The complete download should get you up and running with JDeveloper in no time whatsoever.*

The JDeveloper 10g Preview release notes begin by saying the following about version 10g:

Oracle JDeveloper 10g Preview is a Java 2 Enterprise Edition (J2EE) develop-ment environment with end-to-end support for developing, debugging, and deploying e-business applications and Web Services. Oracle JDeveloper 10g allows developers to build J2EE applications and Web Services either from scratch or by using a J2EE framework.

Oracle certainly seems to believe that JDeveloper has a lot to offer, and I have to agree with it. Having said that, the following features of JDeveloper 10g make it such a super offering:

100 percent Java: JDeveloper 9i was a complete rewrite of the IDE in Java, and 10g continues to be 100 percent Java. Earlier versions of JDeveloper could not have made such a claim.

Operating system support: One of the big advantages of being 100 per-cent Java is the operating system independence that applications can achieve. Being pure Java, JDeveloper can boast of being able to run on Windows, Solaris, and Linux.

Application Development Framework (ADF): JDeveloper 10g has intro-duced a new Model View Controller (MVC)–based ADF framework that is meant to make J2EE easier to work with while making great use of the technology's features. ADF in version 10g brings together components that existed in version 9i to form a complete framework. It also intro-duces tools and wizards that make application development as easy as just dragging and dropping components.

Tools for every stage of a project: JDeveloper offers a wide range of tools that suit particular stages of a project. So JDeveloper can now assist you not just during actual coding but also right from design to production. You can manage modeling, coding, debugging, testing, profiling, and deploying using JDeveloper.

Great Unified Modeling Language (UML) support: UML today is being used by most projects and has become as good as a standard. JDeveloper provides good tools for use cases, class diagrams, and activity diagrams. A useful feature is that JDeveloper keeps your code and the class dia-grams in sync, well after you have stopped working on the class diagrams and moved to full-fledged coding. This feature can be a big asset because often you will find that by the time the coding is done, the class diagrams are completely out of sync and no longer represent the code.

Extensible Markup Language (XML), Structured Query Language (SQL), and Procedural Language extension to SQL (PL/SQL) tools: Although JDeveloper is portrayed as primarily a Java IDE, it does have solid support for related technologies such as XML, SQL, and PL/SQL. Oracle's expertise at databases is reflected in the good integration of JDeveloper with the database.

Code-quality tools: A great feature of JDeveloper that makes it stand out from the multitude of IDEs and Java tools available is the existence of code improvement tools. CodeCoach provides relevant code improvement advice and is also capable of automatically fixing many problems that it points out in the code. Memory Profiler comes in handy to trace out objects that are hogging memory or any memory leaks that might exist in the code. Execution Profiler and Event Profiler are tools that have more to do with timing events across application layers.

Powerful EJB features: Rapid generation and deployment of Container-Managed Persistence (CMP) and Bean-Managed Persistence (BMP) entity beans, along with (stateful/stateless) session beans and Message-Driven Beans (MDBs), is now rather easy with the wizards that JDeveloper provides.

Built-in Web Service support: JDeveloper enables easy interaction with Web Service technologies such as Universal Description, Discovery, and Integration (UDDI), Simple Object Access Protocol (SOAP), and Web Services Description Language (WSDL). JDeveloper also simplifies the task of having your existing Java code ready for Web Services and capable of exposing functionality as a Web Service.

Integration with open-source tools: Open source is now an integral part of the Java world. Although many proprietary products are doing well, lots of free and open-source software are used by Java developers day in and day out. The build tool Ant, the MVC-based framework Struts, the Java unit testing framework JUnit, Cactus, and so on are tools that are open source and widely used by the Java community. JDeveloper can easily integrate with many of these tools, so you can use them from within the IDE. I will cover in later chapters how you can do this.

Extension SDK: Unlike NetBeans and Eclipse, which have a community movement to back the development of the IDE, JDeveloper as yet is very much a proprietary product and is not based on any open-source platform. JDeveloper as a result does not enjoy the advantages that some other IDEs have because the platform underneath keeps getting better. As a result, the extension capability of JDeveloper is important to ensure that JDeveloper benefits from open-source developments and partner developments. JDeveloper provides an extension SDK that can be used to customize the IDE. Many popular open-source products have already provided plug-ins for JDeveloper. These products and other plug-ins being developed by Oracle and its partners ensure that the IDE is constantly maturing and evolving.

Installing JDeveloper

Considering the many useful features of JDeveloper, you should now have enough reason to actually try JDeveloper. You will now get down to installing the IDE. Because the 10*g* preview release is available only for Windows, the system requirements for Windows are as stated in the documentation, but the ones for Linux, Solaris, and HP-UX are based on system requirements for version 9*i*. Check the OTN to confirm the system requirements for the 10*g* production release.

You should have JSDK 1.4.1_02 installed on your machine to run JDeveloper 10*g*. Also, for Windows, the requirements are as follows:

- **Operating system**: Windows 2000, Windows NT, or Windows XP

- **Central processing unit (CPU) type and speed**: 1 gigahertz (GHz) Pentium III

- **Memory**: 512 megabytes (MB) of random access memory (RAM)

- **Display**: 65,536 colors, set to at least 1024×768 resolution

- **Hard drive space**: 210MB (for a base install) or 360MB (for a complete install)

For Linux, the requirements are as follows:

- **Distribution**: Red Hat 2.1AS (enterprise), SuSE SLES-7 (enterprise), Red Hat 7.3 (desktop), or SuSE 8.0 (desktop)

- **CPU type and speed**: 1 gigahertz (GHz) Pentium III

- **Memory**: 512MB RAM

- **Display**: 65,536 colors, set to at least 1024×768 resolution

- **Hard drive space**: 210MB (for a base install) or 360MB (for a complete install)

For Solaris, the requirements are as follows:

- **Operating system**: Solaris 2.8 or 2.9 using the CDE window manager

- **CPU type and speed**: 333MHz SPARC

- **Memory**: 512MB RAM

- **Display**: 65,536 colors, set to at least 1024×768 resolution

- **Hard drive space**: 210MB (for a base install) or 360MB (for a complete install)

For HP-UX, the requirements are as follows:

- **Operating system**: HP-UX 11.0 using the CDE or VUE window managers

- **CPU type and speed**: 200MHz Hewlett-Packard PA-RISC

- **Memory**: 512MB RAM

- **Display**: 65,536 colors, set to at least 1024×768 resolution

- **Hard drive space**: 210MB (for a base install) or 360MB (for a complete install)

This configuration should get you a smoothly functioning JDeveloper if you intend to develop basic Java classes or do user interface (UI) development. However, if you intend to have an application server or similar memory-intensive software running in the background, performance will fall drastically. On a Windows 2000 machine with a slightly better configuration than stated previously, I tried creating Java Server Pages (JSPs) with JDeveloper while having WebSphere 4 Single Server Edition running in the background to try out my JSPs. Performance soon fell to pretty miserable levels, and memory consumption also shot up drastically. I recommend using a superior configuration than that stated previously.

With JDeveloper being 100 percent Java, Oracle seems to have gone for a simplistic installation that will work similarly across operating systems. You have two download options to choose from while downloading JDeveloper. The full installation for version 10*g* is jdev905preview.zip, and the base installation is jdev905preview_base.zip. Both of these files are zipped archives and can be extracted using any commonly used archive tools such as WinZip or PKZip.

The base installation is more or less the same as the full installation. The difference is that the Windows version of JSDK 1.4.1_02 and the complete JDeveloper documentation are missing from the base installation.

 NOTE *If you do not want to download the full installation because it is a rather large file, you could opt for the base install. However, the base installation requires JSDK 1.4.1_02 to be already installed on your machine. If you can download the full install and spare the disk space to have another JSDK installed, you might as well go for the full install. It should get you going in no time, and you don't have to do any special configuration. Also, you do not risk any JSDK version mismatch. If you are new to Java, the full installation is certainly the mode to choose.*

Doing a Full Installation

The zipped archives do not create a top-level folder. So, if you extract to D:\, you will end up creating many folders right into D:\. Instead, create a new folder and extract the contents of the zip file into it. I will refer to this folder where you install JDeveloper as <jdev_home>.

Windows

The full installation of JDeveloper on a Windows machine is as simple as it gets. Simply extract the contents of the jdev905preview.zip file into any folder where you want to install JDeveloper.

After extracting the contents of the zipped file, you should have many new folders created in <jdev_home>. There is no standard Windows installation procedure that you have to go through. Extracting files is all it takes.

Unix/Linux

The installation procedure on a Unix or Linux machine is also similar to the procedure for Windows. Just extract the files in the archive into any directory. However, because the full installation ships with a Windows version of JSDK, to install on a Unix or Linux machine, you need to modify the jdev.conf file to tell JDeveloper where to look for a compatible JSDK installation. Next, follow the procedures in the "SetJavaHome Variable" and "Installing Oracle Java Virtual Machine" sections.

Doing a Base Installation

For the base installation, unzip jdev905preview_base.zip into <jdev_home>. Apart from the documentation and the JSDK's absence, the other contents should stay the same as the full installation. Follow the SetJavaHome variable's procedure in the next section to specify the JSDK to be used.

SetJavaHome Variable

Open the file jdev.conf located in <jdev_install>\jdev\bin\jdev.conf in a text editor. To edit this file, you require an editor that recognizes Unix end-of-line characters. Windows Notepad will not do; however, editors such as WordPad or TextPad will work just fine.

In jdev.conf, set the value for the variable SetJavaHome to point to the location where you have the JSDK installed on your machine. Ensure that the line is not commented out with a pound (#) sign. You do not need to set this variable in the full installation procedure discussed earlier because the JSDK comes bundled with JDeveloper.

If you have the full installation of JDeveloper and yet want to use a different JSDK than the one provided by Oracle, changing the value for the variable SetJavaHome in the file <jdev_home>\jdev\bin\jdev.conf should serve the purpose, telling JDeveloper where to look for the JSDK. You also need to set this if you are installing on a non-Windows platform.

The configuration line in jdev.conf should look something like this:

```
SetJavaHome D:\jsdk1.4.1
```

If you are installing on a non-Windows machine, it could be this:

```
SetJavaHome /local/java/jsdk
```

Installing Oracle Java Virtual Machine

JDeveloper comes with a specialized Java virtual machine by Oracle. The Oracle Java Virtual Machine (OJVM) needs to be installed to be able to use CodeCoach and Profiler and to improve debugger performance. With 10g production release, the OJVM is expected to work on non-Windows platforms as well. If this is the case you will not have to configure the JVM for non-Windows platforms and tools like CodeCoach and the profilers that are dependent on the OJVM will also work on non-Wiindows platforms. Check the OTN to confirm.

If you have installed the full version of JDeveloper and are using the JSDK that is part of the full version, you do not need to do anything; JDeveloper will use the OJVM by default. However, if you have installed the base version and have now configured the JSDK you want to use, you need to install the OJVM as well to be able to use CodeCoach, use Profiler, and speed up the debugger. All you need to do is run the InstallOJVM.bat file located in the <jdev_home>\jdev\bin\directory. Pass the directory where you have your JSDK installed as a parameter, and the .bat file will copy and create the requisite files and directories into your existing JSDK. No existing files will be deleted or overwritten. The command will look something like InstallOJVM.bat D:\jsdk1.4, where D:\jsdk1.4 is the home directory of my JSDK installation.

Starting JDeveloper

Once you have JDeveloper installed, to start it on a Windows machine, you could either run the file <jdev_home>\jdev\bin\jdevw.exe or run the file jdev.exe in the same folder. The only difference between these two approaches is that if you run jdev.exe, a console window pops up that displays internal diagnostic information.

To have a Windows-like feel to your application startup, simply create a shortcut on your desktop for either of the two files, and you will get the standard Windows application type of startup.

On non-Windows platforms, the way to start JDeveloper is to run the file <jdev_home>/jdev/bin/jdev.

Summary

This chapter covered the impressive features in JDeveloper and the simple installation procedure for using it on operating systems. JDeveloper has a clean installation procedure that is much better than the platform-dependent installation procedures for most IDEs. With downloading and installing now out of the way, in the next chapter you can move toward actually using JDeveloper, exploring the interface, and creating some simple applications.

Java with JDeveloper

IT HAS BEEN LESS THAN a decade since Java emerged. Although the initial years of Java were marked by more hype than substance, Java gradually managed to build on its user base and has been constantly evolving and maturing. Even a few years ago, it would have been rather difficult to visualize that Java would get to a stage where its complexities and features warranted the use of such powerful tools as JDeveloper. However, because Java 2 Enterprise Edition (J2EE) has gotten Java to that stage, developers today certainly need the assistance of tools such as JDeveloper.

If you followed the installation instructions in Chapter 2, you should now have JDeveloper running on your machine. In this chapter, you will get down to some real Java. I will begin this chapter with a basic Java example, primarily to familiarize you with the JDeveloper user interface (UI). I will follow this with an example of how to create a Java-based UI, where you will explore the UI creation abilities of JDeveloper.

JDeveloper Documentation

If you want more information about any wizards and screens presented in this chapter, you will need the documentation. If you opted for a complete install of JDeveloper, the rather extensive documentation was also copied to your disk.

You also have the option of using a hosted version of the documentation. On JDeveloper startup, choose Tools ➤ Preferences ➤ Documentation. You can then specify the uniform resource locator (URL) where the documentation is hosted. This option is useful if you have it on your local network. You can also opt for directly using the documentation hosted on the Oracle Technology Network (OTN).

Understanding Workspaces and Projects

Working in JDeveloper revolves around the concepts of workspaces and projects. Workspaces and projects help you easily manage your code and other files and also apply certain settings across a number of files. A *workspace* is nothing but a collection of projects. JDeveloper by default will store all workspaces in the folder <jdev_home>/jdev/mywork. Workspaces are stored as .jws files.

A JDeveloper *project* is a simple and logical collection of files. JDeveloper is capable of listing these files categorized by their file extensions. The physical location of the files is not a factor; you can group files residing in distinct locations in a single project. A project file has a .jpr extension.

NOTE *There is no such thing as creating a simple Java class, using it, and then throwing it away. You have to carry the overhead of creating workspaces and projects at all times.*

Using JDeveloper

After starting JDeveloper, you should see a screen similar to that shown in Figure 3-1. You will first look at some key concepts that are integral to all the development you will undertake when using JDeveloper.

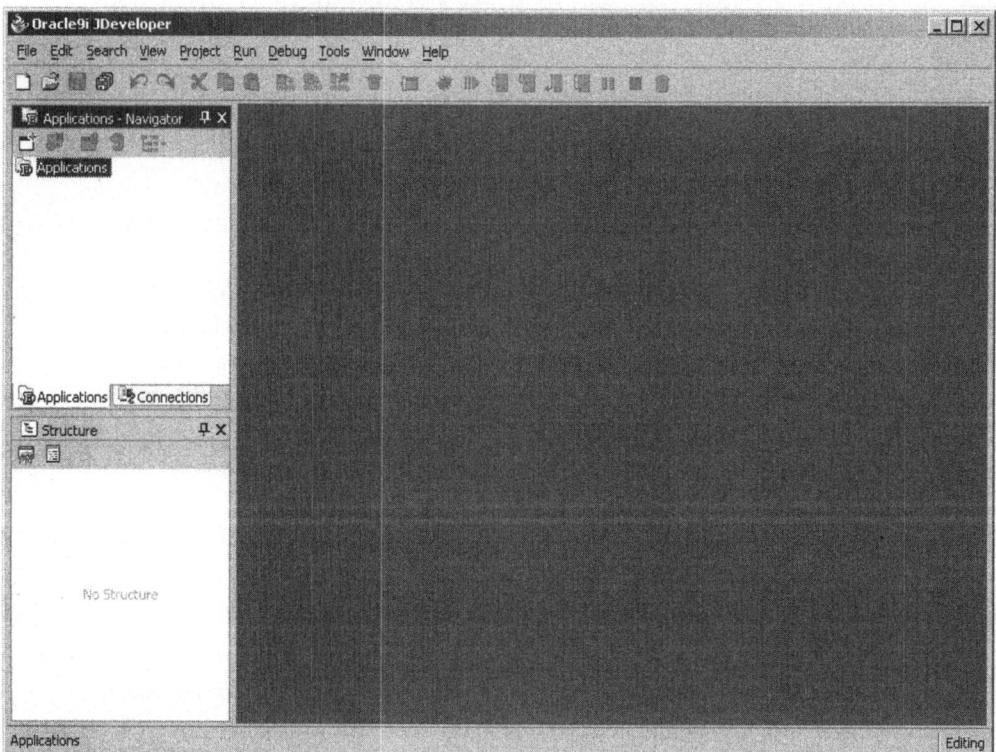

Figure 3-1. JDeveloper display on startup

System Navigator and Applications Navigator

Although earlier versions on startup displayed a System Navigator with two options, Workspaces and Connections, version 10*g* has introduced the Applications Navigator. The Applications Navigator takes a higher-level view than the System Navigator. The System Navigator is more of a file explorer, and the Applications Navigator focuses on the applications being created and the components involved. The System Navigator is still very much present and can be displayed using the View ➤ System Navigator option. However, everything you do using the Applications Navigator can be done using the System Navigator.

You will next look at a couple of other concepts that have been introduced with version 10*g* and have changed the way JDeveloper organizes things.

Technology Scopes and Application Templates

One JDeveloper fundamental is that irrespective of the kind of application you intend to develop, you always have to create a workspace with which to work. A new concept introduced with version 10*g* is that of an *application workspace*. An application workspace is very much like any other workspace except that an application workspace enables you to create an application based on an application template. So instead of manually creating a workspace and then projects within the workspace, in the case of an application workspace, you just select the application template you want to use.

Application templates are based on the idea that displaying things the user may not want to use clutters the interface and confuses the user. For example, if you know that the user is developing a stand-alone Swing application, why display options, toolbars, and such other things that are specific to, say, J2EE and have nothing to do with Swing development?

To add a new application workspace, choose File ➤ New, and in the New Gallery displayed, choose General ➤ Application Workspace. The Create Application Workspace dialog box, as shown in Figure 3-2, will display. Here there are already a few application templates ready for use. These templates are as follows:

- Web Application [Default]

- Web Application [JSP, Struts, EJB]

- Java Application [Default]

- Java Application [Java, Swing]

- Custom Application [All Technologies]

You also have an option to edit existing templates and define your own application templates based on the specific set of technologies you intend to use. An application template not only defines the technologies that you will use but also the projects that will be created automatically when you create the application workspace.

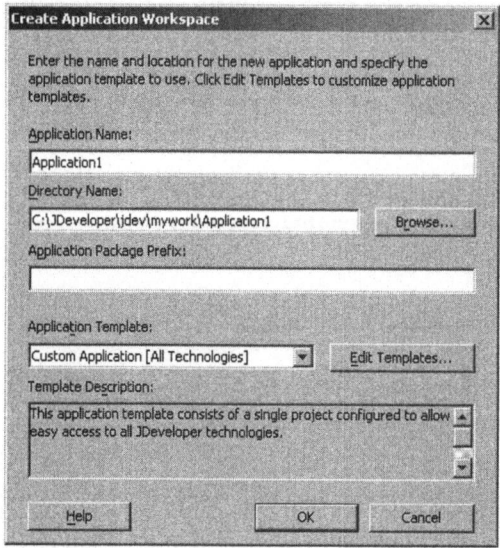

Figure 3-2. The Create Application Workspace dialog box

An application workspace can be both an advantage as well as a disadvantage. When I first used 10g, every time I created a new workspace or a project I was left wondering where the capabilities of JDeveloper's earlier versions had gone. However, for the sake of simplicity and not overwhelming the user with too many options, the new approach does make sense.

For the initial examples, you will not use an application workspace but an ordinary workspace. Using application workspaces forces you to create a new workspace for every technologically different example. Instead of creating new workspaces for every example, you will rather have new projects within a single workspace.

Based on the application template used, the technology scope for a project is defined automatically. However, you have the option of defining the technology scope for a particular project in the Project Properties ➤ Technology Scope section for that project. The new file creation and other options provided to the user are based on these technology scopes.

So, if UML is not listed in the technology scope of a project, the New Gallery displayed for that particular project will not list Unified Modeling Language (UML) diagrams in the list of diagrams you can create.

TIP *In the Filter By drop-down list in the New Gallery, choose the All Technologies option to be able to create files of every type, irrespective of the technology scope of the particular project.*

A Simple Java Application

In the Java application that follows, try to focus on the capabilities of JDeveloper rather than on the application itself. There are innumerable things you can tweak and try out, beyond what I cover. There is no easier way to learn tools such as JDeveloper than to have some fun fiddling with them.

To add a new workspace to the Workspaces list, follow these steps:

1. Choose the File ➤ New command. Very few items are currently listed in the gallery because until you have created a new workspace and project, you cannot get down to creating files and applications.

2. Select the General category, and choose Workspace in the Items list. When selecting any item, a description of that item displays in the grayed-out section below the list. It is well worth going through all the possibilities and reading their descriptions.

3. Click the OK button, and the dialog box shown in Figure 3-3 will display, asking you to fill in the name and location of your new workspace. Workspaces are saved as .jws files, and projects are saved as .jpr files.

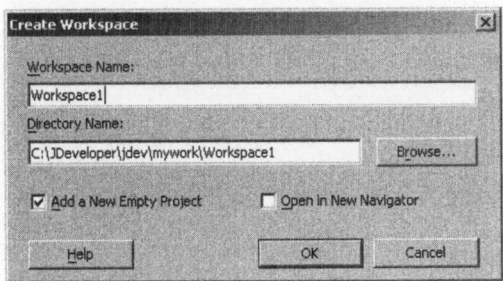

Figure 3-3. The Create Workspace dialog box

4. Name your new workspace and directory *MyJavaApps*. JDeveloper creates a new directory if a directory of that name does not already exist at that location. Also choose the Add a New Empty Project check box. You can add a project later; it is just easier this way.

Choosing the Open in New Navigator option simply displays the new workspace as a separate tab in the System Navigator. However, this option is relevant if you intend to create large projects containing many files. In this case, this is not really useful, so do not choose that option.

A new dialog box asking for project details will now display on your screen, as shown in Figure 3-4.

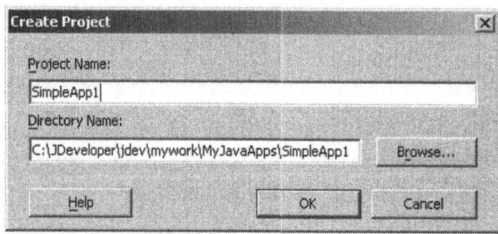

Figure 3-4. The Create Project dialog box

Name your project and the directory involved as *SimpleApp1*. Again, JDeveloper will create the directory if it does not already exist.

So, you now have a new workspace and a new project ready for you. The Applications Navigator displays all workspaces and projects. As shown in Figure 3-5, it currently should display the new workspace and project you have just created.

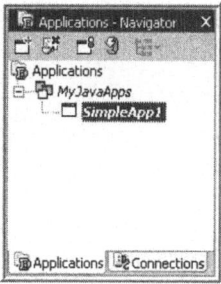

Figure 3-5. Applications Navigator displaying your new workspace and project

If you want to get rid of the project or the workspace you just created, just click the Remove From icon or press Ctrl+Delete. Mind you, this does not delete the directory that was created for the workspace or project. It just removes it from the navigator. To remove a file from the disk as well, you can select the File ➤ Erase from Disk.

If you now want your project to be displayed in a separate navigator, you have the option of clicking the New View icon or selecting the View ➤ New View command. However, this only works in the case of the System Navigator and not for the Applications Navigator. Choosing the New View icon, as shown in Figure 3-6, or pressing (Alt+Shift+N) will do the trick. All workspaces and projects can be moved to a new view at any time.

Figure 3-6. New View icon

Project Properties

You now have the bare minimum in place: a workspace and a project. Next you need to configure the project and then put in some actual code.

To configure the project's properties, you could either double-click the project name or right-click the project name displayed in the Applications Navigator or System Navigator and choose the Project Properties option. You could also choose the Project option from the menu bar and then select Project Properties. To configure the default properties for all new projects that you would create, select the Default Project Properties option on the Project tab.

Choose Project Properties for the project SimpleApp1 you just created. All the options as displayed in Figure 3-7 are certainly worth exploring; however, for the time being, you will deal with only a few of them.

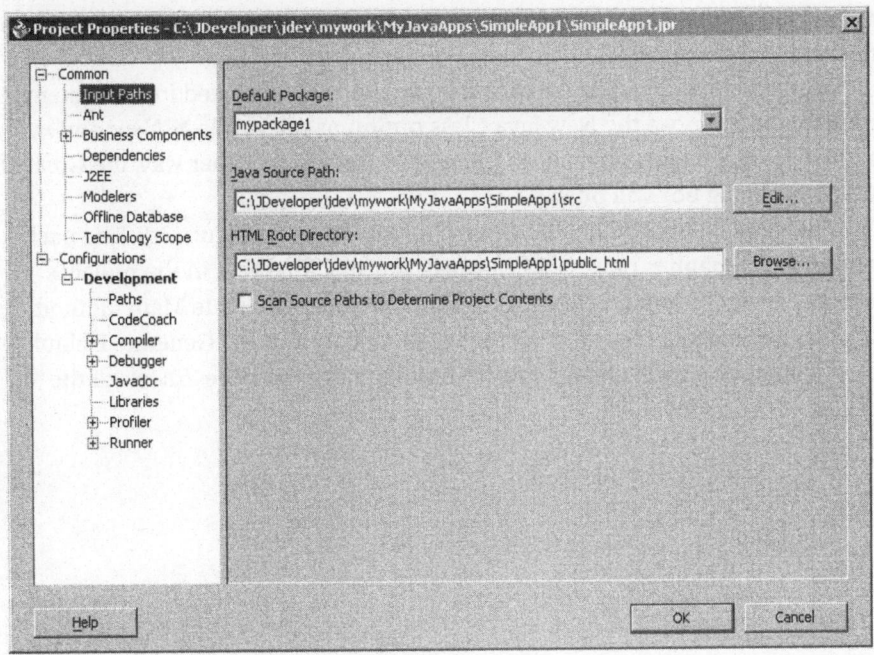

Figure 3-7. The Project Properties dialog box

After selecting the Input Paths option under Common, you will see the Java Source Path field. This is the location where the code you generate using JDeveloper is placed. The HTML Root Directory field shows where all Hypertext Markup Language (HTML) or HTML-based files are kept. By default, JDeveloper names source directories as *src* and the HTML root directory as *public_html*.

Change the Default Package field to *pack1*. If the Scan Source Paths to Determine Project Contents option is checked, JDeveloper will dynamically pick up files from the source directory and will not stick only to files explicitly added to the project. This option is particularly useful if you are one of many developers involved and, unknown to you, new files keep getting added to the source.

Next, select the Paths option that exists in Configurations ➤ Development ➤ Paths. Here you can specify the output directory for the Java code that gets compiled. By default, JDeveloper directs all the class files to the classes directory. The additional classpath comes into play if you want your Java code to access class files or Java archives (JARs) that exist somewhere else on your machine. Because the classpath is the cause for a majority of compile-time errors, this option needs to be handled with care. Because the sample application should not need to refer to any other classes or libraries, you can leave this option alone. Click OK to put all these settings in place for this particular project.

The Code

So you will now finally get your hands into some Java code. The code you will be creating is a simple addition program that takes two numbers as command-line arguments and adds them.

To create a new class, right-click the project name as listed in the System Navigator and choose the New Java Class option or select File ➤ New, and in the New Gallery displayed, choose General ➤ Java class. Either way, the Create Java Class dialog box will open.

Change the class name to *AdditionClass,* as shown in Figure 3-8. The package name by default is now pack1 because you specified that in the project's settings. In the Optional Attributes section, check the Generate Main Method box. The Public attribute will create the class public, and the Generate Default Constructor option will add an empty constructor to the code. Check all the options, and then click OK.

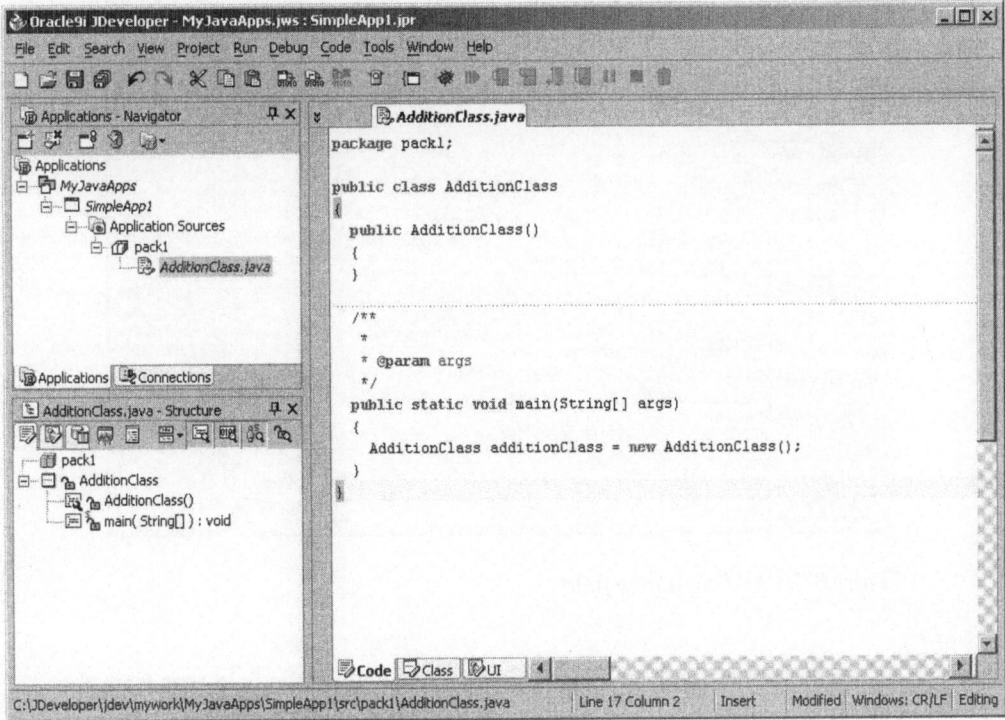

Figure 3-8. The Create Java Class dialog box

The AdditionClass.java file will now be displayed, as shown in Figure 3-9. The Structure window on the left now comes in handy. It displays the structure of the active document. It displays method names, variables, and constructors, each having a distinct icon to represent it. Pointing to any of the listed items in the Structure window displays further details about that item, and double-clicking the item takes you to that line in the code.

Figure 3-9. Viewing the AdditionClass code

Now you will add some variables and a method to actually do the addition for you. If you think you have to do some coding now, hold your horses. There is an easier way. In Figure 3-9, you should notice that below the Java code are three tabs: Code, Class, and UI. These tabs allow you to quickly switch between three types of editors. This tab functionality is a nice addition to version 10*g* because in the earlier versions the different editors were not so obvious. These editors are as follows:

- **Code Editor**: Use this view to display the actual code.

- **Class Editor**: Use this view to visually edit the code.

- **UI Editor**: Use this view to easily create and edit the Java UI.

Choose the Class tab. The Class Editor window displaying some basic details about the class will now appear.

Move to the Fields tab, and click the Add button. The Field Settings Dialog: Add Field dialog box, as shown in Figure 3-10, will now pop up.

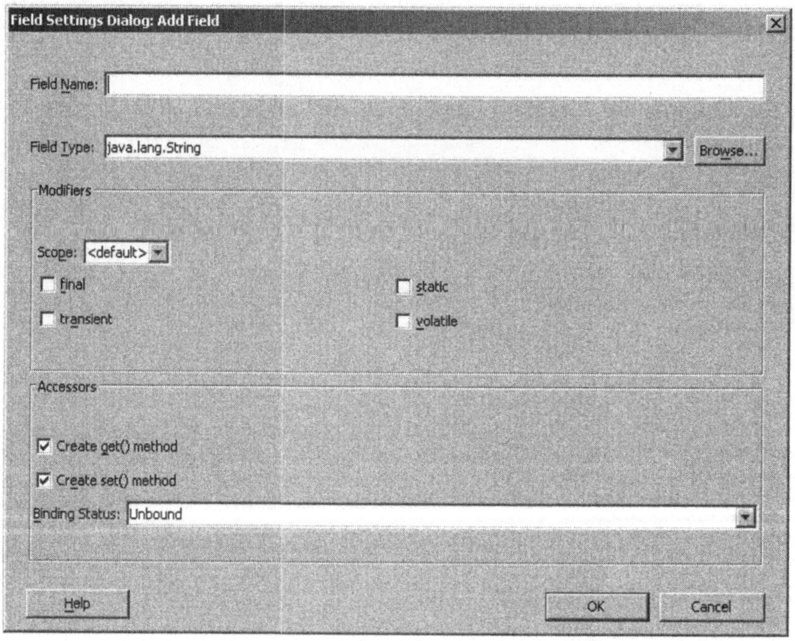

Figure 3-10. Adding a new field

To add a new field, specify the field name, choose the field type from the combo box, and click OK. For this case, add two new int variables named *iValue1* and *iValue2*. The Field Type combo box lists most of the commonly used classes and primitives. Clicking the Browse button can of course get JDeveloper to list even a user-defined class. Uncheck the Create get() Method and Create set() Method options because you will not require getter and setter methods for this example.

 NOTE *Make note of the Create get() Method and Create set() Method options. Although getter and setters are not relevant to this example, this feature will come in handy later.*

Once you are done adding the two variables, move to the Methods tab in the Class Editor. The main method should currently be the only one listed. Click the Add button, and you should get a display as shown in Figure 3-11. Here name the new method *doAddition*, with a return type of int. Move to the Parameters tab and add two int parameters, val1 and val2. Once you are done, choose the Code tab to go back to the Code Editor. Voilà! The code has already been written for you. Check the Structure window that should be at the bottom left of the screen. The methods and variables of the class should be displayed.

 NOTE *The Structure window has tabs that display the code structure, UI structure, or UI model. The Structure window also has the capability to sort listings, show or hide various elements, and create a new view for the structure of a particular class.*

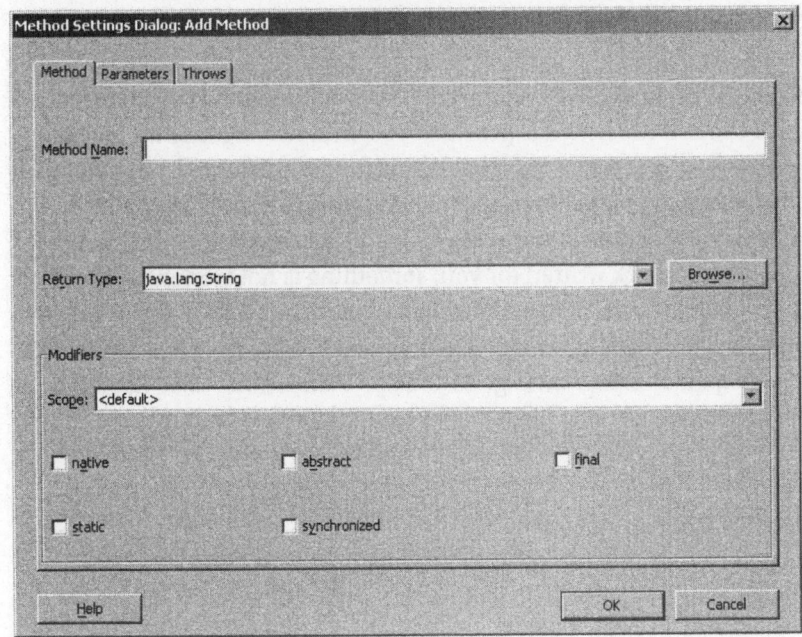

Figure 3-11. Adding a new method

This simple program is meant to take two arguments as input, add them, and print the output. In the meantime, why not check all the classes on which the code depends? Right-click the filename as displayed in the Applications Navigator or System Navigator and choose the Show Dependencies option. The Dependencies log should now pop up at the bottom of the display, as shown in Figure 3-12.

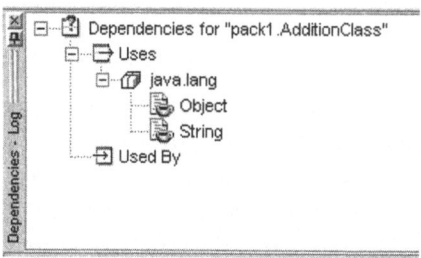

Figure 3-12. Viewing the dependencies

Although in this case this feature is not really useful, it does come in handy when your files contain thousands of lines of code and use various third-party application programming interfaces (APIs). This feature can quickly tell you on which packages and classes the code depends.

Rapid Coding Features

To get the code to do the bit you want it to, you need to make a few changes to it. First, you will check if the user has provided you with two arguments. So if the arguments array is not of size 2, you show a usage message and get out. For this, you need an if block. So on the line after instantiating AdditionClass, simply write *if* and press Ctrl+Enter. If you are not pleasantly surprised to find a nice and well-indented if block written for you, something is not working properly.

This automatic generation of code was an example of what JDeveloper terms as *code templates*. To view a list of all templates that JDeveloper has to offer and to add a few templates of your own, go to Tools ➤ Preferences. Click Code Editor (see Figure 3-13).

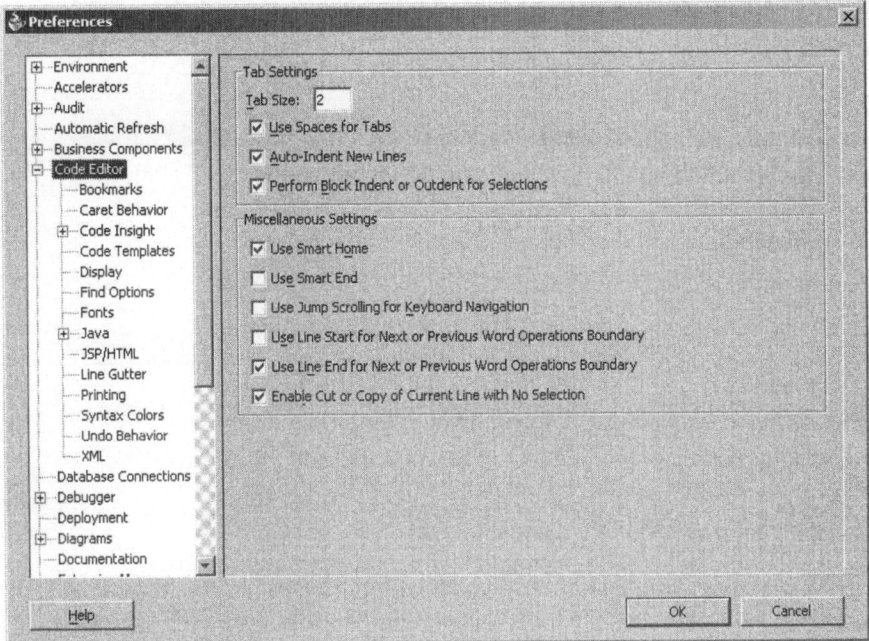

Figure 3-13. The Code Editor settings

 NOTE *As shown in the figure, you can tweak quite a few prefer-ences. Most applications that provide so many options would scare me away from using them; however, JDeveloper does a good job of categorizing preferences, and most options are pretty relevant.*

Next, expand the Code Editor node by clicking the plus (+) sign. In this expanded list, choose Code Templates (see Figure 3-14). In the list that is dis-played, move to the shortcut *if,* and you will see why JDeveloper replaced *if* with a proper *if* block. There are many other useful templates you will use as you progress.

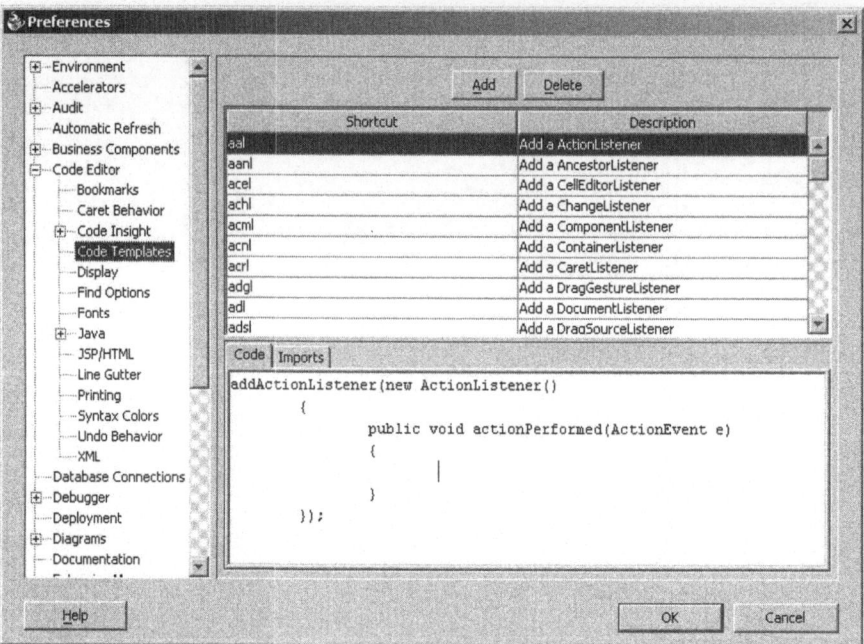

Figure 3-14. The Code Templates settings

 TIP *Explore and use all the available code templates and also try to make it a habit to create new code templates whenever you find that you are repeating a piece of code. This will certainly save a lot of time and will also protect you from Copy/Paste errors.*

You will explore other preferences and settings as they become relevant to the topics covered. Now you will put the *if* logic in place:

```
if (args.length != 2 )
{
    System.out.println("Usage: AdditionClass <argument 1> <argument 2>");
    return;
}
```

A feature of JDeveloper that can be useful if you have hundreds of lines of code is the colored highlighting of braces. Just take the cursor to the starting brace for the if block depicted previously, and JDeveloper will highlight the opening and closing braces for that particular if block. You can have many levels of nested braces, and still this feature will work fine. Keyboard shortcuts for moving to matching braces are Alt+] and Alt+[.

NOTE *All keyboard shortcuts referred to in this book will be based on the default key mapping for JDeveloper. JDeveloper provides five other mapping options, namely Classic, DefaultCDE, DefaultKDE2, Emacs, and Visual C++. These could be useful if you have experience with any of these environments and are comfortable using them. You can configure the KeyMapping option using the Load Preset button in Tools ➤ Preferences ➤ Accelerators.*

If two arguments are provided on execution of the AdditionClass, you will just assume that they are both valid integers. Because you have a separate method to do the addition, you then just call this method and get the result of this addition:

```
else
{
    System.out.println(args[0] + " " +args[1]);
    int iResult = additionClass.doAddition(Integer.parseInt(args[0])
      , Integer.parseInt(args[1]));
    System.out.println("Result of addition = "+ iResult);
}
```

To use JDeveloper's Code Insight feature, in this code snippet, just type *additionClass* followed by a period (.), and JDeveloper will list all the possible method and variable references that can be invoked using this particular reference. A thing to note is that methods and variables in this particular class are depicted in bold, but those inherited from superclasses are not.

An even easier Code Insight option would be to type *additionClass.d* and then press Ctrl+Space. If there is only a single method or variable that starts with the letter *d* and is accessible using this particular reference, JDeveloper writes out that method or variable name. So in this case, JDeveloper will write doAddition() for you. Instead, if you just type *additionClass.i* and then try the Ctrl+Space combination, you will see all the options that begin with *i*, and you will have to choose the one relevant.

Once you have additionClass.doAddition() written for you, just move your cursor to the opening parenthesis, and JDeveloper will open a list of parameters that the method accepts. In this case, you should see int val1, int val2.

Changes to the Code Insight settings are possible by modifying the Code Editor ➤ Code Insight section in the Preferences dialog as well as the Code Editor ➤ Java ➤ Java Insight section in the Preferences dialog.

The doAddition method is as simple as it comes:

```
int doAddition(int val1, int val2)
{
        return val1 + val2;
}
```

Converting Code to ByteCode

Now that you have the code ready, you will compile it. You could right-click somewhere within the Code Editor and choose Make AdditionClass. The second option is to choose the Projects option in the menu bar and then choose the Make or Rebuild option as desired.

NOTE *The Make option does an optimized rebuilding of the application and compiles only whatever it finds has changed and needs to be recompiled. The Rebuild option, on the other hand, does a complete rebuild, ignoring creation dates and so on. Make should do in most cases; however, choose Rebuild if you want to check that whatever compiled fine earlier still does compile.*

Running the Application

Once you compile AdditionClass.java, the class should end up in the output directory as specified in the Project Properties dialog box.

The next task is to run the program, which you can achieve in multiple ways. First, you could choose Run ➤ Run AdditionClass.java from the menu bar; second, you could right-click anywhere in the Code Editor and choose Run AdditionClass.java. Another alternative is to right-click the filename as listed in the Applications Navigator or System Navigator and choose Run AdditionClass.java. Finally, you can click the Run icon shown in Figure 3-15.

Figure 3-15. The Run icon

Running the application using any of these options, however, will not get you the desired result because you are not providing the required arguments to the program. On execution, a new tab will appear in the log window at the bottom of the screen, as shown in Figure 3-16. The log should display the usage message that you provided earlier.

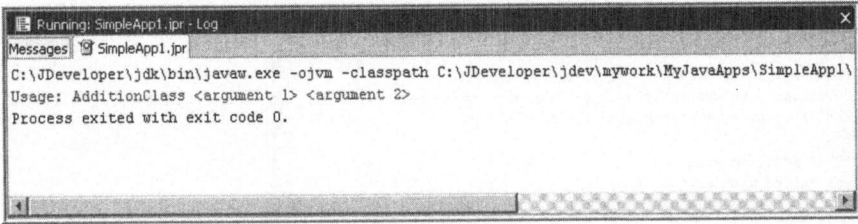

Figure 3-16. Log display on running the project

To pass run-time arguments and to change run settings for this project, go to the project's properties and choose Configurations ➤ Development ➤ Runner (see Figure 3-17).

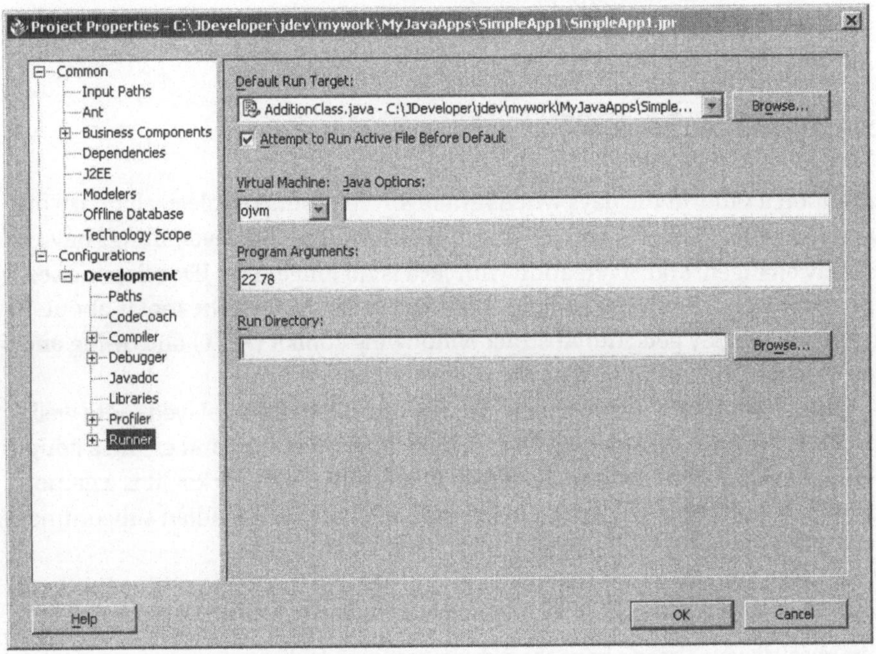

Figure 3-17. The Runner settings

In this dialog box, the Program Arguments option is the one you are currently concerned with. Specify the values here as you normally would on the command line. All other options can remain as they are by default.

Enter *22 78* for the program arguments, click OK, and then run the program. You should now see Result of addition = 100 in the log window (see Figure 3-18).

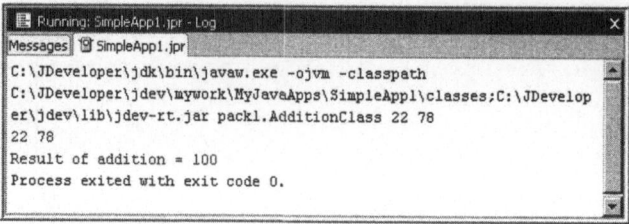

Figure 3-18. Log as displayed on successful execution

 NOTE *Note the line that states the classpath, JVM, and other details of this particular run. You could right-click anywhere in the log window to get a display offering copy, clear, close, and other useful options. With version 10g, you also have the option to wrap the text displayed in the log.*

Developing a Java UI

Once upon a time, in the days when Java revolved around applets, all books on Java were primarily dedicated to Java UI development. However, things have certainly changed, and UI creation with Java is no longer hot. JDeveloper does have some great UI-related features, but it is not really what the tool is about. So this section quickly gets into Abstract Windowing Toolkit (AWT) and Swing and references a couple of sample applications.

The Cricket World Cup was held this year in which India played quite well but lost in the finals to Australia. We will now have some fun and create a couple of cricket-related applications. For those not familiar with cricket, it is a game invented by the British and is the most popular sport in the Indian subcontinent. It is somewhat similar to baseball.

To create your first Swing application, the first step is of course to create a new project to hold the application. You do not need to create a new workspace all over again because you already have the one you created earlier.

The easiest approach to use in this case is to right-click the workspace name and choose New. Alternatively, you can choose File ➤ New. To use the option in the File menu, you need to have the workspace selected in the System Navigator.

In the dialog box that appears, choose General ➤ Projects. Here choose the Java Application Project option. This is more a case of grouping the two wizards for project and application creation to make it even easier to have an application up in minutes. After clicking OK, you should see the welcome screen for the wizard.

This isn't the most useful screen to have popping up every time, so you might as well uncheck the Show This Page Next Time option. After clicking Next, the screen shown in Figure 3-19 appears. This is the first step of the wizard.

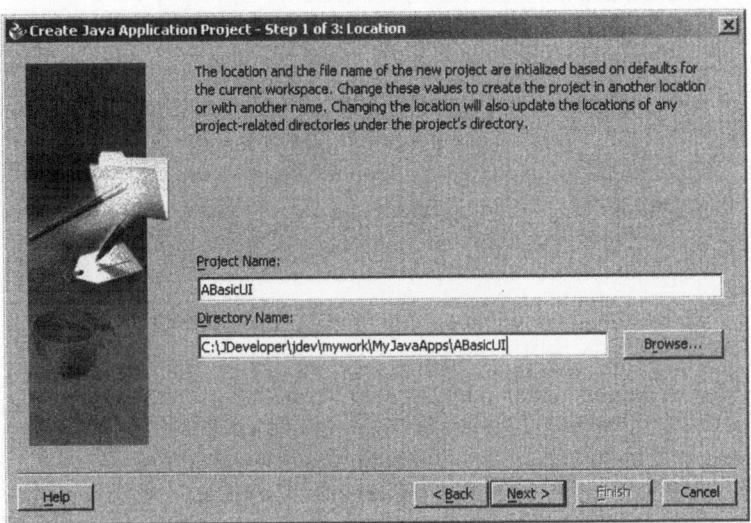

Figure 3-19. Setting the location of the project

Name the project *ABasicUI*. The directory name will change automatically. You could click the Help button to get more information about any options provided by the wizard. The Cancel button can get you out of the wizard at any stage, with no damage done.

NOTE *The project name and directory name do not need to be the same. I am using this convention only for convenience.*

Click Next to get to step 2, as shown in Figure 3-20. Here change the package name to *myui*. Note the path that JDeveloper will be using for the sources of the project and for the output.

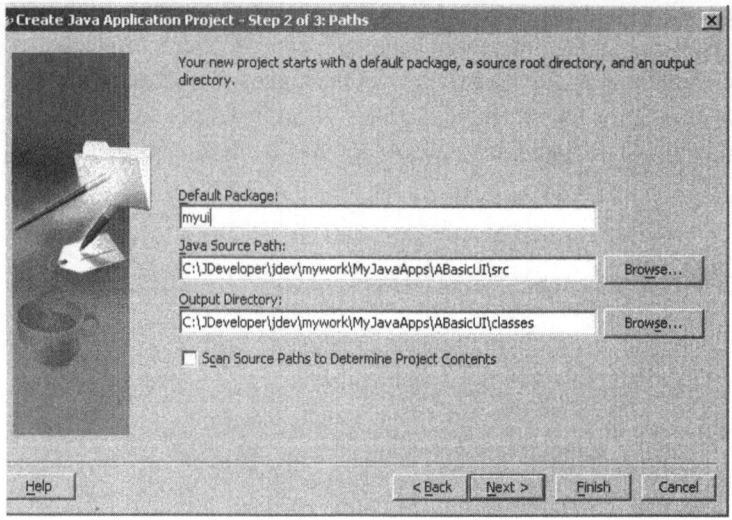

Figure 3-20. Setting the package name

Click Next. In step 3, as shown in Figure 3-21, you do not need to make any changes because you will not be using any of the libraries provided. However, you should look at the libraries available because these will play a big role as you go along. Libraries are a useful facility provided by JDeveloper. Using a library, you can manage, at a single place, the JAR files, the source path, the documentation path, and the other details for a particular component or API. Select any library you are familiar with, and click the Edit button. This makes it easier to understand what a library is and how you can put it to good use. Using the Manage Libraries tool (Tools ➤ Manage Libraries) is the easiest way to work with libraries.

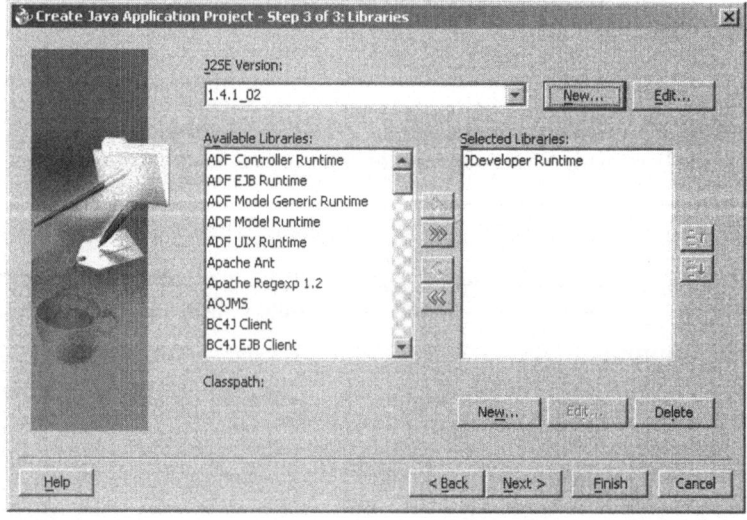

Figure 3-21. Specifying libraries for the application

Click Next. The screen that follows is just a completion screen. Clicking Finish here will fire up the Create Java Application dialog box, as shown in Figure 3-22. This wizard asks for specifics of the application to be created.

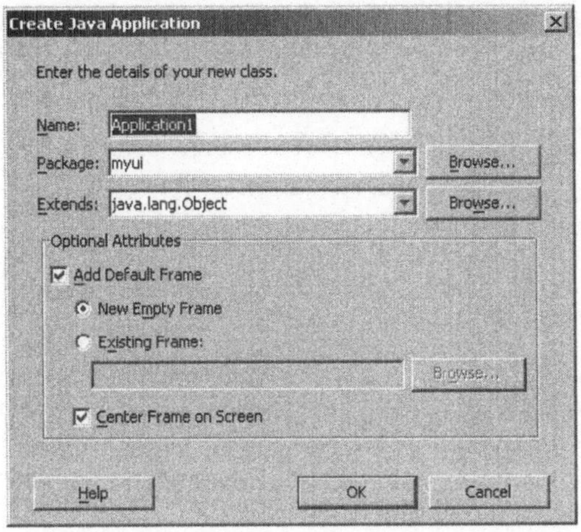

Figure 3-22. The Create Java Application dialog box

Do not modify any values or settings, and click OK. You will now be asked for details of the new class that will form part of the application you just created (see Figure 3-23). Specify the title as *Team Info Application*. Check all the options for creating a toolbar, menu bar, status bar, and About box. Although you will not be using most of these, I am selecting these primarily to familiarize you with the simplistic Microsoft Visual Basic–like creation procedure you have to follow. Click OK, and you are done.

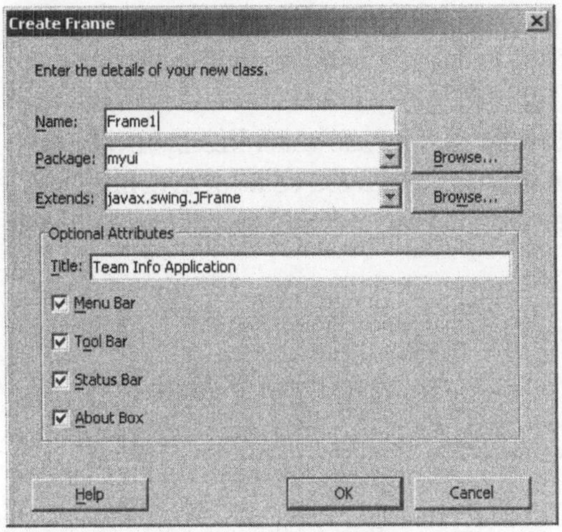

Figure 3-23. Creating a new frame

Now run the application and have a look at what you have managed to create in just a few seconds. As shown in Figure 3-24, you have an application before you, complete with images and an About dialog box. Pretty cool!

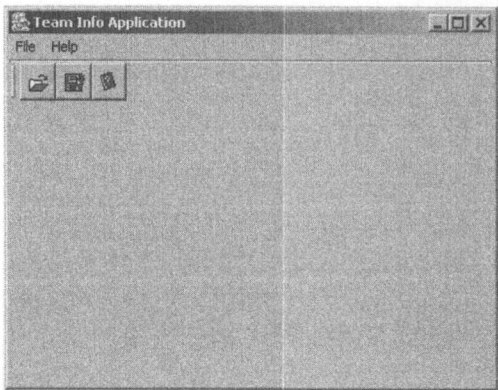

Figure 3-24. The GUI when running the application

JDeveloper should have created six files in the sources folder:

- **Application1.java**: The main application file that has the main method required to run the application.

- **Frame1.java**: This file has the code for the frame that is displayed on application startup.

- **Frame1_AboutBoxPanel1.java**: The frame that is displayed after choosing the About menu.

- **Image files**: Three image files for the images being used in the toolbar.

Before proceeding, you should look at all the code generated by JDeveloper. Unlike some other editors that might generate cluttered code, or in some cases even code you cannot modify, JDeveloper generates clean Java code that you can very well modify.

NOTE   *One aspect where JDeveloper wizards tend to slip is in the lack of proper commenting for the code that these wizards generate. Otherwise, the code is well organized and easily understandable. To add basic Javadoc comments for user-defined methods, simply click the method name in the Code Editor, right-click, and choose the Add Javadoc Comments option.*

Now that you have the base application ready, you will build on it to create a simple application.

The application consists of a drop-down list of all nations that participated in the Cricket World Cup. After choosing one of those listed, you will see the name of the captain of that side and some details about the team.

Java UI development has not always been something I have been fond of. All these components, events, and listeners can be rather perplexing to recall. The only way anyone could manage to remember them is if they intend to take an exam on them. Taking the Sun Certification for Java, for instance, forced me to remember all this. Unfortunately, that learning did not last long. So JDeveloper and other Java integrated development environments (IDEs) of its kind truly make life a lot easier.

Getting back to your application, you will try to do as much as possible while writing the minimum amount of code. Because Frame.java is really the core class for the application, you will begin by making changes to it. Open Frame.java in the Code Editor. You should find some basic window close functionality, UI look and feel, and similar things already taken care of. Now you will try out the fun part of UI development using JDeveloper, the UI Editor.

UI Editor

Instead of editing the code directly in the Code Editor, JDeveloper gives you an option that is a lot easier and effective. To use the UI Editor, simply select the UI tab at the bottom of the screen.

As you are working with Frame1.java, which does actually involve a UI, you should get a proper display of the frame in the UI Editor. Using the UI Editor for nonvisual classes such as Application1.java will display the flashing message "Non Visual Object."

Along with the UI Editor, try and organize the various windows to have a comfortable interface where the most useful pieces are displayed. In Figure 3-25, for instance, I have moved windows and resized them to get an interface with which I am comfortable. If any of the displayed windows is not being displayed, just choose the View option from the menu bar and select the component that is missing. The Property Inspector, the Constraints window, the Structure window, and so on all contribute to make the interface very intuitive.

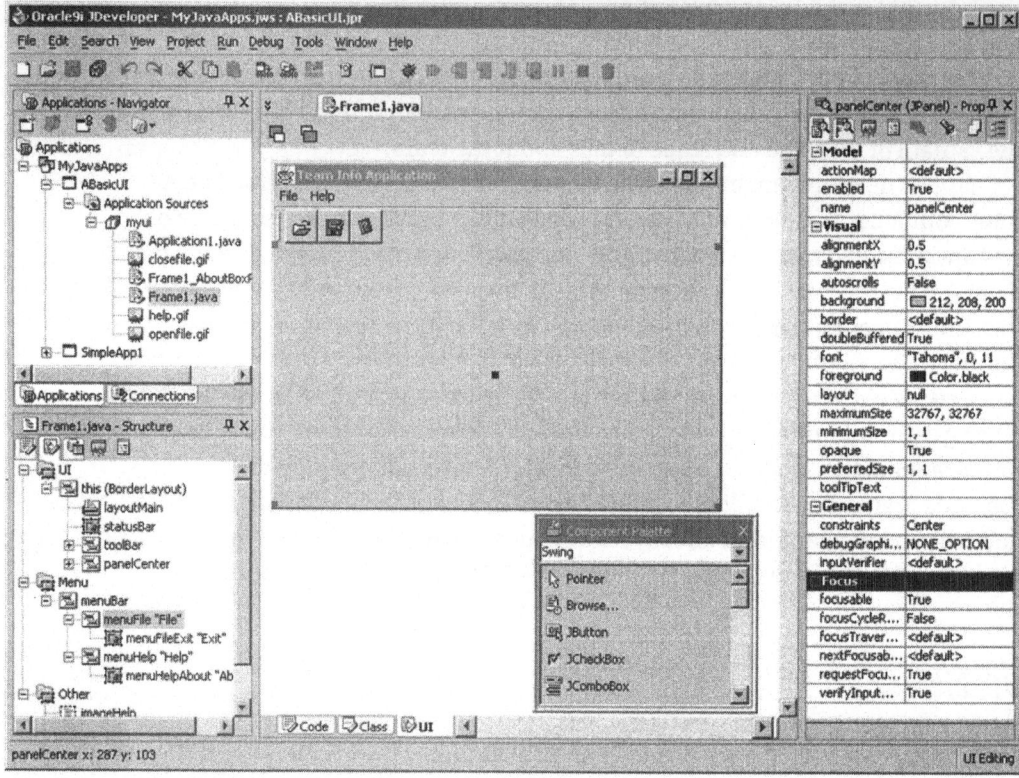

Figure 3-25. Organizing the UI Editor

The Property Inspector is an extremely useful offering of JDeveloper. The display could be alphabetically ordered or can even be properly categorized by clicking the Categories icon (see Figure 3-26).

Figure 3-26. The Categories icon

Another thing to note is that, as shown in Figure 3-27, clicking any of the properties in the inspector displays an explanation of what the property stands for at the bottom of the Property Inspector.

panelCenter (JPanel) - Property	X
⊞**Model**	
⊟**Visual**	
alignmentX	0.5
alignmentY	0.5
autoscrolls	False
background	▦ 212, 208, 200
border	<default>
doubleBuffered	True
font	"Tahoma", 0, 11
foreground	▦ Color.black
layout	null
maximumSize	32767, 32767
minimumSize	1, 1
opaque	True
preferredSize	1, 1
toolTipText	
⊞**General**	
⊞**Focus**	

The text to display in a tool tip.

Figure 3-27. Getting help in the Property Inspector

NOTE *Drag windows to get the positioning you find easiest to work with. As you drag, press the Ctrl key to prevent docking or press the Esc key to cancel. Fiddle with this feature. I had some fun creating strange interfaces.*

Creating the UI

To add any Swing component to the UI, the easiest way is to click the relevant component in the Component Palette window (see Figure 3-28). Then click the container into which you want to add that particular component. In this case, the container will be the panel named *panelCenter* that the wizard has created for you.

Another option to add components is to click the component you want to add and then click the container entry as displayed in the component tree in the Structure window. This option could be useful if you already have many panels and components and a cluttered UI to work with or if a component is not being displayed in the UI Editor.

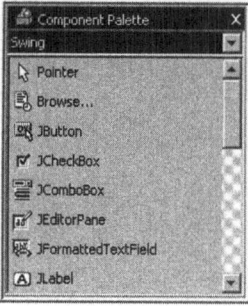

Figure 3-28. The Swing Component Palette

To add multiple instances of a component, hold down the Shift key when you select the component in the palette, and a new instance of that component will appear wherever you click in the UI Editor. To stop this barrage of components, click the Pointer as shown in Figure 3-29; it is the first one displayed in every Component Palette.

Figure 3-29. The Pointer icon

TIP *Once you get familiar with the components available and the icons used, just right-click the palette and select Icon View. In this view, just the icons for the components are displayed, and therefore a lot more fits into the window.*

Adding a Combo Box

First, you will add a combo box to hold the names of all the teams participating in the Cricket World Cup. Click the icon as shown in Figure 3-30 for JComboBox that is displayed in the Swing Component Palette.

Figure 3-30. The JComboBox icon

Second, in the Structure window, expand the components tree (see Figure 3-31). In the expanded listing that is displayed, click panelCenter. The new combo box should now be displayed; also, the Structure window should show it as being contained by panelCenter.

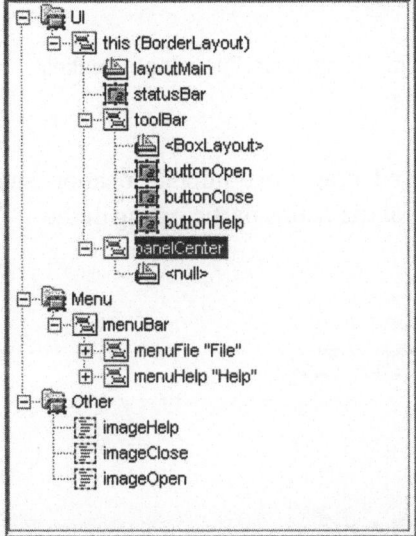

Figure 3-31. The Structure window

 NOTE *When selecting any component listed in the Structure window, the component gets selected in the display as well. You can put the Structure window to good use to understand what the component hierarchy is, which container contains what, and so on.*

Switch over to the Code Editor to look at the code that JDeveloper generated. A new member variable named *jComboBox1* is created, and the bounds for this component are set in the *jbInit* method.

For the UI Editor to work as expected, you need to follow a few guidelines:

- The Java file should be free of syntax errors.

- It must be a public class, and the filename should be the same as the class name.

- The class must have a default constructor.

- The *jbInit* method plays a key role in getting the editor to work properly.

- All UI controls can either be class members or local variables of the *jbInit* method.

- For the UI Editor and the Properties Inspector to reflect changes you make without having to run the application, these changes need to be included in the *jbInit* method.

- To reflect changes made in the Properties Inspector, JDeveloper makes changes to only the *jbInit* method code.

Now that the combo box is being displayed, drag it to a suitable location (see Figure 3-32). The next step is to add a listing of the teams participating in the World Cup.

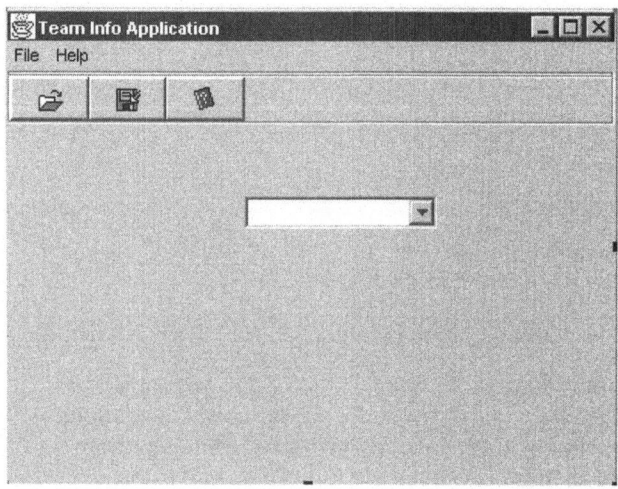

Figure 3-32. The frame after including the combo box

Because you want the additions you make to be displayed in the UI Editor, you will make changes to the *jbInit* method. Right after the line that adds the combo box to the panel—panelCenter.add(jComboBox1, null)—add the following piece of code:

```
jComboBox1.addItem("Select Country");
jComboBox1.addItem("India");
jComboBox1.addItem("Australia");
jComboBox1.addItem("South Africa");
jComboBox1.addItem("England");
jComboBox1.addItem("Pakistan");
jComboBox1.addItem("Canada");
```

Switch back to the UI Editor. You should now see the combo displaying *Select Country* as the selected value. Many other teams participated in the World Cup. I am restricting this application to six teams to maintain simplicity.

Labels and Textboxes

Next you will add some labels. To add a label, you follow a similar procedure to the one you used to add the combo box earlier.

Select the JLabel icon in the Swing Component Palette, and then click panelCenter that is listed in the component tree in the Structure window. You need one more label, so just repeat the procedure. You also have the option of selecting the label named *jLabel1* that you just created and copying/pasting it right there. JDeveloper will create a new label now with the name *jLabel2*. Keep pasting as many times as you want, and you will get many exact replicas of jLabel1. This feature is useful when you want multiple labels or, for that matter, any other component with the same height, width, and other attributes.

To change the text displayed in these labels, change the text property as displayed in the Property Inspector. I changed the text property for JLabel to *Country*, jLabel2 to *Captain Name*, and jLabel3 to *Odds*.

I also changed the foreground color for all labels to blue and the font to 13-point Arial (see Figure 3-33).

Figure 3-33. Changing the font

You do not need to make this change separately for each label. You can use the Shift or Ctrl key and then select with the mouse all the labels for which you want to modify a property. Then change the property details in the Property Inspector, and the changes will be applied across all the labels.

Now with all the labels in place, as shown in Figure 3-34, you will add a JTextField to display the captain's name and another to display the odds of the country winning the Cricket World Cup.

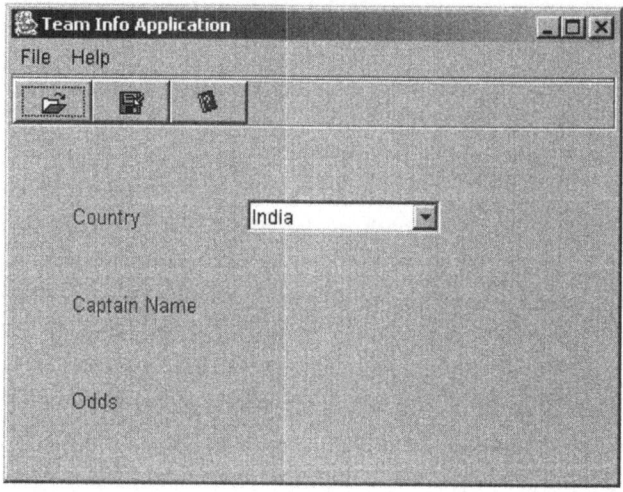

Figure 3-34. Basic application layout

The Status Bar

As yet, you have not used the status bar that the wizard created for you earlier. To access the properties of the status bar, in the Structure window, select the status-bar component. This is just another JLabel that has been placed in the SOUTH region of the content pane.

The content pane is adhering to a BorderLayout. To change this layout, select the entire frame as displayed in the UI Editor and modify the layout property as displayed in the Property Inspector. I will stick with BorderLayout because it serves the current task pretty well.

As for the status bar, even when selecting statusbar in the Structure window, nothing seems to get selected in the UI Editor. This is because you have no text there, and therefore the status bar seems to occupy no space on the UI. So keeping statusbar selected in the Structure window, add the value *** to the text property in the Property Inspector. Now the status bar should be visible, displaying the content ***.

Adding Some Functionality

The basic layout is now more or less done, as shown in Figure 3-35. So you will now add some functionality to it.

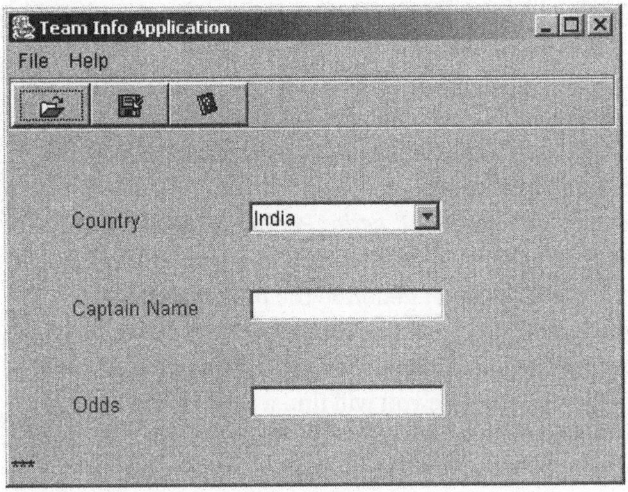

Figure 3-35. The application frame

You will now change the message in the status bar dynamically, based on which country is selected in the combo box. To achieve this, you will listen for the actionPerformed event for the combo box. Event handling is one of the relatively tougher aspects of Java, and I for one certainly took my time to understand how the thing worked and how it is to be used.

However, with JDeveloper, you do not really need to understand the intricacies of the event delegation model while creating simple applications of the kind you are creating currently.

The easiest way to listen to the actionPerformed event of the combo box and perform tasks on its occurrence is to double-click the combo box in the UI Editor. JDeveloper will create an empty method named *jComboBox1_actionPerformed* and will also add code so that when the event triggers, this method gets called.

The following is the event delegation code that JDeveloper adds:

```
jComboBox1.addActionListener(new ActionListener()
    {
        public void actionPerformed(ActionEvent e)
        {
            jComboBox1_actionPerformed(e);
        }
    });
```

Here an anonymous inner class that implements the ActionListener interface is created. This class provides implementation for the abstract actionPerformed method in the ActionListener interface. This method delegates the event handling to the *jComboBox1_actionPerformed* method.

JDeveloper provides event handling for other components and events along very similar lines to this. So even if users do not understand how exactly events are being delegated, as long as they provide proper implementation to the delegated method, their purpose should be served.

If you do not find the name *jComboBox1_actionPerformed* explanatory or it does not conform to the coding conventions you use, you have the option to name the method and yet have JDeveloper generate the previous code.

Select the combo box jComboBox1 in the UI Editor. Next, in the Property Inspector choose the Events tab to get a listing of events associated with that component, as shown in Figure 3-36. Here you will find a list of events associated with the selected component. Because you have already gotten JDeveloper to create the *jComboBox1_actionPerformed* method, the method name is displayed against the property actionPerformed.

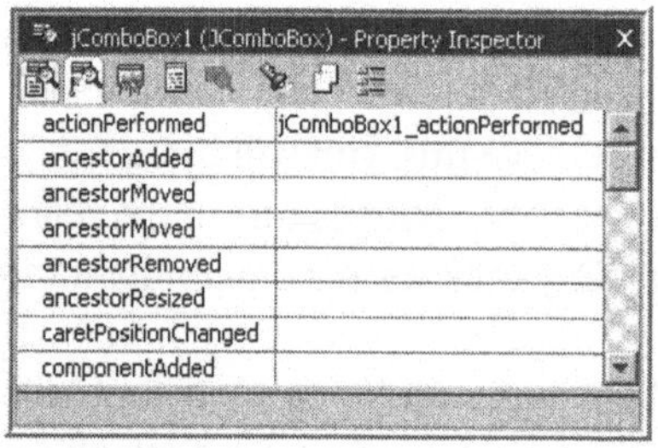

Figure 3-36. Property Inspector (events)

A great feature JDeveloper provides is that the code for this event handling will be modified as many times as you change the name. This is true until you do not provide the implementation for the method. This is good because it ensures that a change of name in the Property Inspector does not accidentally end up deleting all the implementation code you have written.

You will stick with the name that JDeveloper had given to the event handling method and now provide some implementation code for it.

The jComboBox1_actionPerformed method will be called every time an action is performed on the combo box. You trap this event, check what the selected value is, and accordingly modify the status bar text.

Double-click jComboBox1 in the UI Editor, and add the following code to the method *jComboBox1_actionPerformed*:

```java
private void jComboBox1_actionPerformed(ActionEvent e)
{
    String strSelItem= jComboBox1.getSelectedItem().toString();
```

```java
if(strSelItem.equalsIgnoreCase("India"))
{
    statusBar.setText(
        "***Winners in 1983, India have a good chance this time round");
    jTextField1.setText("Saurav Ganguly");
    jTextField2.setText("13 / 2");
}
else if(strSelItem.equalsIgnoreCase("Australia"))
{
    statusBar.setText(
        "*** Australia has won the cup twice before, in 1987 and 1999");
    jTextField1.setText("Ricky Ponting");
    jTextField2.setText("11 / 8");
}
else if(strSelItem.equalsIgnoreCase("England"))
{

    statusBar.setText(
        "*** England has never won the cup. Maybe this time...");
    jTextField1.setText("Naseer Hussain");
    jTextField2.setText("25 / 1");
}
else if(strSelItem.equalsIgnoreCase("South Africa"))
{
    statusBar.setText(
        "*** Have the home advantage. This could be their year");
    jTextField1.setText("Shawn Polock");
    jTextField2.setText("11 / 4");
}
else if(strSelItem.equalsIgnoreCase("Pakistan"))
{
    statusBar.setText(
        "*** As unpredictable as ever. They were champions in 1992");
    jTextField1.setText("Waqar Younis");
    jTextField2.setText("12 / 1");
}
else if(strSelItem.equalsIgnoreCase("Canada"))
{
    statusBar.setText(
        "*** Very new to international cricket. Their time will come");
    jTextField1.setText("-------");
    jTextField2.setText("5000 / 1");
}
else if(strSelItem.equalsIgnoreCase("Select Country"))
```

```
        {
            statusBar.setText("***");
            jTextField1.setText("");
            jTextField2.setText("");
        }
    }
```

Based on the selection in the UI Editor, you update the text in the label named *statusbar*. You also update the text displayed in the text fields for the captain's name and the odds for that team.

You change the editable and enabled properties for both the text fields to *false* because you want the contents to appear grayed out so that the user is not able to change the contents of the text fields.

Menu Management

One feature of Microsoft Visual Basic that I have always been rather fond of is the ease with which you can work with menus. JDeveloper has managed to get a similar mix of functionality and simplicity that is pretty impressive.

The wizard created the menu bar for you earlier, so now you will tamper with it and make a few changes. The first rule I learned while working with menus was to stick to the Structure window. All my attempts to click and right-click the menu in the UI Editor got me nowhere. However, working with the menu tree in the Structure window is a breeze. You can see the menu tree as displayed in the Structure window at the bottom left of Figure 3-25.

Select menuBar in the Structure window's menu listing. Expanding this node reveals two levels of child nodes. On double clicking any of these nodes, the UI Editor will change and display only the menu bar and options related to it (see Figure 3-37).

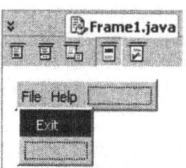

Figure 3-37. Managing menus

On selecting the JMenuItem File ➤ Exit or Help ➤ About, a set of icons appear at the top of the UI Editor. These icons can be used to insert a menu item, insert a separator or submenu, disable a menu item, and make an item checkable. These options are also available when right-clicking any menu item. To change the text of a menu item, all it takes is a double-click to make the menu item text editable.

The Property Inspector is also useful for quickly modifying a few properties for the menus and menu items. Because the existing menu does serve the purpose of the simple application, you will just change the foreground color property for the menu item's File and Exit to Color.Blue.

About Panel

After selecting Help ➤ About, a new panel meant to display some information about the application will pop up. Look at the following helpAbout_ActionPerformed method that provides implementation to handle any action performed on the About menu item:

```
void helpAbout_ActionPerformed(ActionEvent e)
{
  JOptionPane.showMessageDialog(this, new Frame1_AboutBoxPanel1()
    , "About", JOptionPane.PLAIN_MESSAGE);
}
```

This method pops up a JOptionPane using Frame1_AboutBoxPanel1. To edit this frame that pops up, you now need to edit Frame1_AboutBoxPanel1.java. This file is also located in the same directory, which you can easily find in the System Navigator.

Open the file in the UI Editor. GridBagLayout is used to display the information about the application in a proper tabular format. The Constraints window that as yet has not played much of a part now comes into its own. In Figure 3-38, I have arranged my on-screen widgets to try to make the best use of the display space available. You can display the Constraints window using View ➤ Constraints.

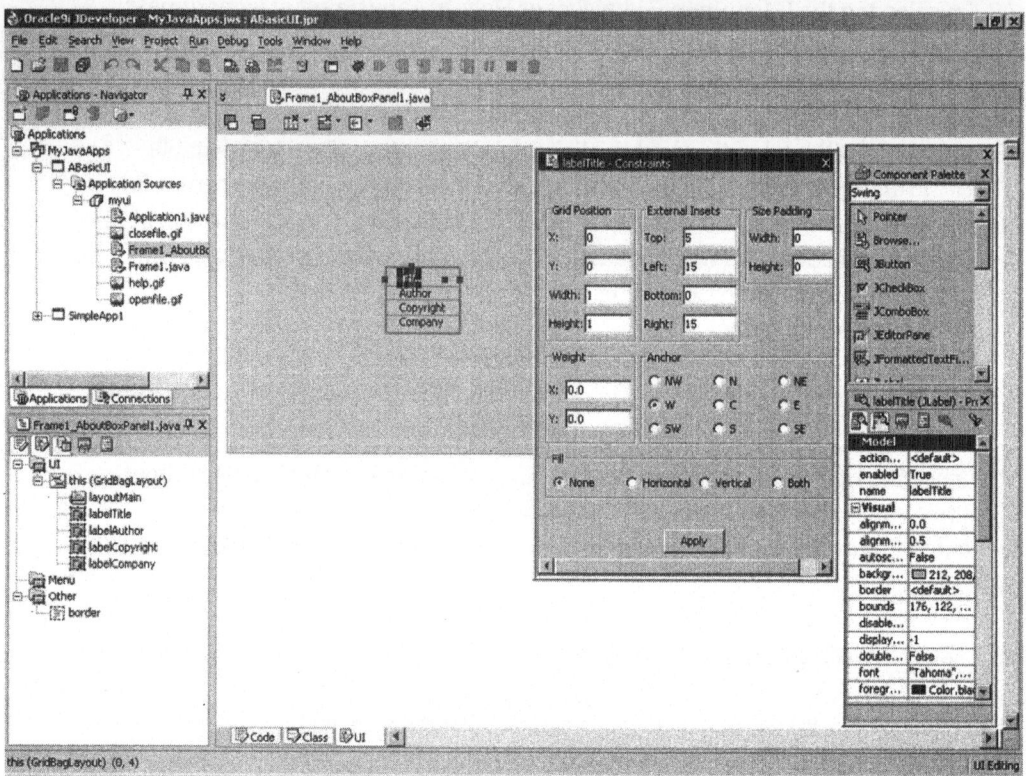

Figure 3-38. Working with the GridBagLayout

I have always found the GridBagLayout to be a powerful yet rather difficult layout to work with. However, with the Constraints window, the toolbar that appears at the top (see Figure 3-39) and the options available when right-clicking any cell in the grid do not require you to even touch the code.

Figure 3-39. The GridBagLayout toolbar

What you will do is to swap the title and the company name displayed in the About panel so that the company name now appears first and the title last. Select the first cell of the grid that displays *Title*. Here, pay attention to the Grid Position and External Insets options as displayed in the Constraints window. Because it is a single-column grid and the row and column count begins with zero, the Grid Position> X and Grid Position> Y options both display zero. Change the Grid Position> Y value to 3, and click Apply. Next, select the Company cell that is barely visible in the grid because the Title cell now overlaps the Company cell. You can always select the exact component by using the tree display in the Structure window. For this selection, the Grid Position> Y now displays the value 3. Change this to zero. The swap is done. You adjust the insets for both and enter the relevant text (see Figure 3-40). If even this procedure is a little too tedious for you, you can always drag and drop cells to the desired location.

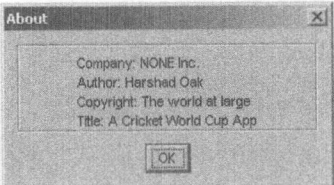

Figure 3-40. The About box

Because this application will not be using the toolbar, you can just select it and delete it. JDeveloper handled clearing most of the code for the toolbar. You have to remove the image files separately.

Now run the application using any of the run alternatives mentioned earlier. The application should be up and running, dishing out cricket team details as shown in Figure 3-41.

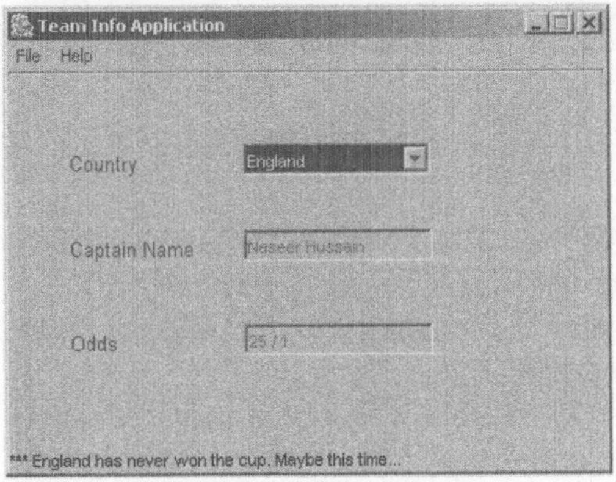

Figure 3-41. The running application

Maximize the application window. Yikes! Not a pretty sight, eh? Fix this by setting the resizable property for Frame1 to *false*. This property is listed in the Property Inspector for that frame.

Exploring Applet Capabilities

In the previous example you looked at a frame, panel, dialog box, and so on, all of which were already part of an existing application created by the wizard for you. However, creating these individually is also possible (see Figure 3-42).

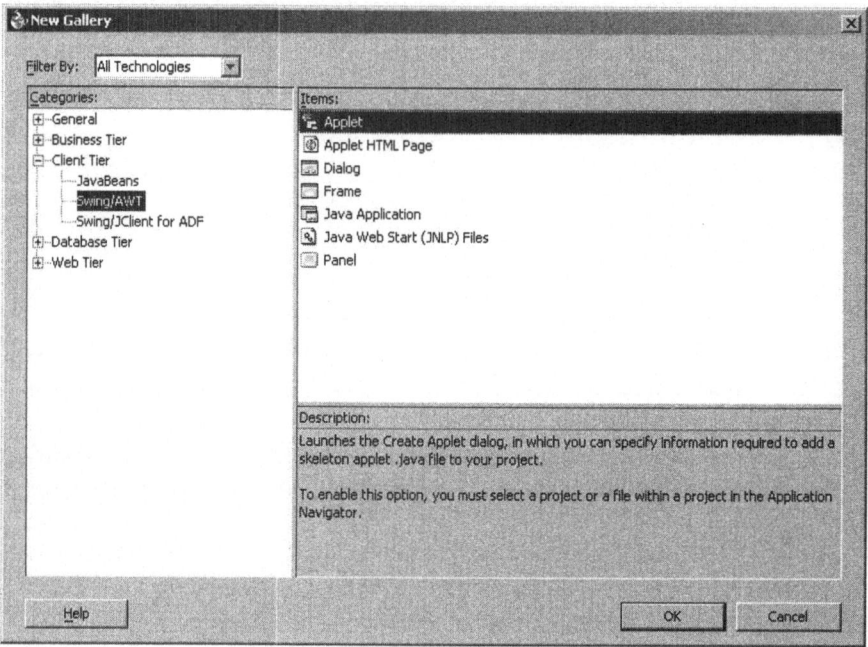

Figure 3-42. The New Gallery's Swing/AWT alternatives

Apart from creating Swing and AWT applications in a jiffy, JDeveloper can also do a great job of creating applets. JDeveloper can add a main method so that running the applet as an application becomes possible. It can also generate code for some of the basic applet methods.

The option to create a new applet HTML page is also a comprehensive offering. The wizard provides you with the option to specify a template for the HTML page, as shown in Figure 3-43. You can also specify the code and codebase for your applet.

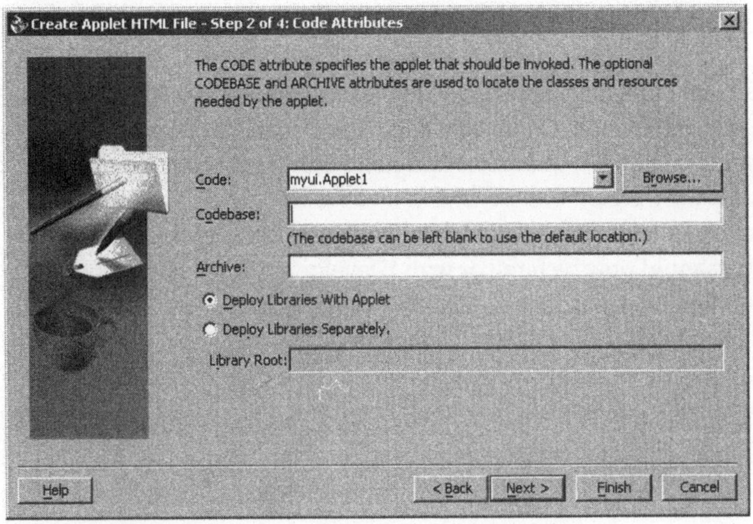

Figure 3-43. Create Applet HTML File Wizard, step 2

As shown in Figure 3-44, the wizard also provides a step where you could specify HTML tag attributes to control how the applet would be rendered on the screen. You could also specify the parameters that the applet takes and create a deployment profile to enable deployment of the applet as a Web application.

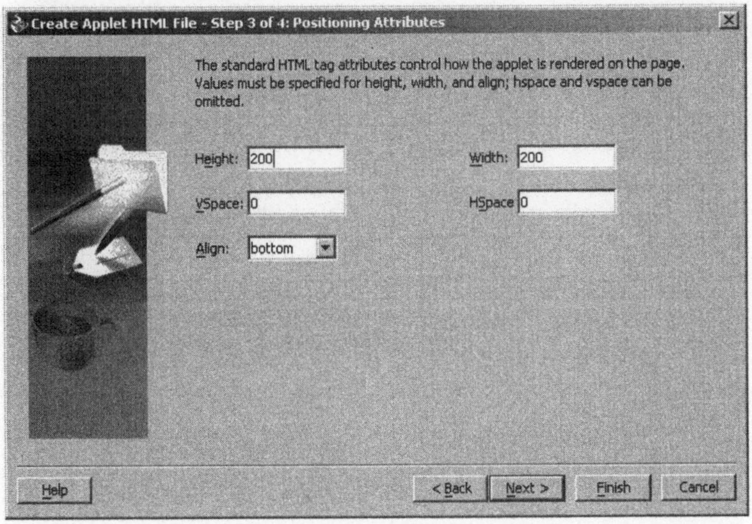

Figure 3-44. Create Applet HTML File Wizard, step 3

Summary

In this chapter, you created a Java application and a Java Swing application. Although the applications were rather simple, I covered all the features of JDeveloper that you should be aware of and that might come in handy in the chapters to follow.

This completes the quick startup to Java and some basic Java UI using JDeveloper. You should now be familiar with JDeveloper and the JDeveloper way of working with Java. As you move to J2EE and other cool things in the chapters to follow, this understanding of JDeveloper will certainly help.

CHAPTER 4

UML Modeling

In the earlier chapters, you got a feel of JDeveloper and tried your hand at creating a basic Java application and a couple of Java user interface (UI) applications. In this chapter, you will look at Unified Modeling Language (UML) and use the UML modeling features that JDeveloper offers. Most Java projects these days use UML, and UML modeling capability is a great feature to have in an integrated development environment (IDE); it eliminates the need for another application to care for the modeling needs.

Unified Modeling Language

UML is the most prevalent modeling language today and is used along with Object Oriented Analysis and Design (OOAD) methods to depict the flow and various other aspects of systems that need to be easily understood. Even after the application is developed, UML diagrams serve as a quick reference and an easy-to-use guide to the application developed. This can be a great help during the maintenance phase of any application.

For detailed coverage of UML, I recommend the book *UML Distilled: A Brief Guide to the Standard Object Modeling Language* by Martin Fowler (Addison-Wesley, Third Edition: 2003). This is a concise and to-the-point book that quickly gets you familiar with the concept and usage of UML. If you have been part of Java 2 Enterprise Edition (J2EE) projects, you have probably encountered some, if not all, aspects of UML.

JDeveloper does not support all the features of UML but only a subset of it. JDeveloper as of version 10*g* supports use case diagrams, class diagrams, and activity diagrams. What this means is that you do not need a separate tool for UML diagramming. JDeveloper's support for use case diagrams, class diagrams, and activity diagrams is good enough for most projects. An important plus for using a tool that has both UML and Java capabilities is that the tool can ensure that the Java code and the UML diagrams stay in sync. Often it happens that the UML diagrams you created using a UML tool depict something different from what the Java code that was actually written does. Because you are using one less tool, the cost saving can also be significant.

For UML to be of any assistance to you, the most important thing is to be able to do your own thing. Two different people consistently will draw diagrams that are different. So just accept this fact and move on. What is important is that the diagrams should simply and visually depict useful information about the system.

You will now look at what use case diagrams, class diagrams, and activity diagrams are and then explore JDeveloper's diagramming capabilities.

Use Case Diagrams

A *use case diagram* shows the actors that interact with a system and the use cases that these actors are involved in. I need to define what I mean by a *use case* and an *actor*, for this definition to make any sense:

> **Use case**: *Use* is the most important aspect of a use case. A use case states what the use of a system is to a particular actor. Because there can be more than one flow of events involved in deriving this use, these flows are depicted as basic and alternate flow of events. If there are any preconditions that need to be fulfilled before the use can be derived, these are also stated.

> **Actor**: An actor is an external entity to the system and can be human or nonhuman. It can be a person or even another system that is interacting with the system in question.

Unlike some other UML tools, use cases generally also have a lot of text to add more value to the diagram. If your requirement is straightforward enough and the diagram does convey all you need, you do not need to take the trouble of writing the text.

Use cases suffer from a problem that is present in many UML tools: huge amounts of jargon being thrown at you. On first glance, use cases might seem harmless enough, but the more books you refer to on the subject, the more it seems to get confusing. What one book refers to as a *use case* suddenly becomes a *scenario;* and a third reference might call it a *use case scenario.* What works for me is to not care about the jargon. As long as I have a diagram before me that conveys useful information to me as well as anybody else looking at it, I am happy.

Use cases can suffer from too little as well as too much. If you have too little, it does not convey all that should be part of a requirements document. If you have too much, nobody ever reads it. Use cases should not drill down to the lowest level of use that the system can be to an actor. To identify a use case, just ask yourself the question, "What use will the system be to an actor to enable him to achieve a desired goal?"

The book *Writing Effective Use Cases* by Alistair Cockburn (Addison-Wesley, 2000) defines three degrees of use cases:

- **Brief**: Just a few sentences or a paragraph

- **Casual**: A few paragraphs of text

- **Fully dressed**: A long and detailed template talking even of open issues, frequency of occurrence, performance constraints, and so on

Based on the individual case you are covering, you can decide which one to use. A combination of casual and fully dressed cases is often used. In such situations, fully dressed cases are used only where detailed coverage of a requirement is expected.

JDeveloper supports casual and fully dressed use cases. Now you will look at an example where you create a use case diagram for a system at a small bookstore.

The system for which you will be drawing a use case is meant to be a basic one, where the system enables an administrative user at a bookstore to check if a certain book is available and to process an order for a book. Also, an external reports system is using data from this system to generate its reports.

To begin, you will create a new project within the workspace: MyJavaApps that you created in Chapter 3. You can find the option to create an empty project using General ➤ Projects in the New Gallery. Name the project *BookStoreUseCase*. To create a new use case diagram for this project, browse to the General ➤ UML Diagrams section in the New Gallery. Here, select the option UML Use Case Diagram, and click OK. In the next dialog box, as shown in Figure 4-1, name the package *com.jdevbook.chap4* and name the diagram *BookStore System*.

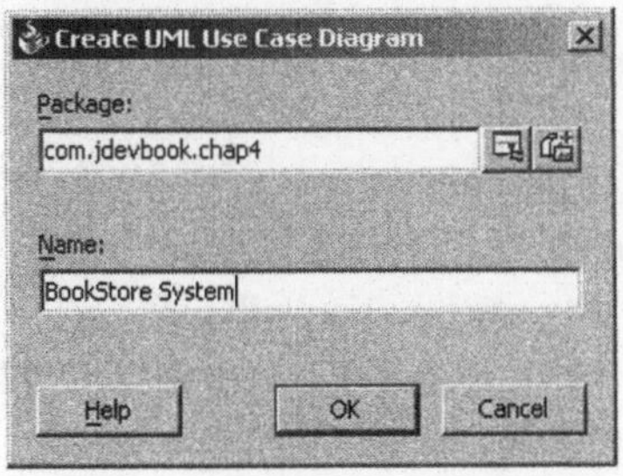

Figure 4-1. Creating a UML Use Case diagram

You should now have a blank display and the UML Use Case Component Palette displayed, as shown in Figure 4-2, which lists all the elements of a use case diagram that you might require.

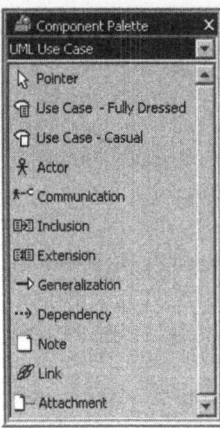

Figure 4-2. UML Use Case Component Palette

Before you get down to drawing the use case, I will quickly describe the various relationships that can be depicted in a use case diagram:

- **Inclusion**: An *include* relationship means that a certain use case will also include the behavior of the other use case that is being included.

- **Extension**: An *extension* is used where one use case extends behavior of another use case.

- **Generalization**: A *generalization* depicts specialization among use cases.

- **Communication**: A *communication* relationship depicts communication of an actor in a use case.

There are just two actors for this example: the administrative user and the reporting system that retrieves information from this system. You will just plot these two actors on the diagram. Simply click the Actor option in the palette, and then click anywhere in the diagram to insert an actor. To edit the name of an actor, just click the name currently displayed to make it editable.

Once you have plotted the actors on the diagram, you will define the use cases for the actors. The use cases for the administrative user are Check Book Availability and Process Book Order. The use case for the reporting system is Get Order Details. You will use the Use Case Casual option for these use cases. The casual and the fully dressed use cases both appear the same except you have to provide a lot more information for the fully dressed use case.

Next depict the communication between the actors and the use cases using the communication component on the UML Use Case Component Palette. You can draw lines anywhere on the diagram, and can easily extend and reduce the communication lines.

 TIP   *If the display you have created is not proper visually, try using the Optimize Shape Height and Lay Out Shapes options when right-clicking any element or a set of elements. You can also access these options from the Model menu.*

Once you get to diagram as shown in Figure 4-3, the next step is to add details and descriptions for the use cases.

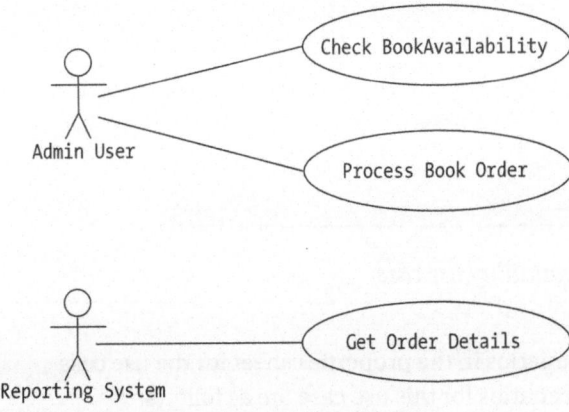

Figure 4-3. Bookstore use case diagram

Double-click the Check Book Availability use case, or right-click and select the Properties option to display the screen shown in Figure 4-4. Although some segments in this display are populated automatically, others need to be manually filled.

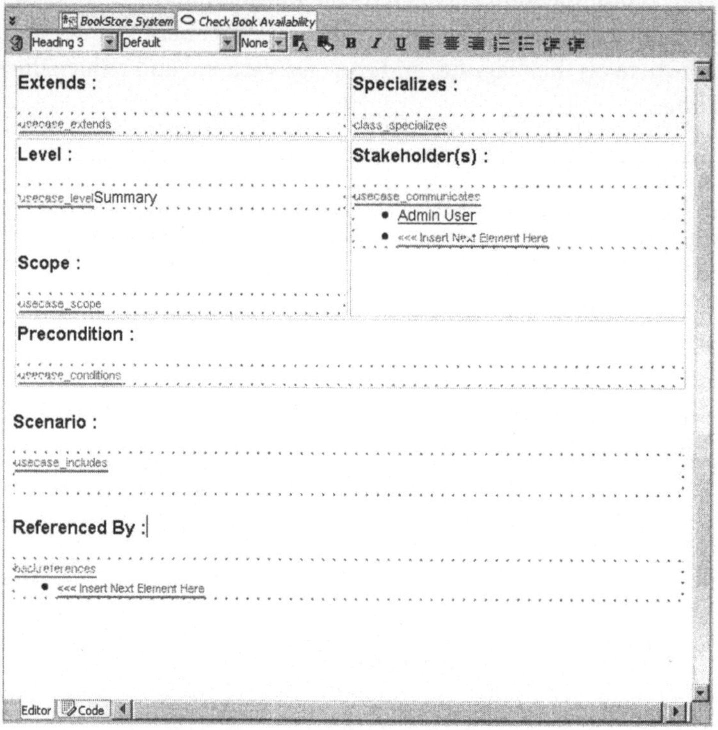

Figure 4-4. The Check Book Availablity use case

You will now define the scenarios in the properties sheet for the use case Check Book Availability. The scenarios for this use case are as follows:

Main Success Scenario:

1.   The user queries based on a book name.

2.   The book is available, and the details are fetched.

Alternate Scenario:

1.   The user queries based on a book name.

2.   The book is not available, and an appropriate message displays.

A precondition that can be stated in the use case would be that the system is running properly. Select the Code tab to see the Extensible Markup Language (XML) that is being created to represent the details of the use case. Changes made to the code directly are reflected in the editor. You will not be changing any of the other properties for the use case. However, based on individual cases, these properties can be used to create detailed use cases.

NOTE *The listing in the Applications Navigator is updated as you keep adding or removing elements from the use case diagram.*

You can double-click the actors, or you can right-click and choose Properties to provide more details about the actors.

NOTE *Use case diagramming is a recent addition to JDeveloper's feature list, and although it does its tasks well, it still does not have a refined feel like some of the other tools.*

You will now look at another popular UML tool, the class diagrams.

Class Diagrams

The class diagram plays a key role in object-oriented system design. Object-oriented design involves identifying the various objects that play a part in the system. Class diagrams depict these objects, their attributes, their operations, and their relationships with other objects in the system.

Class diagrams are used quite widely in projects, and although the usage does not appear to be consistent across people and organizations, the basics stay the same. If you have come from the entity relationship diagram (ERD) way of identifying entities and their relationships, understanding the difference between an ERD and a class diagram can be difficult at times. My way of going about it has been to keep telling myself to keep away from the relational database management system (RDBMS) kind of thought and not think of databases, tables, or relationships between tables and instead think about objects that play a part in the system. This is easier said than done because for simple systems, the ERD would often look similar to what a class diagram depicts.

Class diagrams can be used as a diagrammatic representation of objects, their composition, their capabilities, and their relationships. This is done using distinct notations to depict object-oriented concepts such as inheritance, aggregation, and composition.

Class Diagram Elements

You will now look at some of the key concepts for understanding and using class diagrams.

Generalization

Generalization is where you move from a more general concept to more specific elements. For example, a tree is a general term, and a mango tree, banyan tree, or a pine tree is a more specific example of a tree. So if you generalize the various types of trees, you will get a common general concept of just a tree. What happens in generalization is that attributes and operations specific to a certain type are lost and what remains are just the things common to all types. In the Java context, generalization is depicted using the extends keyword.

If you take the example of doctors, they can be classified as dentists, psychiatrists, neurosurgeons, and so on. If you generalize, you get to the concept of just a doctor. If represented using Java, then the Java classes for the specific types of doctors will all extend the general class Doctor.

If you look at things the other way round, it can be termed as *specialization*, where you move from the general concept of a doctor to more specialized cases that have all the basic features of a doctor but also have some specialized attributes and are capable of performing specialized operations.

Realization

Realization is where a Java class implements a Java interface. If you take a Java input/output example, all objects that you intend to serialize and maybe write out to a file need to implement the java.io.Serializable interface. What this implementation conveys is that the class implementing the interface is suitable for being serialized.

TIP *By convention, interface names end with* able—*for example, Serializable, Runnable, and so on. In other words, all classes implementing that interface are* able *to do what is specified in the interface.*

Dependency

A *dependency* relationship only says that another class depends on this class, and so if a change is made to this class, the other class will also be affected. For example, say you have a method in a DateHelper class that formats strings in the format mm/dd/yy to dd/mm/yy. If another class is using that method to format strings, there is a dependency on the DateHelper class, and so any change to this formatting logic will affect the dependent class.

You will now create a simple class diagram with JDeveloper to understand the concept of class diagrams.

A Class Diagram Example

You will now create a simple class diagram using an easily understood example about automobiles. First up, using the steps shown in the previous chapter, create a new workspace and project. For this example, use the workspace MyJavaApps you created in an earlier chapter and use the Add New Empty Project option that JDeveloper provides to create a new project named *ClasDiagSample* within that workspace.

Creating a New Class

For this project, select the Class Diagram option in the New dialog box, as displayed in Figure 4-5.

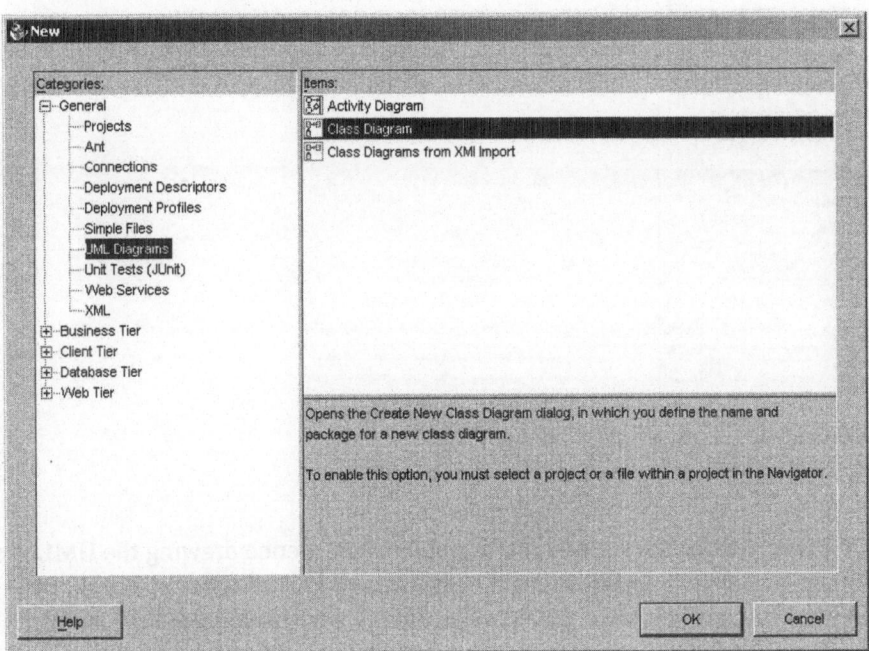

Figure 4-5. The Class Diagram option

In the Create Java Class Diagram dialog box, name the package *com.jdevbook.chap4* and the class diagram *AutomobileClassDiag* and then select OK (see Figure 4-6).

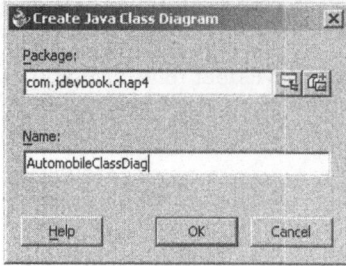

Figure 4-6. Creating a new class diagram

A blank window will now be displayed along with the Component Palette. The Component Palette has Business Components, Database, EJB, Java, UML Class, UML Use Case, and Web Service options. If not already selected, select the Java option in the drop-down list to display the Java Component Palette (see Figure 4-7).

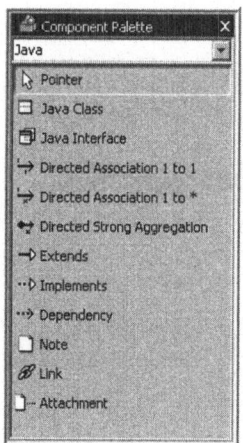

Figure 4-7. Java Component Palette

Now you have your canvas ready and can commence drawing the UML diagram. The class diagram you will be drawing depicts a relationship that is commonly taught as part of OOAD training—an example about vehicles and specific types of vehicles.

This class diagram depicts the relationships among different vehicles, the operations they perform, and the attributes of the different types of vehicles. If you begin at the top of the heap, consider a vehicle. Cars, buses, and trucks, if generalized, can all be termed as *vehicles*. However, because there is nothing on the road that is just a vehicle, what exists are specific instances of vehicles that you might refer to as, say, a Honda Accord or a Ford Escort. So if you own a Honda Accord, it "is a" car as well as a vehicle. So Vehicle is the top-level class for this hierarchy; add the Vehicle class to the class diagram.

Because there is nothing that is just a vehicle, this class is incomplete and hence abstract, and specific implementations such as a Honda Accord or a Ford Escort are not abstract. With reference to the generalization concept you saw earlier, what you are doing is that you generalize many kinds of cars to just a car and you generalize many kinds of vehicles to just a vehicle.

To add the Vehicle class, just click the Java Class option listed in the Java Component Palette and then click anywhere in the blank modeling window. A new class with the name *JavaClass1* will now be introduced in the diagram. Note that the corresponding Java file will be automatically created and is listed in the source tree in the System Navigator.

TIP *To add multiple classes, hold down the Shift key when you click the element in the Component Palette and then click repeatedly in the modeling window. This tip also works for other elements of the Component Palette.*

Now you need to change a few properties to create the abstract class Vehicle. To change the properties for a class, you can directly write into the class as displayed in the diagram. The other option is to double-click the class to display the underlying Java code. You can either manually edit the Java code or use the Class Editor you used in Chapter 3 to add and remove attributes and methods. These changes will automatically be reflected in the class diagram. If you are aware of UML conventions, the easiest way is to directly write into the class as displayed in the diagram. To drag the class to a specific location in the class diagram, you can use the handle at the top-left corner of the class to drag it.

You will first rename the JavaClass1 class to *Vehicle*. Click the name displayed in the diagram, change it to *Vehicle*, and press Enter. Because JDeveloper has a capability to keep the class diagram and the code in sync, such changes to the class involve some refactoring work on part of JDeveloper.

NOTE *The word* refactoring *in the extreme programming context suggests that some improvements are made to the code. However, the JDeveloper usage of the word is just related to modifying the associated Java code. These do not have to be improvements to the code.*

In this process, you might encounter a pop-up window asking if the Update Imports property should be set, if so select Yes. Voilà! Your class has been renamed. To make the Vehicle class abstract, you need to edit the code. Just add the word *abstract* to the class definition. The diagram will get automatically updated, and the class name will display in italics.

The icons at the bottom right of the modeler window, as shown in Figure 4-8, provide view options that could come in handy, particularly when your class diagrams get complex and messy. Try these out, and you will soon get the hang of when and where to use them.

JDeveloper provides many options that enable you to get a proper display and layout of elements in a diagram. When selecting a single element and then right-clicking, you will encounter Optimize Shape Height, Layout Images, and other options. When selecting multiple elements and then right-clicking, two more useful options of Align and Distribute are also offered. Because class diagrams having many classes can appear to be a grand mess at times, these tools can be a big help to make class diagrams easier to understand.

Figure 4-8. Class diagram viewing options

Adding Attributes

You will now introduce attributes into the Vehicle class you created. The attributes of the class have to be attributes that would exist across all vehicles, and the operations are those that can be performed by all vehicles. A couple of attributes that are present in all vehicles are color and registration code. So you will put these two attributes into the Vehicle class.

The class displayed in the diagram is split into the following four rows:

- Class details

- Attributes

- Methods

- Inner classes

To add new attributes, select the second row that lists the attributes of the class. Add these two lines:

```
# color : String
# regcode : String
```

You have now defined two protected String attributes.

NOTE   *In the Visibility drop-down list, the various symbols denote the visibility of the attribute. These symbols are what are actually shown in the diagram, so remembering what they signify is important. The paragraph mark is Package, the hyphen is Private, the pound sign (#) is Protected, and the plus sign stands for Public visibility.*

CAUTION   *If you check the Vehicle.java file, you will find that the two new attributes are now reflected in the Java code. Do not forget to save your changes when you close the code window because if you do not, JDeveloper goes back to the Java code version before you added the new attributes. Because JDeveloper then synchronizes the class diagram with the code, even the attributes in the class diagram are lost.*

Adding Operations

All vehicles are supposed to move. Thus, you can take this as a basic operation that will be present in all vehicles. In other words, the move operation should be present in the Vehicle class. However, the way the vehicle will move might change; for example, a ship would not move in the same fashion as a bus. Providing an implementation for the move operation in the Vehicle class would not make sense. Instead, the move operation should be an abstract method that all concrete subclasses have to implement. Remember that a subclass is *concrete* only if it provides implementation to all the abstract methods in the superclass. If it does not, the subclass also has to be declared abstract.

An easy way to add operations is to click in the third row of the class in the class diagram and just write the details for that operation in a format that JDeveloper understands. The operation will be automatically created. However, for setting some properties of the attribute or operation, you might need to edit the Java code.

So to add a new stop operation, which again is something that all vehicles possess, and the move operation, you need to write the following into the operations row of the class displayed in the class diagram:

```
# move (): void
# stop (): void
```

You have thus defined two protected operations that return void. To make these methods abstract, edit the code and add the word *abstract*. The method signature would now be as follows:

```
protected abstract void move();
protected abstract void stop();
```

You should now have a Vehicle class like the one shown in Figure 4-9. Note the three compartments that appear in the class. The compartments are for attributes, operations, and inner classes and interfaces—in that order. Pointing your mouse anywhere in the class pops up some useful tips.

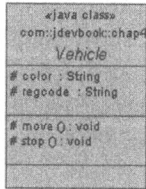

Figure 4-9. The Vehicle class

Now that you have created the Vehicle class, you will add new classes named *Car*, *Boat*, and *Bus* that will extend the Vehicle class. You could also put in an intermediate level of Land, Air, and Water classes. Because cars, boats, and buses are all types of vehicles, they also inherit from the Vehicle class the operations and attributes common to all vehicles. To depict this generalization in the class diagram, you will use the *Extends* component in the Java Component Palette. Extends is depicted using an arrow that points from the subclass toward the superclass. So draw three *extends* arrows that point from the classes Car, Bus, and Boat toward the superclass Vehicle, as shown in Figure 4-10. JDeveloper will generate code for these three classes and also depict the inheritance in the Java code generated.

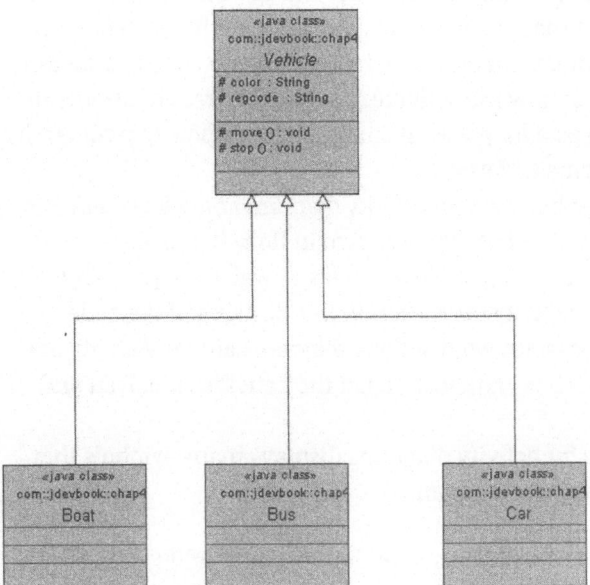

Figure 4-10. Vehicle inheritance

With version 10g, JDeveloper has introduced a distinction between Java class diagrams and UML class diagrams. If you do not intend to generate Java code from your class diagram, you can consider using the UML class diagram because it is a little easier to define properties for classes and relations using the various displays and dialog boxes provided.

Apart from class diagrams, another UML feature that JDeveloper supports is an activity diagram. You will now look at what activity diagrams are and how you can create these diagrams using JDeveloper.

Activity Diagrams

An activity diagram is the closest thing to flowcharts that exists in UML. Activity diagrams are the easiest way to visually depict what a certain system does and the flow of things in the system. A great thing about activity diagrams is that they are easily understandable by all parties involved in a project—everyone from the developers to the testers to even the management folks who might not understand anything else about the system.

Activity diagrams are the next logical step after the use cases for the system are in place. You can in most cases have one activity diagram for each use case, and if the case is a little complex, there can be more than one activity diagram per use case. The depiction of how the activities have to progress to be able to fulfill a certain use case can go a long way in enabling developers to understand the system and testers to frame test cases.

An important distinction between an activity diagram and a flowchart is that things do not always happen sequentially as shown in flowcharts. Activity diagrams have the capability to depict parallel activities as well as sequential flow. The key to drawing a proper activity diagram is in not thinking of the code. Depicting object interactions is not what activity diagrams are for. Activity diagrams should stay at a higher level and just depict the activities involved and their flow.

The Component Palette for activity diagrams displays many symbols that can be used in drawing an activity diagram:

- **Activity**: Any action that is performed in the system to fulfill a certain use case is shown using a rounded rectangle as an activity. The dictionary meaning of *activity* does convey what an activity is in the context of UML; an activity can be one time or be repeated multiple times.

- **Object flow state**: An object flow state is depicted in the diagram when a certain activity causes an object to change state. This notation is perhaps the only one that can be a little confusing, and I do not suggest using it unless it really does convey something useful.

- **Initial state**: This is where the flow begins. Every activity diagram should depict this initial state. There can be only one initial state.

- **Or decision point/join**: This notation can be used as either a decision point from where two new flows fork out based on a decision or as a join where two flows come in and only one flow continues.

- **And fork/join**: And notation can be used as both a fork and a join. It is used where a single flow forks out into two parallel flows. As a join, it is used where two flows come in and once both are in, only one flow continues.

- **Final state**: A final state is where the flow of activities ends. An activity diagram can have more than one final state even though it has only a single initial state.

- **Swimlane**: Swimlanes are used to group activities based on various entities in the system responsible for performing those activities. For example, you can group activities based on departments or distinct systems.

- **Transition:** Transitions depict the actual flow of activities. You can also place guard conditions to denote that the transition occurs only on fulfillment of a certain condition.

- **Note:** Notes are used to add an explanatory note.

- **Attachment:** Attachments are used to attach a note to any other notation.

You will now see a real-world example and draw an activity diagram before you move into the virtual world and think of software solutions. Consider that you have gone to your local bookstore to buy *Harry Potter and the Order of the Phoenix*. What are the activities involved, and how would the flow of events work?

You will first create a new empty project named *ActivityDiagExample*. For this project, use the UML Activity Diagram option in the New Gallery General ➤ Diagrams list to get a blank diagram and UML activity components listed in the Component Palette. Name the activity diagram *Book Order* and the package *com.jdevbook.chap4*.

An activity diagram begins with the initial state symbol because this is where the story begins. There can be only one initial state; however, there can be multiple final states because based on conditions, the flow of activities is bound to vary.

An optional feature of activity diagrams is the swimlane. Swimlanes are used where there is a distinction between the performers of the activities. Using swimlanes also make your activity diagrams easier to comprehend.

The three parties to the Book Order process are the customer, the sales desk, and the stores. So you will draw three swimlanes. Because the process begins with the Customer, the initial state lies in the Customer's swimlane. Click the activity component in the activity diagram Component Palette, and then click in the Customer's swimlane to insert an activity. Change the name of this activity to *Request for Book*. You can make this change by directly editing the activity displayed in the diagram or by double-clicking and editing the name displayed in the Properties dialog box. Now keep adding new activities in the appropriate swimlane. Figure 4-11 depicts a possible flow of activities in the process of buying the book.

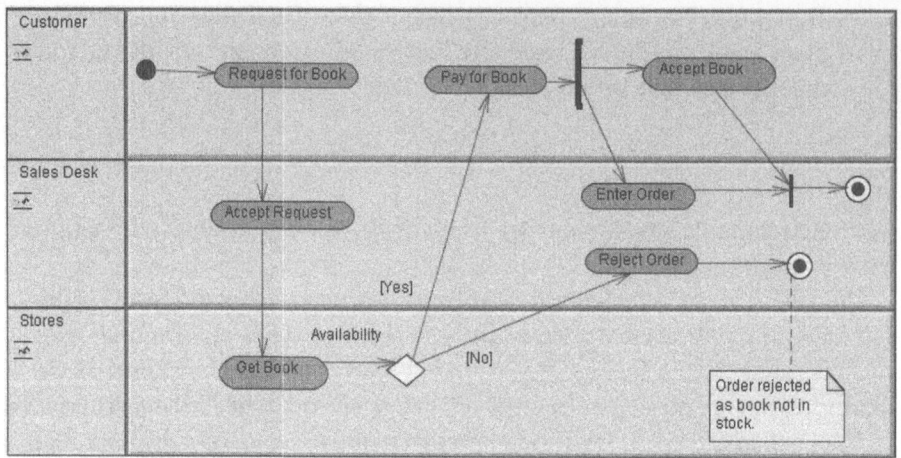

Figure 4-11. Book Order activity diagram

Note the use of the 0r notation to denote that if the book is available, the flow continues. If the book is not available, you get to a final state because the activities cannot progress further. The And notation is also used in two cases with different meanings associated. In one case, you fork out two flows because once you know that the book is available and the customer pays for the book, the two activities of a salesperson entering the order details and a customer accepting the book are parallel activities. The next usage of the And notation is as a join because only after both activities of the order details being entered by the salesperson and the book being accepted by the customer can the activities be termed as being in a final state.

In this case, you have used three swimlanes to depict the responsibilities of the three parties involved and the demarcation of activities performed by each.

Summary

In this chapter, you looked at the UML capabilities of JDeveloper. Although class diagram and activity diagram support existed in earlier versions, use case support is a new feature introduced with version 10g. Using these three diagrams together should give any application development a good OOAD foundation to build on.

The UML support and the ability to sync code with the diagrams is an important feature of JDeveloper that you need to consider before choosing an IDE.

Servlet and JSP Development

THIS CHAPTER INTRODUCES Servlets and Java Server Pages (JSPs) and then presents a simple example to display how to use JDeveloper in creating Servlets and JSPs.

JDeveloper provides excellent support for the Apache Struts framework, which I believe is the most popular Web framework around. I will delve into how you can easily create Struts-based JSPs and other files of relevance to Struts. Some of the most useful enhancements to JDeveloper introduced in version 10g are related to JSP and Struts development.

The thing about Servlets, and to a certain extent JSPs, that I like the most is that they represent an age when Java was meant to be simple. Before the dawn of Enterprise JavaBeans (EJBs) and the n number of application programming interfaces (APIs) that exist today, Servlets and JSP kept things nice and simple. You did not need to read and reread books to try and comprehend the subject and still be left wondering if you have really understood it.

There are many good things about EJBs, but if misused, they can be a real pain. A majority of projects do not need to venture into EJB territory. Servlets and JSPs used in tandem with ordinary Java classes can do a far cleaner and faster job for you.

Web Applications

Before you get into Servlets and JSPs, you need to understand the "why" and "what" of Web applications. Even Java 2 Enterprise Edition (J2EE) Web applications that do not delve into EJB territory are not always easy to comprehend. There are predefined directory structures, specific locations where libraries or code need to be kept, and key files that provide the container with deployment instructions. So although integrated development environments (IDEs) such as JDeveloper can make it a cinch to create and deploy Servlets and JSPs, if you are not aware of the intricacies of Web applications, it would be rather difficult to understand how the whole thing works and how to fiddle with it.

All containers that support deployment of J2EE applications need to adhere to certain rules and expect a Web application to be in a certain format. Unless the right things are in the right location, your application will not work.

I will show an example of a simple Web application named *simplewebapp* that you will create. If you presume that this application will have one Servlet and a Hypertext Markup Language (HTML) page, the most likely Web application structure would look like that depicted in Figure 5-1. Here the directory simplewebapp is the top-level directory and can hold any files that are meant to be publicly accessible, either directly under it or under a subdirectory other than WEB-INF. So if you create an HTML file named *index.html* and want the file to be accessible publicly, you can place the file either directly under the simplewebapp directory, or you could create a new directory by any name other than WEB-INF. The files placed here are generally HTML files, image files, and JSPs.

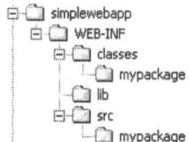

Figure 5-1. Web application structure for simplewebapp

The WEB-INF directory is the directory that holds the meat of the application, and the contents of this directory and its subdirectories are not publicly accessible when deploying the application. Public and private access does not mean that the files cannot be read or modified on the server. Access is only referring to a user trying to access the application after it has been deployed on a server. The WEB-INF directory has three elements, discussed next.

classes

The classes directory under the WEB-INF directory holds the compiled Java files. As shown in Figure 5-1, there exists a mypackage directory under the classes directory. This directory is where the class file for a servlet or Java class mypackageTest Servlet would have to be placed. The directory structure under the classes directory is strictly based on the package names used for the Java files involved. Normal usage is that during development, class files are maintained in the classes directory because the server can be configured to keep checking for changes to this directory and automatically update the reference if it finds that the file has changed. This can be a useful feature because you do not need to restart the server for any changes to be reflected.

lib

The lib directory holds packaged Java archive (JAR) files. The big advantage of the classes and the lib directory is that they eliminate the need to fiddle with the classpath for the container to be able to locate any of the requisite classes. Unlike the classes directory, the container does not check for changes to this directory; and so if a new JAR file is placed, the container needs to be restarted for changes to be reflected. The lib directory is useful when you are using third-party code in your application such as an Extensible Markup Language (XML) parser or a Java database connectivity (JDBC) driver. In this case, you can just dump the JAR file into the lib directory and get going.

web.xml

The deployment descriptor for a Web application needs to be named *web.xml* and should be placed right under the WEB-INF directory. The web.xml file is the only place where you can provide the container with deployment instructions specific to a particular Web application. A web.xml file can specify the following:

- **Servlet declarations**: Declare names and classes for key Servlets in the application. All Servlets used in the application do not need to be declared. Servlet mappings use the names specified in the declaration.

- **Servlet mapping**: Specify the Servlet to invoke when encountering a specific uniform resource locator (URL) pattern.

- **Session configuration**: Specify session configuration details such as time-out period.

- **Listeners**: Specify classes meant to listen for the occurrence of specific events.

- **Tag libraries**: Declare the custom tag libraries being used in the application.

- **Welcome file list**: Welcome files are files that are to be used even if only the context root is specified in the URL and no file is mentioned.

- **MIME types**: Specify the MIME types that are to be used in the application.

- **Filters**: Specify any filters used in the application. Servlet API 2.3 introduced the concept of filters.

Context Root

The context root defines how the application will be accessed. So the simplewebapp as shown in Figure 5-1, although would be generally accessed using a URL such as http://localhost:8080/simplewebapp, can very well be accessed using a URL such as http://localhost:8080/toughwebapp. Here toughwebapp is the context root that you have set to access simplewebapp using a different name. The context root configuration procedure differs between various J2EE servers.

Now that you have looked at concepts that are relevant across all J2EE Web applications, you will move into the specifics of Servlets and JSPs.

Servlets

Until a few years back, applets were the most popular feature of Java. So the first definition of Servlets that I came across was "Servlets are applets that run on the server." Although I did not understand it much, I thought that would be pretty cool. I would now say that a Servlet is Java code that runs on the server where the server does all the hard work of networking and other underlying tasks involved in processing client requests and sending an appropriate response. The Servlet code that you write sits at a higher level and deals with just application-specific tasks. The Servlet is concerned more with picking up input and generating output; there is no messing with protocols, sockets, and networking stuff.

Servlets are a great attempt to free application developers from having to worry about things they really should not be worried about. Like many of the other Java APIs, the Servlet API is also just a set of interfaces. The API provides no implementation, and it is solely up to the server vendor to actually code the implementation that will get the result as stated in the API. So the way an Oracle server internally provides Servlet support can be very different from, say, the Apache Tomcat server. However, the developer is just concerned with the Servlet API and does not need to worry about how the vendor complies with the API. As long as the developer is told that X server is Servlet API 2.3 compliant and Y Server is also compliant with that version of the API, he can rest assured that his code will work on both servers and get the same result. Because this same concept applies to all J2EE APIs, you ideally do not need to worry about vendors and implementations as long as you strictly adhere to the API.

A Servlet is pure Java, so everything that can be done with an ordinary Java class can be done using Servlets. A Servlet has to implement the javax.servlet.Servlet interface, either directly or indirectly by extending a class that implements the interface (see Table 5-1). The basic handling expected from a Servlet has to be specified in the methods of the interface that are implemented in the Servlet (see Table 5-2).

Table 5-1. Key Interfaces

Name	Description
javax.servlet.Servlet	This interface defines the life-cycle methods for a Servlet to initialize the Servlet, service requests, and then destroy the Servlet.
javax.servlet.ServletConfig	This interface defines methods meant to provide information about the Servlet such as its initialization parameters, name, and so on.
javax.servlet.ServletContext	This interface defines methods that can tell the Servlet more about the environment it is being run in. The Servlet can use this to get information such as initialization parameters for the application or the container being used.
javax.servlet.httpHttpServletRequest	This Hypertext Transfer Protocol (HTTP)–specific interface extends the javax.servlet.ServletRequest interface and defines methods to retrieve information from the request received.
javax.servlet.http.HttpServletResponse	This HTTP-specific interface extends the javax.servlet.ServletResponse interface and defines methods to create an appropriate response to a request received.
javax.servlet.http.HttpSession	A HTTP-only interface that provides ways to track a user across multiple requests and share information across a particular session.

Table 5-2. Key Classes

Name	Description
javax.servlet.GenericServlet	This class provides a generic Servlet that is independent of any particular protocol. The abstract method service needs to be implemented by any subclass of the GenericServlet to be able to process requests.
javax.servlet.http.HttpServlet	This is a class meant specifically for HTTP. It provides many method implementations that can make HTTP request handling a lot easier for any of its subclasses. HttpServlet extends GenericServlet.

For a Servlet to be independent of protocol, you can extend the javax.servlet.GenericServlet class and provide your implementation in the service method overridden in your Servlet. However, because Servlets are generally used to communicate over HTTP, the common usage is of extending the javax.servlet.http.HttpServlet class and, based on the nature of the request, overriding the appropriate methods. You will stick to extending HttpServlet for all these examples.

For the various types of HTTP methods, there are corresponding methods in the HttpServlet interface. The methods are doGet, doPost, doHead, doPut, doTrace, doOptions, and doDelete. Because GET and POST are the two most commonly used HTTP methods, the doGet and doPost methods are the most important ones provided by the HttpServlet class:

GET: A GET request is where the request information is sent as part of the URL. The request parameter names and their values appear as part of the URL. In the URL http://localhost:8080/TestServlet? paramOne=Oracle&paramTwo=JDeveloper, the two request parameters are paramOne and paramTwo and their values are Oracle and JDeveloper, respectively. Note the use of the ? and the & sign. The doGet method of the Servlet is automatically invoked when the Servlet encounters a GET request.

POST: In a POST request, the data is sent as part of the message body and not as part of the URL. POST requests are generally encountered in case of HTML form submissions. The values of the form fields are sent usin0g POST and do not appear as part of the URL. The doPost method of the Servlet is automatically invoked when the Servlet encounters a POST request.

Most Servlets do not go beyond the interfaces and classes stated in Table 5-1 and Table 5-2. A good understanding of these is essential to understand how Servlets work. This is especially true when you use advanced tools such as JDeveloper because the tool makes creation so simple that people often fail to understand the underlying fundamentals.

 TIP   *Spend some time understanding the key Servlet interfaces and classes before you leap into Servlet creation using JDeveloper. There are few classes involved, and the Javadocs can be very useful.*

New Web Module and Servlet

You will now dive into an example where you will create a Web application and a basic Servlet that will be a part of the application. The Servlet will accept a first name and last name as input and flash a welcome message.

Before you create anything in JDeveloper, you need a workspace and project. In this case, you will use the workspace MyJavaApps that you created in Chapter 3. You are free to use any other workspace. No settings for the workspace are relevant to this project. You will next create a new project meant specifically for Web applications. Follow these steps:

1. Select the MyJavaApps workspace, and select the New option to take you to the New Gallery, as shown in Figure 5-2.

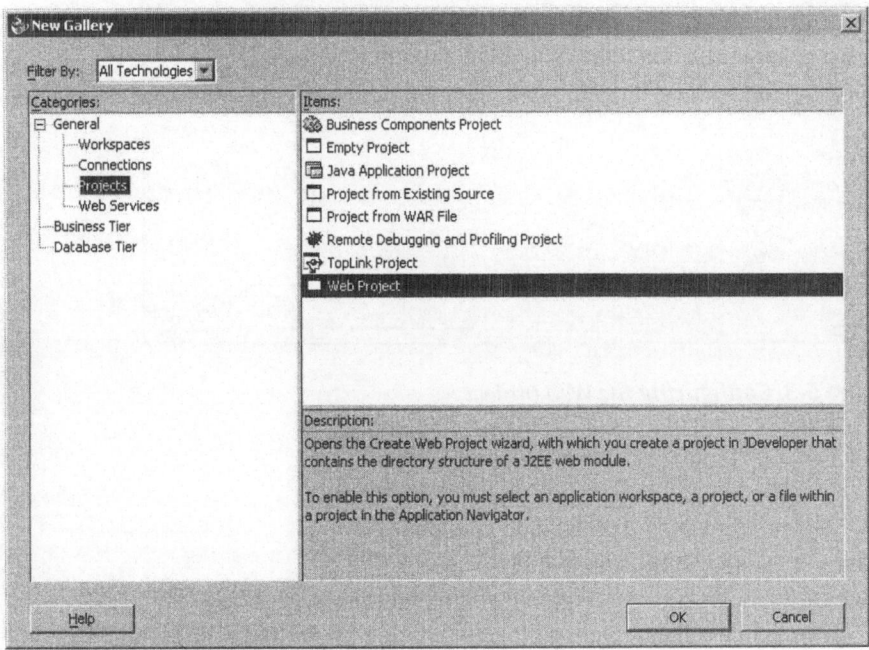

Figure 5-2. Creating a new Web project

2. In step 1 of the wizard that follows, name the project and the directory *BasicWebApp*.

3. In step 2, as shown in Figure 5-3, the wizard populates a default document root, Web application name, and context root. The document root directory specified will serve as the base reference that the container will use to access files in the Web application. Change the context root to *basicwebapp*. You need not change any of the other settings.

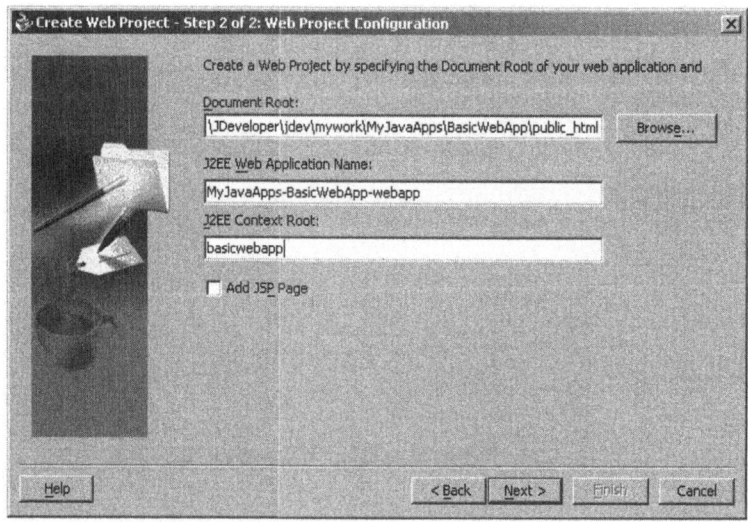

Figure 5-3. Configuring the Web project

4. Click Next.

5. Click the Finish button.

Web Module Project Settings

Now that you have created a new Web module, you need to look at the project properties relevant to a Web module. In the Project Properties dialog box, choose the Common ➤ Input Paths option. In the screen shown in Figure 5-4, change the default package to *com.jdevbook.chap5*. Note the directory where the Java source path is maintained and the HTML root directory. This directory forms the base for any links HTML, JSPs, and images. You do not need to change these settings.

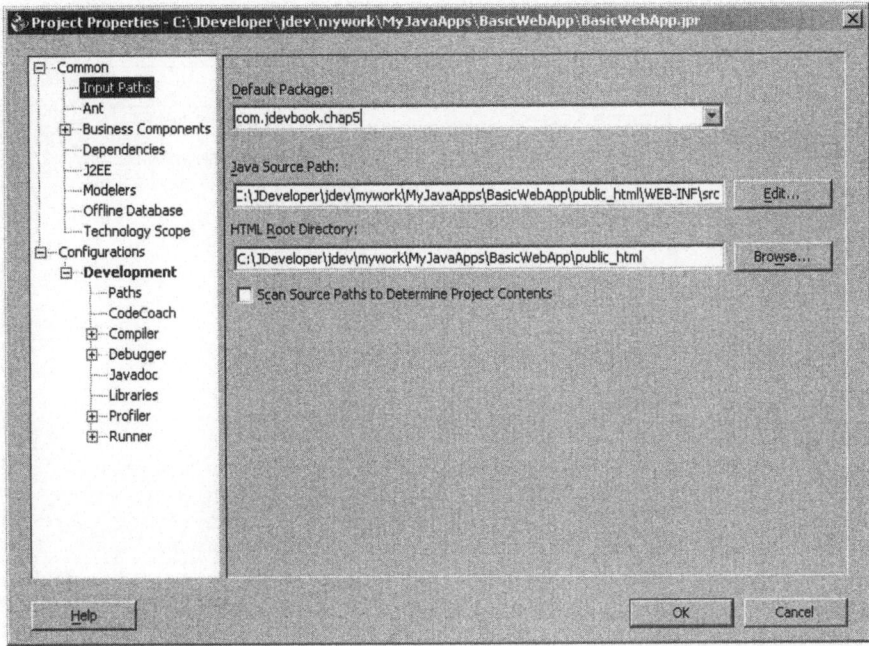

Figure 5-4. Setting the project input paths

> **NOTE** *Naming the Java source directory* src *and having it under the WEB-INF directory is a matter of convention. The specifications do not force the name* src *or the location because after deployment, the location of the source code is immaterial to the container.*

Next, choose the option Common ➤ Technology Scope in the project's properties. In the screen shown in Figure 5-5, you can see the Technology Scope page for a Web project. Because you only intend to use a Servlet, you do not need to make any change to the technology scope of the project.

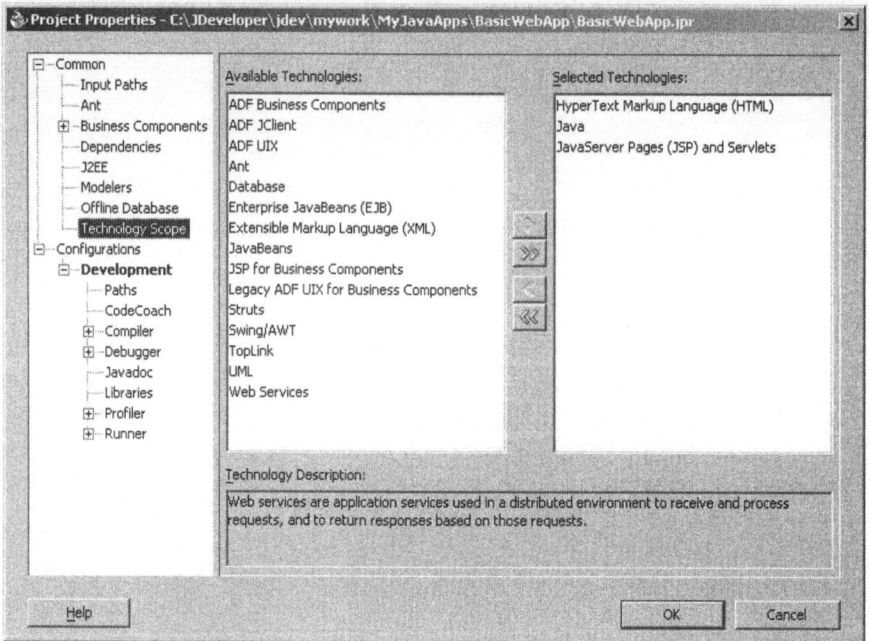

Figure 5-5. Setting the project's technology scope

You now have a proper Web module in place and can proceed to add Servlets and JSPs to the application. Select the project BasicWebApp.jpr in the Applications Navigator or System Navigator, and select the New option either by right-clicking or by using the File menu. In the New Gallery displayed, move to the Web Tier section. Here, select the Servlet option. You will find that JDeveloper is capable of creating a new HTTP Servlet, Servlet filter, and Servlet listener. Choose HTTP Servlet, and click OK.

Servlet Creation and Deployment

In step 1 of the wizard, enter the Servlet name as *WelcomeServlet*; the package name should be the same as the default package you stated in the project settings, *com.jdevbook.chap5*. As shown in Figure 5-6, check the Generate Header Comments option to have JDeveloper insert comments in the generated Servlet code. Choose doGet as the only method to be implemented.

NOTE *The Single Thread Model option will get the Servlet class to implement an empty marker interface named javax.Servlet.SingleThreadModel. Servlets by default use multi-threading so as to have one instance of the Servlet handling multiple requests. However, if you want one instance to process only one request at a time, implementing SingleThreadModel serves the purpose. Such usage is not advisable and is unnecessary in most cases.*

Note the various options displayed in the Generate Content Type drop-down list. Choosing WML or XHTML will only change the content type for the response sent and the default tags generated by JDeveloper. For this example, you will stick with HTML.

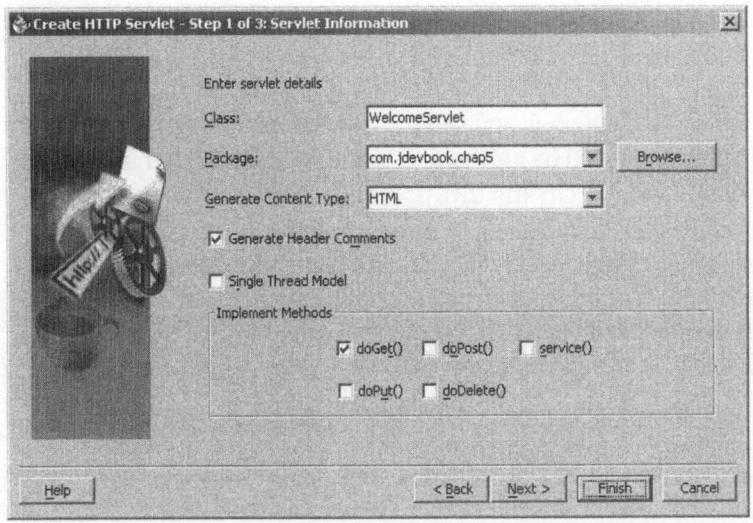

Figure 5-6. Create HTTP Servlet Wizard, step 1, setting the Servlet information

Step 2 of the wizard is what drastically cuts down the amount of code you need to write. The details specified in Figure 5-7 convey that you will be getting two parameters named *fname* and *lname* as part of the request. The value of these parameters will be picked from the request and stored in two String variables named *strFname* and *strLname*, respectively. Note the Type drop-down list; if you specify a type other than String, JDeveloper will also create code to convert the data type from the String received in the request to, say, an int or double. Enter these details, and click Next

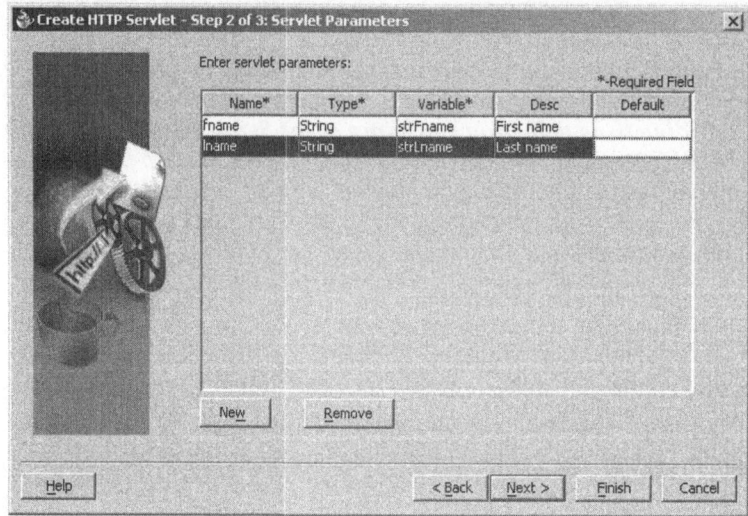

Figure 5-7. Create HTTP Servlet Wizard, step 2, setting the Servlet parameters

In step 3, shown in Figure 5-8, you can provide the mapping information. By specifying a mapping, you will be able to access the WelcomeServlet using the pattern you specify. Here, specify the URL pattern as *.welcome*. In this case, it means that any request that matches the pattern *.welcome* will be directed to the WelcomeServlet. This setting will be reflected in the Web deployment descriptor. So requests in the form of <context root>/abcd.welcome or <context root>/.welcome will be directed to the WelcomeServlet. Click the Finish button, and voilà! You have your Servlet code as well as the Web deployment descriptor prepared for you.

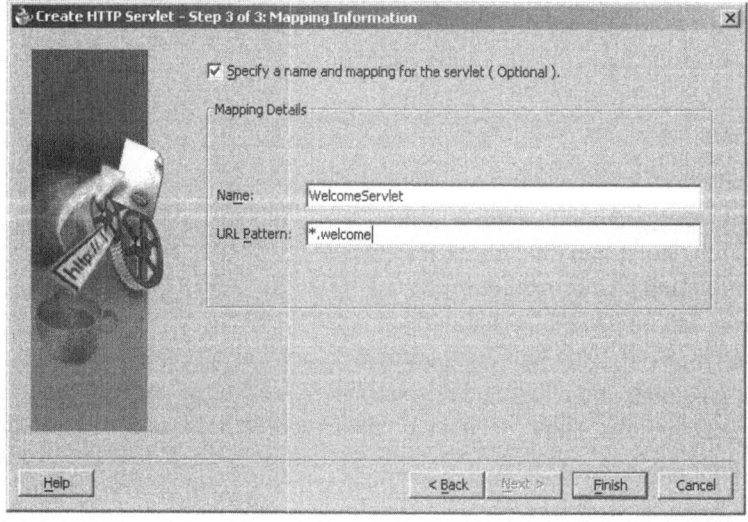

Figure 5-8. Create HTTP Servlet Wizard, step 3, providing mapping information

The files web.xml and WelcomeServlet.java will be listed in the System Navigator. Open the web.xml file to check how the various steps in the Create HTTP Servlet Wizard have led to specific tags being inserted in the file. The file WelcomeServlet.java is almost in its final form. Open the file WelcomeServlet.java in the Code Editor. Apart from the code to get request parameters, even the basic HTML generation code is in place. The only change you will make is to insert the following line:

```
out.println("<p>Welcome "+strFname+" "+strLname+"</p>");
```

This line will create a new paragraph in the HTML page displayed and flash a welcome message using the first and last name fetched from the request. So the HTML generation code looks like this:

```
out.println("<html>");
out.println("<head><title>WelcomeServlet</title></head>");
out.println("<body>");
out.println("<p>The Servlet has received a GET. This is the reply.</p>");
//Use the First and Last name received as part of the request.
out.println("<p>Welcome "+strFname+" "+strLname+"</p>");
out.println("</body></html>");
out.close();
```

Next, choose the Run WelcomeServlet.java option, either by using the Run menu or by right-clicking the file listing in Applications Navigator or System Navigator and choosing that option in the pop-up list. JDeveloper will compile and deploy the code to the embedded OC4J server that I will talk about in the next section. Your default browser will also be executed and the URL that will be accessed is http://127.0.0.1:8988/basicwebapp/*.welcome. As you probably have figured out, this URL is a result of the context root and the mapping you specified during Servlet creation. Replace the * with anything from *abcd* to *onomatopoeia*, and you will still get to the same page, courtesy of the mapping you specified.

NOTE *If required, you can configure the Web browser and proxy settings from the Web Browser/Proxy section in the Preferences dialog.*

Note that the message displayed on the page is "Welcome null null." This is because the parameters are not part of the request, so the call to request.getParameter() returns null.

NOTE *The default HTTP method is GET. So even if no request parameters are part of the URL, the doGet method gets invoked.*

To display the expected message, you need to change the URL to pass the request parameters. Try changing the URL to http://127.0.0.1:8988/basicwebapp/ tennis.welcome?fname=Boris&lname=Becker. You should now have a message welcoming Boris Becker on the HTML page.

Embedded OC4J

An important feature of JDeveloper is the Oracle Application Server Containers for J2EE (OC4J) server that is embedded in JDeveloper. The server, being embedded and tightly integrated into JDeveloper, eliminates the setup and configuration time involved in setting up the server. Rapid deployment and ease of use are also benefits that cannot be ignored. The OC4J server that is part of JDeveloper comes with EJBs and a Java Servlet container along with a JSP translator and a JSP runtime.

Running Web applications, debugging them, profiling them, and using code enhancement tools such as CodeCoach on them is all made possible using embedded OC4J. Because production-level deployment is not the purpose of the embedded OC4J container, it does not provide too many configuration possibilities within JDeveloper.

The embedded OC4J server is automatically started when running, debugging, and profiling or while using CodeCoach on a J2EE component such as an EJB, Servlet, or a JSP. To stop OC4J, you can terminate the process from the Run manager using the View ➤ Run Manager option.

NOTE *Only one instance of the embedded OC4J server can be run at a time. If you try to start another instance, the earlier instance gets terminated.*

OC4J configuration until version 9.0.3 was quite straightforward; however, with version 9.0.5, things have changed. OC4J configuration now has a separate tool listed under setting when choosing Tools ➤ Embedded OC4J Server Settings, as shown in Figure 5-9. OC4J configuration provided through this interface is stored in a file named *server.xml* that can even be edited manually.

In most scenarios, you will not have to tamper with any of the default settings of the server. However, if you want to use an OC4J installation other than the one bundled with JDeveloper, you could specify the directory for that installation. The change of port options can prevent port conflicts with other running instances of OC4J or a different server. The Load All System JARs and Lookup All EJBs During Startup options could slow down server startup and are not recommended.

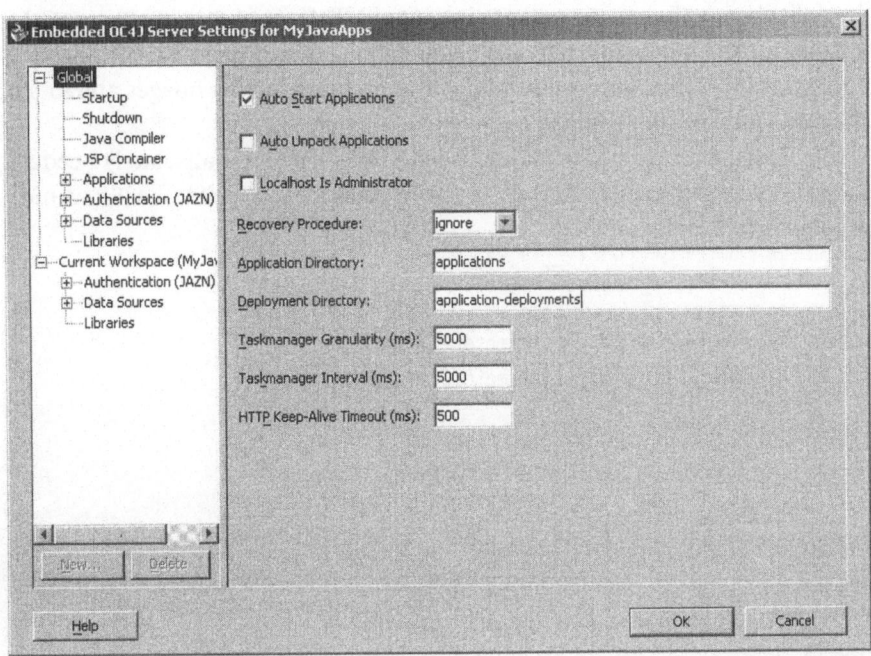

Figure 5-9. Configuring the OC4J server

When choosing the Shutdown option in the Embedded OC4J configuration, you can specify the shutdown methodology to use. A graceful shutdown is the best option; however, in some circumstances, a forced shutdown becomes essential.

You are provided configuration options for OC4J at two levels, Global and Current Workspace. I will explain some of the configuration elements when you encounter them in the example. Now that you have had a feel of J2EE applications and OC4J, you will move on to what is the most widely used element of J2EE, JSPs.

Java Server Pages

JSPs came a lot after Servlets had emerged; however, today JSPs are all over the place, but not many new Servlets are being developed. The primary reason for the decline of Servlets and for the emergence of JSPs was that Servlets were just not good enough to generate a lot of HTML output.

In the "Servlet Creation and Deployment" section earlier, you created a basic Servlet that flashed a welcome message. Note that in this Servlet, apart from the logic of displaying the message, there is a lot of HTML output being generated that is not directly relevant to the purpose of the Servlet. Imagine if your Servlet had to generate HTML for hundreds of complex pages having images and lots of JavaScript. Quite a scary thought.

JSPs changed things such that Java is used only where it is absolutely needed. If that same Servlet functionality were to be implemented as a JSP, the JSP would look something like this:

```
<%
  String strFname = request.getParameter("fname");
  String strLname = request.getParameter("lname");
%>
<html>
  <head>
      <title>Hello</title>
  </head>
  <body>
      <p>Welcome <%=strFname%> <%=strLname%> </p>
  </body>
</html>
```

If you are wondering when you have to write the Java class and do all the extending classes and implementing methods, then surprise! This is all it takes. There is no need to create and compile any Java class. Just embed whatever Java you need right into the HTML, and you are on your way. This embedding is done using special tags; you can even create your own tags.

How JSP Works

The nature of Java demands that to execute anything written in Java, it needs to undergo a conversion to bytecodes, which can then be executed by the Java virtual machine (JVM). You are not writing and compiling the Java code in your JSP; it is your container that does that for you. In the translation phase, the container generates Java code for all content in a JSP and also generates a corresponding *.java file. The file is compiled to generate a Servlet class file, and it is this Servlet that actually does the job for you.

Although a JSP developer does not really need to be aware of the methods generated in the Java code or the interfaces implemented, it always helps to understand them. The package javax.servlet.jsp is what holds the Servlet API's JSP-related classes and interfaces. The interface javax.servlet.jsp.JspPage needs to be implemented, and the _jspService method is the method that corresponds to the body of the JSP page. The JSP developer should not define the _jspService method in the JSP because the container defines this method.

NOTE *The Java files created for JSPs, although a somewhat scary sight, can be extremely useful for debugging purposes. Strangely enough, all container vendors seem to fancy creating these files in the most obscure of locations. Searching for the pattern *<filename> *.java is the easiest way to locate these Java files. OC4J creates a new directory named .jsps in the WEB-INF/classes directory of the Web application to which the JSP belongs.*

Most containers, unless instructed otherwise, compile the JSP into a Servlet only on the first invocation of the JSP. So you will notice a slow response the first time you invoke a JSP. However, because your next request will be serviced by the compiled Servlet already in place, the response will be much faster. Once the Servlet generates the appropriate HTML, it is only the HTML that goes across to the client. So any JSP tags you use are not visible at the client side; what appears is just HTML.

JSPs files are treated more like ordinary HTML files than like Java code. For the JSP to be publicly accessible, it can be placed in any directory other than the WEB-INF directory or its subdirectories.

JSP Elements

For the container to be able to convert a JSP that includes HTML, embedded Java code, and special tags, it is imperative that the JSP has to follow a definite syntax for the container to be able to convert it into a Java file and compile it.

Under the JSP specification 1.2, many tags underwent a change to make them compliant with XML standards. Using these new XML-like tags, it is now possible to write a JSP adhering to the rules for well-formed XML. You will first quickly look at the various JSP elements and then create a new JSP in JDeveloper that uses all of these elements.

Directives

Directives are instructions for the container that are to be processed while translating the JSP into a Servlet. The directives play a part in the Servlet code that gets generated. The types of directives are as follows:

- **page**: The page directive is meant to specify the properties of the JSP. Things such as the classes to import, the error page to use, and the content type to be generated are specified in the page directive.

- **include**: JSPs have a capability to include text and/or code right when the page is being translated; the content in the JSP along with the included content is translated into a single Servlet and then compiled. The include directive can be used to specify the resource to be included.

- **taglib**: To use custom tag libraries in a JSP page, you first need to specify the tag libraries to be used in the page directive.

This is the normal syntax:

```
<%@ page import="java.util.ArrayList" language="java" %>
```

This is the XML syntax:

```
<jsp:directive.page import="java.util.ArrayList" language="java"/>
```

Declarations

Declarations are used to declare new variables and methods that can be used throughout the JSP. Variables declared in a declaration are converted into instance members of the Servlet created, and methods defined are reflected as new instance methods in the Servlet.

If you look at the Java file created for the JSP page, you will notice that the methods and variables declared in a declaration appear independent of the _jspService method that has most of the other request processing and response generation logic in it. The contents of a declaration have to just follow normal Java rules and syntax.

This is the normal syntax:

```
<%!
int i=0;
%>
```

This is the XML syntax:

```
<jsp:declaration>
int i=0;
</jsp:declaration>
```

Scriptlets

Scriptlets are perhaps the most used as well as misused feature of JSP. Although the usage of scriptlets is declining because of the growing popularity of custom tag libraries, scriptlets are still ubiquitous in the JSP world. Scriptlets are Java code snippets that are embedded right into the JSP. The way to go about it is to believe that you are writing Java code within a method and have a few predefined objects such as session, page, and application to work with.

 NOTE *The easiest way to distinguish between scriptlets and declarations is that scriptlet code ends up in the _jspService method of the Servlet generated for the JSP, and the code for declarations appears outside this method.*

Scriptlets were quite popular in the early days of JSP; however, these days, any developer who codes using scriptlets is given what I believe is the Microsoft treatment. You know the thing will work well initially but will cause headaches later. And even if it does not, you hate it anyway. So to stay popular and appear smart, stay away from scriptlets and use custom tags wherever possible. Using tags created to accomplish a certain task instead of writing the Java code for it keeps the JSP easy to understand and maintain. Standardized and well-tested tags are also unlikely to throw unexpected errors at runtime.

This is the normal syntax:

```
<%
    System.out.println("In a Scriptlet");
%>
```

This is the XML syntax:

```
<jsp:scriptlet>
    System.out.println("In a Scriptlet");
</jsp:scriptlet>
```

Expressions

An *expression* is just an out.println statement. In the Servlet code generated, the contents of the JSP expression are parameters to an out.println method call, where *out* is the implicit JspWriter object provided. So the expression `<%= new java.util.Date() %>` would be represented in the _jspService method of the Servlet code as `out.print( new java.util.Date() );`.

A variable you declare in a declaration or a scriptlet can be used in an expression to get the value out to the display. A common mistake is to end the expression with a semicolon. This will give you a compilation error because putting semicolons in a println call is just incorrect Java.

This is the normal syntax:

```
<%= new java.util.Date() %>
```

This is the XML syntax:

```
<jsp:expression> new java.util.Date() </jsp:expression>
```

Actions

Actions are some of the smartest tags that form a part of the core JSP specification. Based on attribute values, actions accomplish specific tasks. The standard JSP actions are as follows:

- **jsp:include**: Include another JSP in a JSP. This is different from the include directive because this include is processed at request time, unlike the directive include, where the two JSPs form a single translation unit.

- **jsp:forward**: This forwards a request to another JSP.

- **jsp:useBean**: This declares a JavaBean to be used in the JSP.

- **jsp:setProperty**: This sets property values of the Java bean being used.

- **jsp:getProperty**: This gets property values of the Java bean being used.

JSP Implicit Objects

For anything to be accomplished in the JSP, you need to be able to access and use the user's session, fetch request details, set response information, and so on. However, writing the code to get these things in every JSP does not make sense. So the container declares and initializes variables that could provide the requisite functionality.

Again, if you refer to the Servlet code, you will find that the first few lines of the _jspService method have nothing to do with the JSP's output or logic. These lines of code only create these variables for use by code specific to the JSP.

So within the JSP, the developer can just presume that these variables are there and use them. For a JSP named *MyTestJSP.jsp*, OC4J generates a file named *_MyTestJSP.java*. The _jspService method in this Servlet code would begin with these lines (the variables are in bold):

```
public void _jspService(HttpServletRequest request, HttpServletResponse response)
        throws java.io.IOException, ServletException {

    response.setContentType( "text/html;charset=windows-1252");
    /* set up the intrinsic variables using the pageContext goober:
    ** session = HttpSession
    ** application = ServletContext
    ** out = JspWriter
    ** page = this
    ** config = ServletConfig
    ** all session/app beans declared in globals.jsa
    */
    PageContext pageContext = JspFactory.getDefaultFactory().getPageContext( this
            , request, response, null, true, JspWriter.DEFAULT_BUFFER, true);


    // Note: this is not emitted if the session directive == false
    HttpSession session = pageContext.getSession();
    if (pageContext.getAttribute(OracleJspRuntime.JSP_REQUEST_REDIRECTED
                , PageContext.REQUEST_SCOPE) != null) {

        pageContext.setAttribute(OracleJspRuntime.JSP_PAGE_DONTNOTIFY, "true"
                , PageContext.PAGE_SCOPE);
        JspFactory.getDefaultFactory().releasePageContext(pageContext);
        return;
    }

    int __jsp_tag_starteval;
    ServletContext application = pageContext.getServletContext();
    JspWriter out = pageContext.getOut();
    _MyTestJsp page = this;
    ServletConfig config = pageContext.getServletConfig();
```

The following is the list of variables:

- **request**: This holds the details for the current request.

- **response**: The response details are to be set into this object.

- **pageContext**: As shown in the previous code, the other variables in question are derived out of the pageContext. The pageContext is what stores references to all other implicit variables.

- **session**: This object refers to the user's session and can be used to store many details about the user and the current session.

- **application**: The application object holds details about the environment in which the JSP is being run.

- **out**: This is a reference to JspWriter that is used for all generation of output.

- **page**: This refers to the current object of the Servlet generated for the JSP in question.

- **config**: This object is used to fetch configuration parameters for the JSP.

Now that you have gone through most JSP concepts, you will move on to creating a JSP using JDeveloper.

A JSP Example

With JSP being the most extensively used component of J2EE, it becomes a critical element for the success of any J2EE development tool to provide good JSP features. JDeveloper does a good job at creating and editing JSPs. An important addition to version 10*g* is the introduction of visual editors for HTML and JSPs. This is a significant step because these tools are quite competent and work toward making a separate What You See Is What You Get (WYSIWYG) editor usage unnecessary.

Earlier in this chapter you created a new Web module named *BasicWebApp* (refer to Figure 5-2). You will use the same Web module to create a new JSP. Considering that all J2EE developers willingly or unwillingly have to work with HTML and JavaScript as a part of Web development projects, JDeveloper provides good HTML editing features as well. You will quickly look at the HTML editing features of JDeveloper while creating your JSP.

Open the New Gallery for the BasicWebApp project, and choose Web Tier ➤ JavaServer Pages. Of the options listed, JSP Document will create a JSP adhering to XML standards having a <jsp:root>, and the JSP Page option will create a free-flowing JSP that does not need to adhere to XML standards.

NOTE *If you intend to transform the JSP using Extensible Stylesheet Language (XSL) or parse it using an XML parser, you can go for the JSP Document option. If not, go for a JSP Page because it has less clutter and is easier to work with.*

Choose the JSP Page option, and name the new JSP *Welcome.jsp*. JDeveloper creates a bare-bones JSP that has a title and displays the current time. The JSP appears in two views, Design and Code. The Design view is the WYSIWYG editor, but you always have the option of directly editing the code. The WYSIWYG features are similar to using any other word editor. The toolbar provided makes changing text formatting, using lists, colors, and so on a simple task. What you intend to do in your JSP example is take user input of first name and last name and call the WelcomeServlet with these values as part of the request.

For this you need to create an HTML form. As per normal HTML usage, the form has to be enclosed between the body tags of the HTML. With JDeveloper you hardly need to write any HTML. While in the Design view, choose the HTML option in the Component Palette to display the HTML palette shown in Figure 5-10.

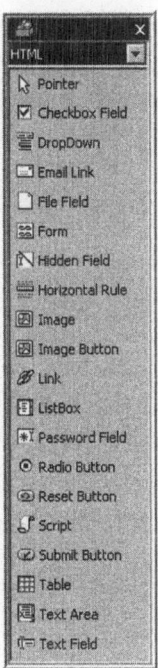

Figure 5-10. HTML palette

In this palette, choose the Form option. Double-clicking the form displayed in the Design view or right-clicking and selecting the Edit Tag option will take you to the dialog box shown in Figure 5-11. Here state the action name as *name.welcome* and the form name as *NameForm*. The form name does not really matter in this particular case; the action matters. Based on the Servlet mapping you provided in the web.xml file earlier, all requests matching the pattern *.welcome will be directed to the WelcomeServlet. Thus, the action *name.welcome* will have the request directed to the WelcomeServlet.

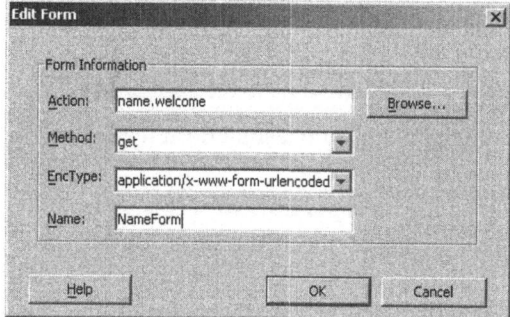

Figure 5-11. The form details

 TIP *The HTML palette options provide for specifying event handling as well as styles to be applied. It is always advisable to use these features, especially in the case of JavaScript where it can be a real pain debugging the simplest of problems. The IDE will not make the silly mistakes that humans regularly commit.*

Now to get the user's first name and last name as input, you need a table that will hold the requisite input fields. The Table option presents a user interface (UI) that will take all parameters that an HTML table can take. After this, place two text fields into the table to get the first and last name from the user. Next, use the Submit Button option in the HTML palette to insert a new Submit button for the form.

 NOTE *The text fields have to be named* fname *and* lname *because these are the request parameters expected by the WelcomeServlet. The input fields and the submit button have to be within the form tag structure—in other words, after <form> and before </form> for the data to be submitted as part of the form.*

Welcome.jsp should now look like this:

```
<%@ page contentType="text/html;charset=windows-1252"%>
<html>
  <head>
    <meta http-equiv="Content-Type" content="text/html; charset=windows-1252">
    <title>
    Hello World
    </title>
  </head>
  <body>
    <h2>
      The current time is:
    </h2>
    <p>
      <%= new java.util.Date() %>
    </p>
    <form action="name.welcome" name="NameForm">
      <table  cellspacing="2" cellpadding="1" border="1" width="40%">
        <tr>
            <td>First Name</td>
            <td><input type="text" name="fname"></td>
        </tr>
        <tr>
            <td>Last Name</td>
            <td><input type="text" name="lname"></td>
        </tr>
      </table>
      <p>
        <input type="submit" name="Submit" value="Submit Name">
      </p>
    </form>
  </body>
</html>
```

The Structure window is a handy feature while working with JSP and HTML. This window shows the structure of the page as a tree of tags. It becomes even more useful if you commit blunders. For example, if you misspell the contentType attribute in the page directive, the Structure window immediately points out the error, as shown in Figure 5-12. The window constantly keeps getting updated while you work. You do not even need to save the file to have the errors pointed out.

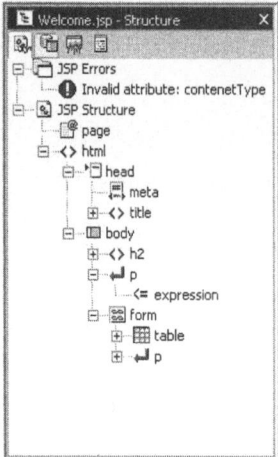

Figure 5-12. Structure window

To run the JSP, choose the Run Welcome.jsp command. The embedded OC4J server will start, and your default browser will open to the URL for the JSP. On the page displayed, input your first name and last name and then click the Submit button. The WelcomeServlet should be invoked, displaying a welcome message with your first and last name entered.

This example was more about HTML than JSP, but you will use and explore JSPs further while dealing with JDeveloper's integration with Struts.

JSP Standard Tag Libraries

Custom tag libraries hold a set of tags that are used on very similar lines to normal HTML tags but perform special functions that are beyond what HTML tags can achieve. These tag libraries provide tags that can format dates, modify strings and perform other similar tasks. Some Java code runs in the background to get these tags to perform the task.

With the growing adoption and usage of custom tag libraries has arisen the need to have tag libraries provide functionality in a standardized fashion. Although free third-party tag libraries are available, a need existed for the standardization of some commonly used tags.

The JSP Standard Tag Libraries (JSTL) is a specification and not an implementation for tags; you can find it at http://java.sun.com/products/jstl. JDeveloper provides Component Palettes for JSTL Core, Formatting, SQL, and XML. Using the JSTL tags wherever possible is a far better alternative than developing your own tags or writing code in your JSP.

Jakarta Struts

With the ever-growing complexity of Web applications has arisen the need to have frameworks in place that can handle the mundane and can streamline the application as a whole. Most frameworks are based on the Model-View-Controller (MVC) pattern and are primarily meant to have a clear distinction between the presentation and the logic in an application. Many frameworks go way beyond these humble targets and provide tons of other features. Some of the more popular frameworks are Apache Struts, Apache Cocoon, Expresso, and WebWork.

Apache Jakarta Struts is by far the most popular of the frameworks in use, so most of the newer IDEs have some degree of built-in Struts support. JDeveloper also provides great integration with Struts and has wizards and tools to enable the creation and development of various Struts components.

Figure 5-13 depicts a common Struts architecture. The struts-config file is the file that the controller Servlet in Struts refers to in order to determine which Action class to use. All requests should go through the controller Servlet, and it is this Servlet that should determine the flow of the application. On finding the appropriate Action class, the Action class can either do the necessary processing on its own or can pass on to a core logic class. Then based on conditions, the Action class can tell the controller Servlet where the request should be forwarded. No JSP names are stated in the Java code; the actual JSP to use is stated in the configuration file.

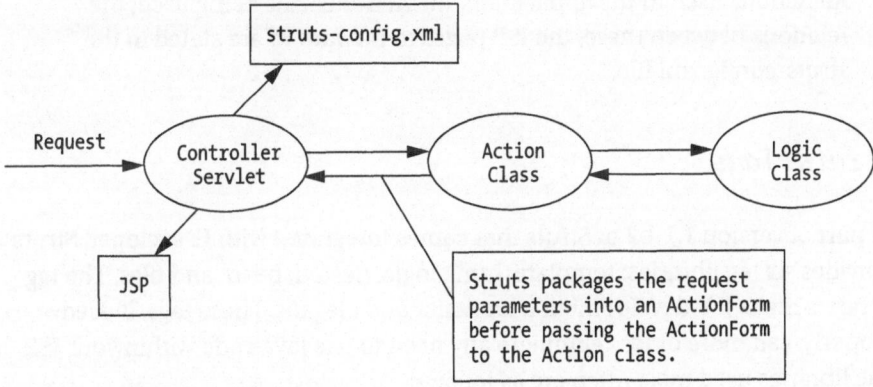

Figure 5-13. Struts architecture

The Struts framework provides the controller Servlet, and the user is expected to create the struts-config.xml file that adheres to a certain set of rules specified in a document type definition (DTD). Apart from this division of tasks that forms the core of the Struts framework, it also provides many other features to make Web development easier.

Elements of Struts

The key elements of the Struts framework that you need to understand to use the framework well are as follows:

Action: The controller Servlet based on the request received and on referring to the flow instructions stated in the struts-config file passes control to the action class stated in the struts-config file. Custom development using Struts begins with the Action class. The Action class can perform all the required logic and handling or in turn call a core logic class and then forward to the appropriate page.

ActionForm: Because all Web development revolves around the request parameters received from the client, Struts has the concept of an ActionForm to make things simpler. An ActionForm is an ordinary Java class adhering to JavaBean conventions. That is basically having the variables as private members and providing public get and set methods for the variables to get the value and set the value, respectively. The framework invokes the setter methods for all parameters that it finds in the request. Resultantly, the Action class does not need to work with the request as such but just a prepopulated ActionForm.

struts-config.xml: This file is the heart of Struts. For any development with Struts, this is the file to fiddle with and make it do things you want. All Actions used in the application, the ActionForms being used, the relations between these, the JSP pages to forward to are stated in the struts-config.xml file.

Struts Tags

As part of version 1.1-b2 of Struts that comes integrated with JDeveloper, Struts provides six tag libraries: template, html, logic, nested, bean, and tiles. The tag libraries make JSP development a lot easier and elegant. These tags, if used properly, can more or less eliminate any need to use Java code within your JSP. The libraries used most often are as follows:

- **bean**: This library provides many tags to make using and defining new beans possible.

- **logic**: This library provides tags that, based on conditions, can perform various actions. It is mostly used as a better option to using Java if else statement or for loops.

- **html**: This library provides tags to replace most core HTML tags and enable the creation of dynamic HTML pages.

NOTE *Before you use any scriptlets and end up having Java code in your JSP, look at all the tags available. In all probability, you will find the functionality you need. Also have a look at the JSTL at http://java.sun.com/products/jstl. In the long run, using standardized tags is a smarter option to using the existing Struts tags.*

You will now create a Struts application where you use the concepts discussed previously to create a simple login scenario.

Struts Application

Most Struts applications use JSPs extensively; there rarely arises the need to use Servlets. You will now create a Struts application where the flow is as follows:

1. Submit data from one JSP page.

2. Pass the request information encapsulated in an ActionForm to an Action.

3. Based on the userID and password entered, direct the user to a JSP that displays the appropriate message.

An addition to version 10*g* is the Struts page flow diagram. Because the primary task of Struts is proper and conditional management of flow, having such a flow diagram can be a valuable asset to quickly understand the workings of a Struts-based application.

Create an empty project named *StrutsApp.jpr* in a new directory named *StrutsApp.* Change the default package to com.jdevbook.chap5 using the Common ➤ Input Paths section in the Project Properties dialog box. For this project, from the New Gallery, select the item WebTier ➤ Struts ➤ Struts Controller Page Flow and click OK. The name is a little deceptive because what happens in reality is that JDeveloper completes all the groundwork required for a Struts application. The files created are struts-config.xml, web.xml, and ApplicationResources.properties. I have already talked of the first two files. ApplicationResources.properties is an ordinary text file that makes application internationalization a simple affair. You never need to hard-code any messages; just pick the messages from the properties file using simple Struts tags.

Struts Configuration in `web.xml`

To understand what JDeveloper has done for your Struts application, look at the web.xml file created for you. Because you want all requests to come through the controller Servlet, the web.xml file declares a new Servlet named *action* and has a mapping in which all requests that fulfill the URL pattern *.do will be directed to the action Servlet declared earlier. The tag libraries used in the application are also declared in the web.xml file.

 NOTE *Using the URL pattern *.do is more of a convention than a rule. You can of course change it to anything you want. The pattern *.twinkle (read as star dot twinkle . . . humor intended) would be nice.*

However, one thing that JDeveloper does not do is that it does not add tag library declarations in the web.xml file for all the tag libraries that Struts provides. So for other tag libraries that you intend to use, the tag libraries have to be declared using the following bit of code and also the .tld file has to be placed in the corresponding location. However, if you use Struts Logic Component Palette to write the tags, JDeveloper does the rest automatically:

```
<taglib>
  <taglib-uri>/WEB-INF/struts-logic.tld</taglib-uri>
  <taglib-location>/WEB-INF/struts-logic.tld</taglib-location>
</taglib>
```

Creating the Application

The only action involved in this example is that of receiving a login request. For this action, you need to create an Action and an ActionForm as well as add a corresponding entry in the struts-config.xml file.

With the Struts page flow diagram, you can even get a base application running by just visually depicting how you want the flow of the application to be; just draw actions, forwards, and pages in the diagram and depict their relationships. JDeveloper will automatically generate the Java code as well as make the necessary modifications to the struts-config.xml file.

On the blank Struts page flow diagram, first use the page component to add a page to the diagram. In the diagram, name this page */login.jsp*. The / symbol before login.jsp is required. Next, add an Action to the diagram. Change the action name in the diagram to */Login*. Right-click, and select the Go to Code option or double-click the action. As shown in Figure 5-14, change the action name to *LoginAction*. As a convention, Action classes end with *Action*.

After you click OK, the class LoginAction will be created for you. As per usage, the class extends the Action class and overrides the execute method.

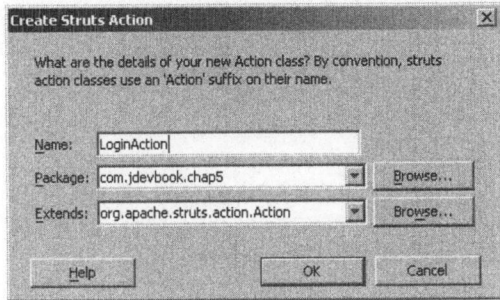

Figure 5-14. Viewing the Action details

Now that you have your Action class defined, you will define the form associated with the action. Right-click the action displayed in the diagram, and select the Go to Bean option. Change the form name to *LoginForm*, as shown in Figure 5-15.

The LoginForm class created extends ActionForm and overrides the reset and validate methods.

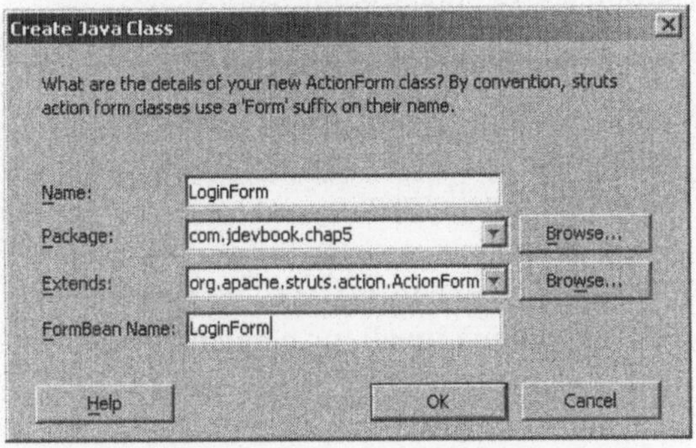

Figure 5-15. Viewing the ActionForm details

Now right click the struts-config.xml file, and choose the Edit Struts-Config option. The Struts Configuration Editor dialog box, as shown in Figure 5-16, should open. In the Form Bean tab for the action /Login, add login.jsp as the value of the input attribute. This value means that in case of an error, Struts takes the user back to the input page. Make it a point to explore most of the options provided in the Struts Configuration Editor dialog box.

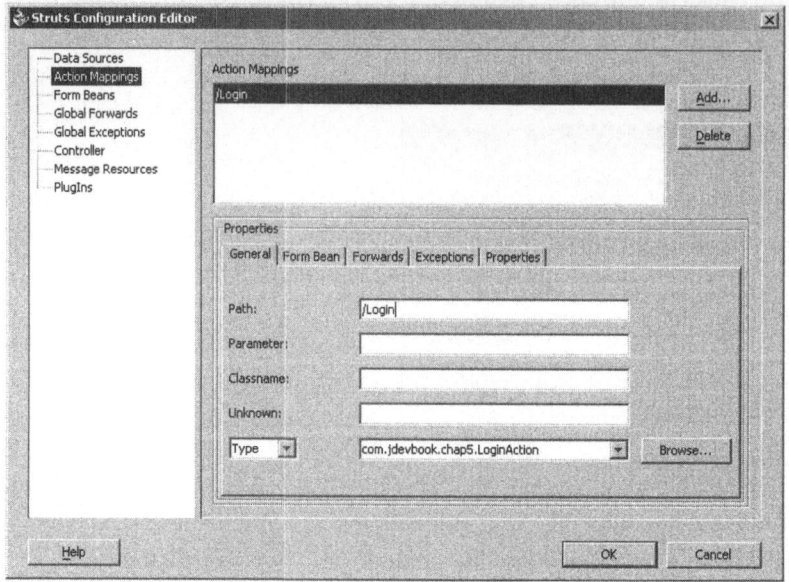

Figure 5-16. Using the Struts Configuration Editor dialog box

Now that you have the Action and ActionForm in place, you will move on to putting the JSPs in proper shape. Next you need to add a JSP to depict the successful flow. The Action will forward the request to this JSP if the request is successful. Add a new JSP to the diagram, and name it */result.jsp*.

 NOTE *Double-click the JSPs depicted in the diagram for the files to be actually created. Only after the files are created can the JSPs be linked to actions or other JSPs in the diagram.*

Now use the Forward/Link component to link up all the elements you have drawn on the diagram, as shown in Figure 5-17.

Figure 5-17. Struts flow diagram

You will now edit the login.jsp file to provide for submitting a form to the Login action. Open the login.jsp, file and choose the Struts HTML palette in the Component Palette list, to view a long list of all the HTML tags provided by Struts. The Struts HTML tags are replacements for many ordinary HTML tags. The Struts tags not only generate the relevant HTML tag, but also perform some additional Struts-specific functionality. You need a new HTML form to take a userID and password as input and submit the same. As per normal HTML usage, the form has to be enclosed between the body tags of the HTML. Click the Form option in the palette and name the form *LoginForm* to match the form entry you created in struts-config.xml. The action would be named *Login*. You do not need to append the .do extension to the action because the tag will do that.

> **NOTE** *Based on the Servlet mapping in the web.xml file, Struts determines the extension to be used. In this example, you have mapped the extension *.do to the ActionServlet, so the .do extension to the action name is inserted automatically by the <html:form> tag. Changing all links to, say, *.twinkle involves only a simple Servlet mapping change to the web.xml file. View the source of the HTML generated to check the complete action name being used.*

You now need to create a text field to get the login userID and a password field to get the login password. Use the tags <html:text> and <html:password> to do this job for you. You can create the form's Submit button using the Submit option in the HTML palette.

Form Field Validations

Validating form input can at times be an especially annoying task. Struts provides many features that make validating user input a lot easier. With version 1.1, the Validator framework has also been integrated into Struts, making validations even easier. However, you will stick to validations using some of the concepts that the framework uses and not dwell on the validator framework as such.

The form is what carries the input to the action, so the ideal place to validate input is just after the form has been populated based on the values received in the request. For this, Struts provides a mechanism by which it calls a validate method in the form before actually calling the action class and passing the populated form instance to it. So if a validation fails at the form level, an appropriate error is returned and the user is taken back to the input page based on the value of the input attribute for the action.

The things you need to do to validate the userID and password are as follows:

- **Modify the validate method:** JDeveloper automatically created a validate method in the LoginForm class; however, you need to provide proper implementation to check the values received and act accordingly. If the validation of the fields fails, this method returns ActionErrors that holds the details of the exact errors that occurred.

- **Add an input attribute to the action stated in struts-config.xml:** The input attribute is what conveys to Struts the page to be displayed when an error occurs. In most forms, you go back to the same page, display the exact validation error, and allow the user to resubmit.

- **Use the <html:errors> tag to display the message on the JSP**: The ActionErrors returned by the validate method can be displayed in the JSP using this tag. The tag uses the key, which is part of the ActionError object, and fetches the corresponding message from the ApplicationResources.properties file.

- **Add appropriate error messages to the ApplicationResources.properties file**: This file holds the various messages to display. This particular filename is not mandatory and can be changed by editing the <message-resources> tag in the struts-config.xml file.

You will first provide an implementation to the validate method. You want to check that if the username or password is null or empty, you return ActionErrors and take the user back to the input page. You will take the names of the request parameters as the userID and password. So you have to define these variables and their corresponding getter and setter methods in the LoginForm class. Next you edit the validate method as follows:

```
 public ActionErrors validate(ActionMapping mapping, HttpServletRequest request)
{
  //return super.validate(mapping, request);
    ActionErrors actErrors= new ActionErrors();
    if(userId==null || "".equals(userId))
    {
        actErrors.add("userId", new ActionError("error.userid"));
    }
    if(password == null || "".equals(password))
    {
        actErrors.add("password", new ActionError("error.password"));
    }
    return actErrors;
}
```

The values you are setting in theActionError objects are keys against which you maintain appropriate messages in the properties file. For the error.userid and error.password keys that are set into the ActionError object, you also need corresponding messages in the properties file. The properties you require are as follows:

```
error.userid=<LI>Invalid UserId</LI>
error.password=<LI>Invalid password</LI>
errors.header=<font color="red">Validation Errors</font><UL>
errors.footer=</UL><HR>
neo=Mr. Anderson! Welcome to the JTricks.
agent=JTricks likes you no more. Go away!
```

The login.jsp page has to undergo a small change with the <html:errors/> tag now appearing at the top of the page. If this tag finds any ActionError objects, it iterates through all the ActionError objects and displays all the error messages. The login.jsp will be as follows:

```
<%@ taglib uri="/WEB-INF/struts-html.tld" prefix="html"%>
<%@ taglib uri="/WEB-INF/struts-bean.tld" prefix="bean"%>
<%@ page contentType="text/html;charset=windows-1252"%>
<html>
<head>
<meta http-equiv="Content-Type" content="text/html; charset=windows-1252">
<title>untitled</title>
</head>
<body>
  <html:link page="/Login.do">
    <bean:message key="link.Login"/>
  </html:link>
  <br/>
      <html:errors />
      <html:form action="Login">
          <table  cellspacing="2" cellpadding="1" border="1" width="40%">
            <tr>
                <td>UserId</td>
                <td>
                  <html:text property="userId" maxlength="10" />
                </td>
            </tr>
            <tr>
                <td>Password</td>
                <td>
                  <html:password property="password" maxlength="8" />
                </td>
            </tr>
          </table>
          <p>
            <html:submit title="Submit" value="Submit" />
          </p>
      </html:form>
</body>
</html>
```

So whenever the validate method returns one or more ActionErrors, Struts takes the user back to the login.jsp page while displaying all the errors that occurred. The login.jsp page will appear in the Design view as shown in Figure 5-18.

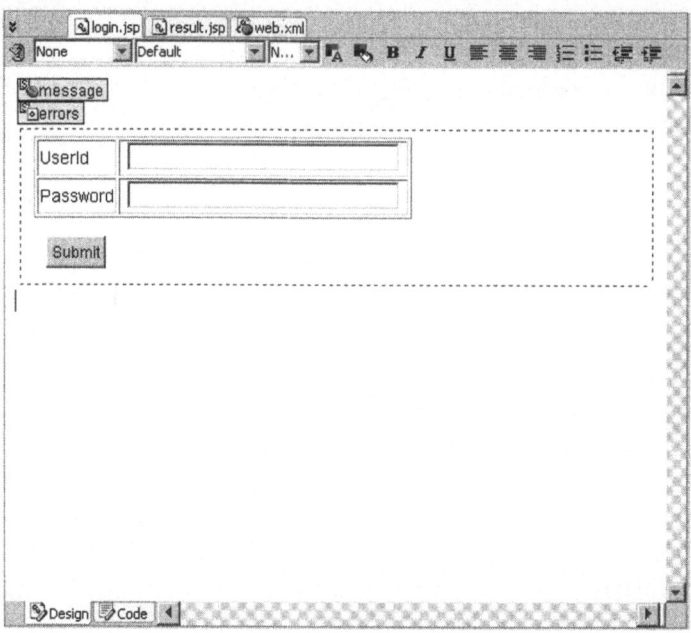

Figure 5-18. Accessing the Login.jsp Design view

Next you create another JSP named *result.jsp* to display a welcome message only if the user manages to log in successfully. You place the logic to check whether the access is legitimate in the LoginAction class. The execute method shell that JDeveloper has already created takes the validated form as input. The action fetches the userID and password, checks if the user is valid, and sets a flag into the request that states whether the access is valid. This flag is then used by result.jsp to display the appropriate message. The execute method in LoginAction is so modified:

```
public ActionForward execute(ActionMapping mapping
  , ActionForm form
  , HttpServletRequest request
  , HttpServletResponse response) throws IOException, ServletException
{
    String userId=((LoginForm)form).getUserId();
    String password=((LoginForm)form).getPassword();

    String accessFlag="NO";
```

```
        if("neo".equals(userId) && "trinity".equals(password) )
        {
            accessFlag="YES";
        }

        request.setAttribute("ACCESS", accessFlag);
        return mapping.findForward("success");
}
```

Here you fetch the details from the form, and if the user is valid, you set the request attribute ACCESS value to YES. Otherwise, it is set to NO. The method then calls mapping.findforward. This call takes a string as input and forwards the request to the corresponding forward as stated in the struts-config.xml file. You now add a new forward to the action you created in struts-config. Because the forward tag is <forward name="success" path="/result.jsp"/> , returning success takes the user to the result.jsp page.

You next create a result.jsp page:

```
<%@ taglib uri="/WEB-INF/struts-html.tld" prefix="html" %>
<%@ taglib uri="/WEB-INF/struts-bean.tld" prefix="bean" %>
<%@ taglib uri="/WEB-INF/struts-logic.tld" prefix="logic" %>
<%@ page contentType="text/html;charset=windows-1252"%>
<html>
<head>
<meta http-equiv="Content-Type" content="text/html; charset=windows-1252">
<title>
Hello <bean:write name="LoginForm" property="userId"/>
</title>
</head>
<body>
    <logic:equal name="ACCESS" value="YES">
        <bean:message key="neo"/>
    </logic:equal>
      <logic:notEqual name="ACCESS" value="YES">
        <bean:message key="agent"/>
    </logic:notEqual>
</body>
</html>
```

Because you are using three tag libraries, these are specified in the taglib directive. The <bean:write> tag is capable of displaying values fetched from the request and the session. Because the same request that was fired from the login.jsp page is being forwarded to the result.jsp page, the request object can be used even in this JSP. Struts stores the form instance in the request or the session based on the scope attribute value of the action tag defined in the struts-config.xml file. Because in this particular case the form is in the request, the userID is fetched from the form.

Next you use the logic tags to check if the ACCESS value is YES or NO. Based on this value the corresponding message is fetched from the ApplicationResources.properties file using the <bean:message> tag. The login functionality is now in place. Run the login.jsp file. In the input form displayed, only the userID *neo* and password *trinity* will get you a welcome message shown in Figure 5-19. If both values are invalid, you will get the screen shown in Figure 5-20.

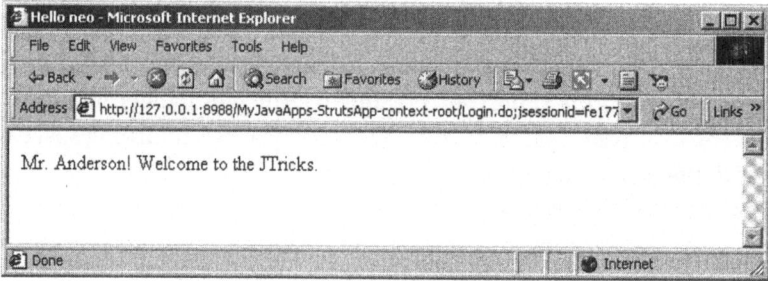

Figure 5-19. A valid login

If either or both values are incorrect, you will get the login page again with the appropriate messages displayed at the top of the page.

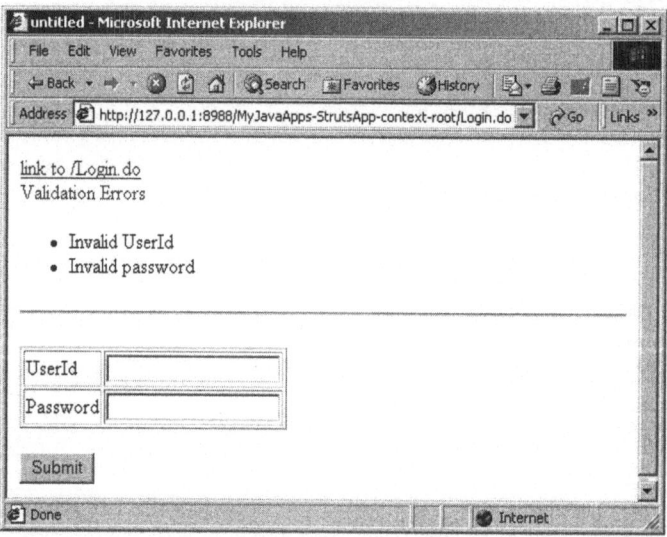

Figure 5-20. Invalid input values

An important feature of J2EE applications is the ease with which they can be ported across operating systems and application servers. Web applications are packaged as Web archive (WAR) files. You will now look at how you can get this packaging done.

Deploy to a WAR File

A WAR file is a single file that holds all the files that are part of a Web application. The WAR file maintains the exact directory structure as required for Web applications. You can use the *jar* command to create a WAR file, either compressed or not. However, JDeveloper eliminates the need to manually create WAR files.

To simplify application deployment, JDeveloper has introduced the idea of creating deployment profiles. These profiles hold all the information required to easily deploy the application on various severs and to package the application into archives. Although enterprise applications consisting of EJBs are packaged as enterprise archive (EAR) files, Web applications such as StrutsApp that you created are packaged as WAR files.

The web.xml file in a Web application plays an important role in the deployment of the application. JDeveloper provides a neat visual environment to configure your web.xml file without having to manually edit the XML. To get this display, right-click the web.xml file listing and select the Settings option. The screen shown in Figure 5-21 should be displayed, making it easier to edit the web.xml file without having to worry about committing XML mistakes or using tags that are not valid as per the DTD concerned.

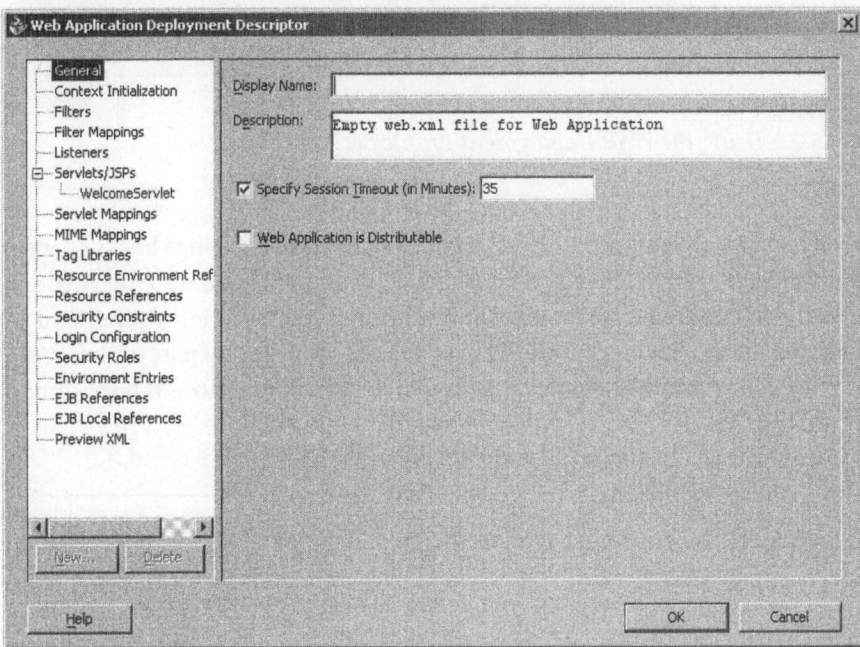

Figure 5-21. The Web Application Deployment Descriptor dialog box

For a Web application, the deployment depends greatly on the web.xml file. To create a deployment profile for StrutsApp, simply right-click the web.xml file as listed in the System Navigator and choose the Create WAR Deployment Profile option. Save the file in the StrutsApp directory as *StrutsApp.deploy*. You should now see the WAR Deployment Profile Settings dialog box, as shown in Figure 5-22. If you create a new Web application using the wizard provided, a WAR deployment profile is created by default and stored as webapp.deploy.

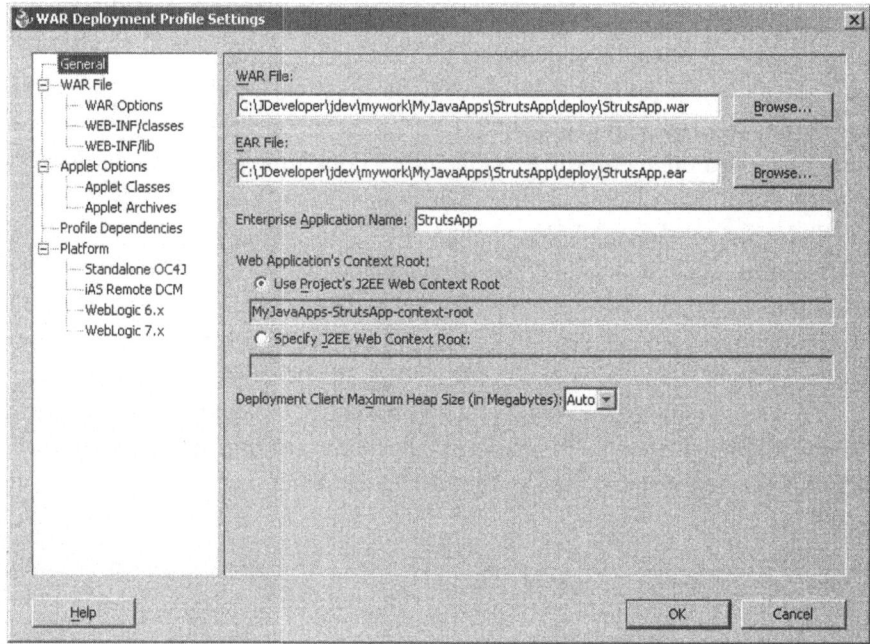

Figure 5-22. Using the WAR Deployment Profile Settings dialog box

In most cases, you do not need to change any of the settings because the default settings ensure that all the relevant files are packaged into the WAR. However, you can exclude certain files by choosing the WAR File option and deselecting all the directories and files you do not want to be part of the WAR file. If you do not want to ship your source files, you can remove the src directory from the list.

NOTE *JDeveloper creates class files for JSP in a directory under the classes directory named .jsps. Remember to remove this directory from the list of directories to be included in the WAR file.*

The Deployment Profile Settings dialog box also lets you tweak and set many other properties with respect to WAR creation and deployment on various supported servers. To actually deploy the StrutsApp application to a WAR file, simply right-click the StrutsApp.deploy file and choose the Deploy to WAR option. As specified in the deployment settings, by default the WAR file is created in a directory named *deploy* under the StrutsApp directory. The WAR file can now be easily ported to any other server, and the application can be up and running in no time whatsoever.

Summary

In this chapter you looked at the fundamentals of Servlets and JSPs and explored JDeveloper's features that enable quick and easy creation and deployment of Web applications.

JSPs are the workhorse of J2EE, and JDeveloper's integration and support for Struts and tag libraries makes JSP development a breeze. Deployment of J2EE applications has always been one of the relatively complex parts of J2EE. JDeveloper's ability to create deployment profiles that can be extensively configured and enable quick deployment to multiple supported servers is certainly a feature to write home about.

Enterprise JavaBeans and Database Interaction

NOW THAT YOU HAVE had a look at web development using Servlets, JSP, and Struts, you can move to the next step and develop web applications that also use Enterprise JavaBean (EJB) technology and interact with the database.

Considering the growing popularity and the inherent complexity of EJB, a Java Enterprise IDE must not only provide good EJB features, but also make using them very easy. JDeveloper does a great job of it. You will soon see what EJBs are, and how you can have a proper application in place with just a few minutes of work.

Because JDeveloper comes from the Oracle stable, databases are its strong suit. JDeveloper provides many useful features to make interaction with the database very simple and eliminates the need for separate client software.

You will look at EJB and its relevance to enterprise Java development, and then create applications using JDeveloper's EJB features. This chapter will get you going with EJB; however, understanding all the intricacies of EJB and their workings is not within the scope of this book. I suggest that you look at a book completely dedicated to Enterprise JavaBeans, such as *Enterprise JavaBeans 2.1*, by Rob Cataneda, Stefan Denninger, and Ingo Peters (Apress, 2003).

Enterprise JavaBeans

EJB is another Java 2 Enterprise Edition (J2EE) component that focuses on making the developer do as little as possible while the server does a lot of things. EJBs are server-side components that encapsulate business logic. EJBs are simply Java business logic classes that are written and deployed in a specific format.

The emergence of EJB can be partially attributed to Model View Controller (MVC) pattern-based applications. These applications placed emphasis on a clear distinction between the components responsible for the view of the application and for the core logic underneath. As these logic components were managing transactions, database interactions and other key aspects of the application, they became ideal candidates for optimizations. EJB is a focused effort on getting the core logic components to perform their best while causing minimum headaches for the developer.

The big news with EJB is that you do not have to handle the transaction management, concurrency, resource management, and other critical aspects of the application. The Java code is innocuous enough. Just tell the container what it needs to do and the container does it for you. Telling the container what to do, however, can be a grand pain at times, but that is another story.

NOTE *The use of the terms* server *and* container *can get quite confusing as they often also end up being used interchangeably. I will use* server *to refer to the software, such as WebSphere Application Server, JBoss, WebLogic, and so on. The term* container *is used to refer to the actual component in the server that is running the EJB or Servlet.*

An important feature of EJB is that it is a standard specification. You are not locked in to the server you have to use. You develop your EJBs adhering to the specification, and they will work fine on any server that supports that specification. So any of the EJBs you develop using JDeveloper and test on the embedded Oracle Application Server containers for J2EE (OC4J) will work fine on an IBM WebSphere, BEA WebLogic, JBoss, or any other server supporting the particular specification.

Another important aspect of J2EE is its distributed nature. EJBs are ideal if you want to use an architecture where you have your client code and the bean running in different Java Virtual Machines (JVMs). One of the commonly used architectures for EJB-based applications is shown in Figure 6-1.

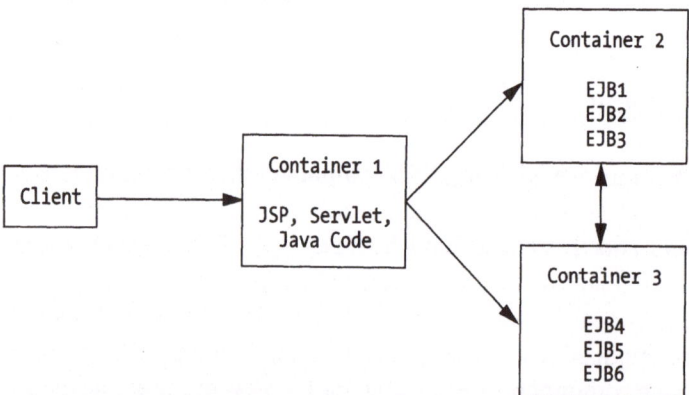

Figure 6-1. EJB-based architecture

In this figure you can see that not only does a client running in a separate JVM and container access EJBs in another container, but even EJBs in one container can remotely access EJBs in another container. I haven't depicted database access in the diagram, so the missing step in the flow depicted here is where the EJBs talk to the database.

The concept of local references has only emerged with EJB 2.0. Before that, even one EJB accessing another in the same container involved a remote call. Because the overhead of a remote call in such cases was unnecessary, EJB 2.0 now provides the option to call EJBs in the same container using a local reference and no remote call.

NOTE *JDeveloper supports development for EJB versions 1.1 and 2.0. Most of the popular application servers today support 2.0, and some even the later versions, so for the purpose of this book, I will stick with version 2.0.*

As depicted in Figure 6-1, the EJBs and the client code can be distributed over multiple containers. There is no means for a container to be able to locate an EJB directly. JNDI lookups are used for this purpose.

Java Naming and Directory Interface (JNDI)

The Java Naming and Directory Interface (JNDI) is an API to access various directory and naming services. Much like the JDBC API, even the JNDI is an abstraction over many different directory and naming services. Using the JNDI API, you can communicate with a directory service provided by Novell, Sun, Microsoft, or any other provider that supports the standard.

Directory services, like a common telephone directory, maintain a structured record of various resources. If you wanted Bill Gates' phone number, you would look in the *G* section in the telephone directory and then alphabetically search for *Gates*. Similarly, if you have to find a bean named *BeanOne*, you use a JNDI lookup, passing the location in the JNDI structure where the record is maintained. Based on this lookup, the JNDI lookup would fetch you the exact location of the bean on the network.

NOTE *The JNDI lookup plays an important part, because other EJB activities can only be performed if the lookup succeeds. The JNDI lookup is also a cause of many of the problems faced while working with EJBs.*

Let's now have a look at the various types of EJBs that exist and the use that each can be put to.

Types of Beans

Enterprise JavaBeans can be classified into different types. Each of these types serves a specific purpose and each is important in its own right. Even these types have evolved with different versions, and while new types were introduced, existing types underwent changes to make their adoption easier. The types of beans are discussed in the following sections.

Session Beans

Session beans are action- or task-oriented. Session beans do not merely represent data, but actually act on data to achieve some end. A session bean for a Student Management application would have methods to add new students to different courses, generate annual reports for a student, accept fee payment, and so on.

Stateful

Stateful session bean instances, once associated to a client, service only that client. They are capable of maintaining conversational state. The most common example is that of a visitor to a shopping site, using a shopping cart to add and remove products as he moves around. A stateful session bean could maintain this state of the cart across multiple pages.

The state is not persisted, but simply maintained in memory, so it will not survive a system crash. Stateful session beans haven't really caught on, and other means of maintaining state are preferred over stateful session beans. Most system architects aren't willing to incur the overhead involved in using stateful session beans.

Stateless

Unlike stateful session beans, with stateless session beans, no bean instance services just a single client. No attempt is made at maintaining state. Instances are used as required from the pool of instances maintained, and released when they are no longer needed. The methods of a stateless session bean have to work with just the data provided to them during a particular invocation.

Entity Beans

An entity bean is a type of EJB that is meant to represent and interact with data. Entity beans are meant to make interaction with the database simpler and object oriented. Entity beans can eliminate the need to write SQL queries in your code, or to use JDBC ResultSets to fetch data and then package that data again into objects based on your application design.

For example, suppose you have a table named Students, and you also have a class Student that is meant to store details for a student. Using the normal JDBC approach of fetching data, you will have to first write a SQL query and then fetch data in a ResultSet. You then need to iterate through the ResultSet and populate objects of the Student class. These objects would be what you actually use in your application.

What if you had an alternative where you just create the class Student and then tell the container to associate this Student class with the Students table? The container does all the querying, inserting, and updating of the database while you interact with Student objects only. Sounds too good? Container-Managed Persistence (CMP) Entity Beans can do that for you.

Container-Managed Persistence (CMP)

CMP Entity Beans are beans where the developer tells the container "Persistence is your problem, not mine." With CMP, once the developer provides an association between classes and tables, no persistence issue after that is the developer's problem. The developer only has to work with Java objects, while the container handles the persistence. While the developer creates Java objects or modifies their values, the container handles the communication with the database to ensure that the changes are also reflected in the associated table or tables.

Bean-Managed Persistence (BMP)

If you have some special cases that make you think that you should handle the data persistence yourself and not delegate it to the container, Bean-Managed Persistence (BMP) is the alternative. Here you will have to handle the DB and SQL bit on your own. With BMPs, entity beans suddenly do not remain as attractive an option as with CMP.

While session beans represent processes, entity beans represent data. A rule of thumb to identify entity beans is that entity beans are nouns like Student, Department, Employee, Course, and so on. Entity beans, until version 2.0, had obtained quite a bad name for themselves. They are not easy to develop, and most felt the overhead of having thousands of entity bean instances created for records in the database was too high a cost to pay.

However with EJB 2.0, CMP not only got easier to develop, but also underwent such a transformation that beans developed for version 2.0 are not backward-compatible. With faster machines, better JVMs, and advanced IDEs like JDeveloper making creating entity beans very simple, they certainly are a great option. If you had given up on entity beans long ago, and you are unsure of the persistence mechanism to use, I certainly recommend CMP entity beans.

Message-Driven Beans (MDB)

Message-Driven Beans (MDB) were introduced in EJB 2.0 and act as listeners for Java Messaging Service (JMS) messages. They are somewhat similar to stateless session beans; the big difference is that unlike session beans, MDBs provide asynchronous processing. There is no request-response process with MDB; the requester sends a request but does not wait for a response.

JMS is an API that is part of the J2EE platform and is used for communication with message-oriented middleware (MOM).

Interfaces

The key to understanding EJBs is in understanding the various interfaces that are involved and the role that each one plays. Creating and working with all these interfaces can be a little strange at times, but you will get used to it once you see them working in an application.

Prior to EJB 2.0 there was just the home and remote interfaces to worry about, but now there are two more local interfaces. Let's look at the various interfaces and understand the need for each. I will discuss these interfaces with reference to session and entity beans.

Remote Home Interface

This interface defines the life-cycle methods for a bean. These include methods to create, find, and remove the bean. EJB client code in the same container as well as code located in different containers can use this interface to access a particular bean. In the EJB client code, when you perform a JNDI lookup, you get a remote reference to the EJB Home object for the bean. You can also refer to this as the EJB home stub. You hold this reference in a variable of the remote home interface as the EJB Home implements the remote home interface. The remote home interface must extend javax.ejb.EJBHome.

Local Home Interface

The local home interface performs a task similar to that of the remote home interface, except the local interface is meant for use by clients in the same container. Client code running in a remote container cannot use the local home interface of a bean to access that bean. Such clients have to use the remote home interface. This interface is an addition to EJB 2.0. The local home interface must extend javax.ejb.EJBLocalHome.

Remote Interface

Once you have performed a JNDI lookup for a bean, you get the remote reference to the Home object for a bean, and use a variable of the remote home interface to refer to that Home object. You next use this variable to create an instance of the bean. Once this instance is created, a remote reference to the EJBObject is returned. This reference is what you use for calling the business methods in the bean. You hold this reference in a variable of the remote interface as the EJBLocalObject implements the remote interface. The remote interface is used to expose the various business methods in the bean. The remote interface must extend javax.ejb.EJBObject.

Local Interface

The local interface is similar to the remote interface; however, EJB client code running in a different container cannot use this interface to access a bean. It exposes the business methods provided by the bean and must extend javax.ejb.EJBLocalObject.

NOTE   *You do not need to choose between using either remote interfaces or local interfaces. An EJB can use both remote as well as local interfaces.*

Now that you are aware of the various interfaces that come in play, let's have a quick look at how the process of using an EJB works.

The Process

Using an EJB isn't as simple as just instantiating a class and using a method. It would be nice if that were the case, but unfortunately you have to follow a definite sequence of steps before you can use an EJB. Let's now look at these steps and try them out using a stateless session bean example.

EJB Usage Steps

As shown in Figure 6-2, you have to follow a few steps before you can use any of the bean's methods.

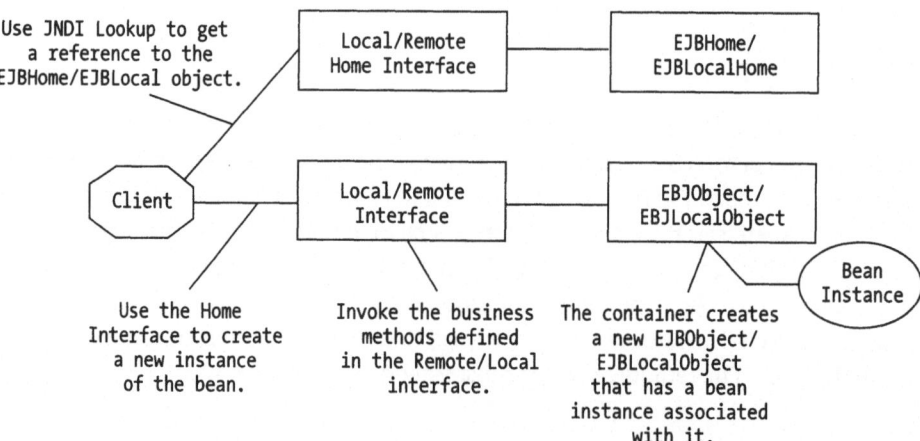

Figure 6-2. EJB usage steps

Assuming that you wish to invoke a method named getCurrentTime that returns a String and is located in a session bean named DateEJB, you would have to perform the following steps.

1. You first have to perform a JNDI lookup for the bean DateEJB using the JNDI name the bean is using.

2. This call will return a reference to the EJBHome / EJBLocalHome object. In case of a remote call, you need to narrow the returned object, and then cast it using the appropriate home interface reference. In case of a local call, the narrowing is not required.

3. Once you have the home interface, you use that interface to actually create an instance of the bean to work with. The EJBObject or EJBLocal Object is created, and you hold the reference to this object using a variable of the remote or local interface.

4. You can invoke a method in the client code only if the method has been defined in the remote or local interface. It is no use if the method is public in the bean class; if it is not defined in the remote or local interface, it cannot be used.

5. You use the remote or local interface variable that holds a reference to the EJBObject or EJBLocalObject to invoke the business method and get the expected return value.

EJBHome and EJBObject

In the earlier section I referred to the EJBHome and the EJBObject as two objects distinct from the bean instance that get created on certain actions being performed.

- **EJBHome:** The EJBHome is a vendor-specific class that is automatically generated on installing an EJB. The actual classes used as the EJB Home will vary across J2EE servers, but it does not really matter to the EJB developer. The EJBHome implements the remote home interface that is provided by the developer and also implements the life-cycle methods involved. On performing a JNDI lookup for an EJB, you get a remote reference to this EJBHome object.

- **EJBObject:** Like EJBHome, the EJBObject is also a vendor-specific class, an object of which is generated by the container. The EJBObject implements the methods in the remote interface. The methods in the EJBObject get invoked whenever you invoke a business method defined in the remote interface.

EJBLocalHome and EJBLocalObject are similar to EJBHome and EJBObject, but are meant for access locally using the local interfaces.

Let's now take up an example where you create a stateless session bean providing just a single method getCurrentTime. You will invoke this method using a java client as well as a JSP. While keeping the complexity of the application low, you can try to understand the elements that play a part.

Stateless Session Bean Example

First up, create a new Application workspace named DateApp using the Web Application [JSP, Struts, EJB] template. State the Application Package prefix as com.jdevbook.chap6. The wizard should now create two projects, Model and ViewController. The naming is based on a distinction between the components of the application based on the Model View Controller (MVC) pattern.

While the Model project will not contain anything, the ViewController project already has some basic Struts and web application files created for you. You will first create your session bean in the Model project and then create a JSP client in the ViewController project.

Select the New option for the Model project. A New gallery listing only files based on your application template selection should appear. Here choose the Enterprise JavaBeans (EJB) section in Business Tier and from the listing, choose Session Bean.

In the wizard that starts up, Step 1 is just a welcome screen, and Step 2 asks for the EJB version that you wish to use. Select Enterprise JavaBeans 2.0 and choose Next. In Step 3 enter the following.

- **EJB Name:** DateEJB

- **Session Type:** Stateless

- **Transaction Type:** Container

Leave the prepopulated values in Step 4 as they are, so that your Bean Class is com.jdevbook.chap6.model.DateEJBBean, and the source directory is C:\JDeveloper\jdev\mywork\DateApp\Model\src, and select Next. In Step 5, as shown in Figure 6-3, check the Include Remote Interfaces option as well as the Include Local Interfaces option. Click Next.

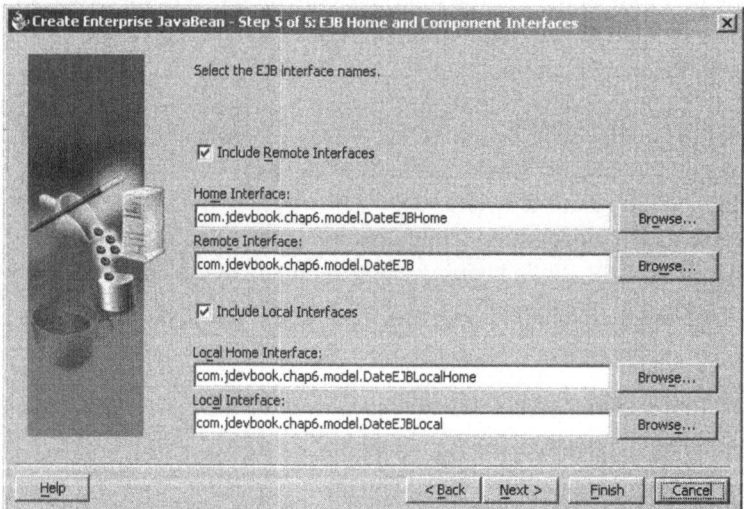

Figure 6-3. Step 5, Session Bean Interfaces

NOTE *The naming convention used for EJBs is important, because there are so many files to create and manage. A consistent naming convention at least makes it easier to figure out which file contains what.*

The Summary Screen, as displayed in Figure 6-4, is useful for a quick roundup of what is created. Changing things later on can be a little trouble, so ensure that what is being displayed is what you want. Click Finish.

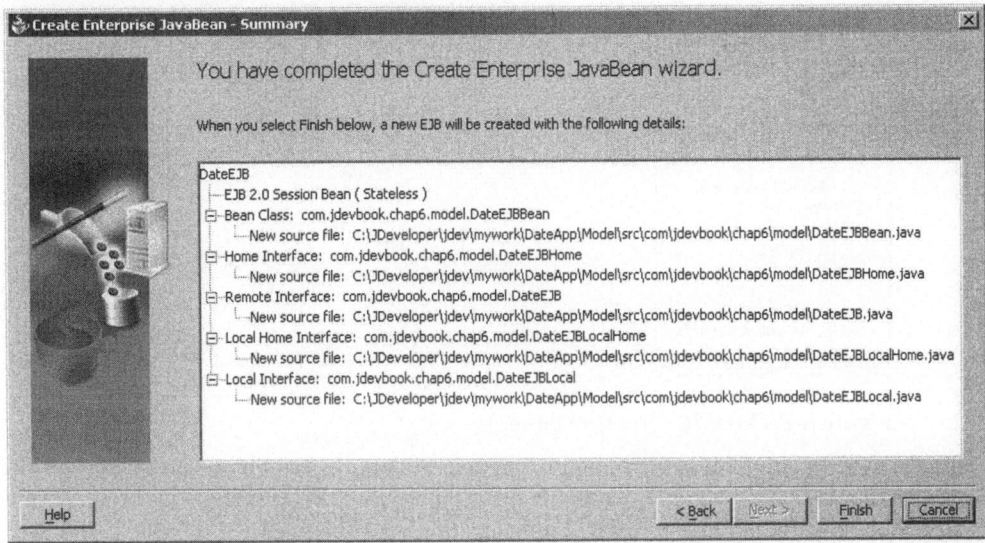

Figure 6-4. Create EJB summary screen

The Applications Navigator, shown in Figure 6-5, now shows that although all you have done is click a few times, the entire structure and all the files that you require are already in place.

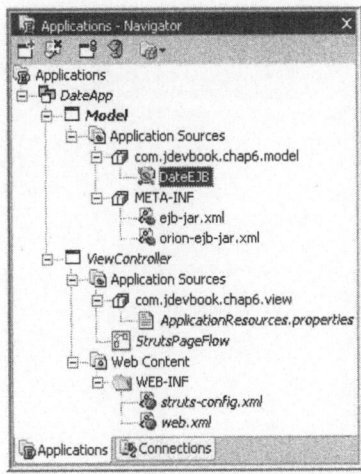

Figure 6-5. DateEJB Applications Navigator

If you are wondering where the interfaces and bean files have disappeared to, just click DateEJB, and all the files associated with DateEJB will be displayed in the Structure window, as shown in Figure 6-6.

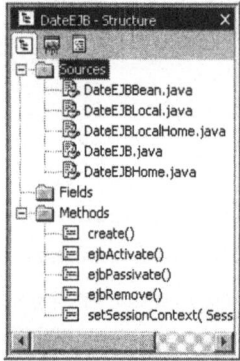

Figure 6-6. DateEJB Structure window

Now let's add the method getCurrentTime to the bean. The easiest way to do this is to double click DateEJB in the Applications Navigator. You could also right-click and select Properties to get the EJB Module Editor display shown in Figure 6-7. Although you could explore the various options provided here, for the time being I will stick to just adding one business method.

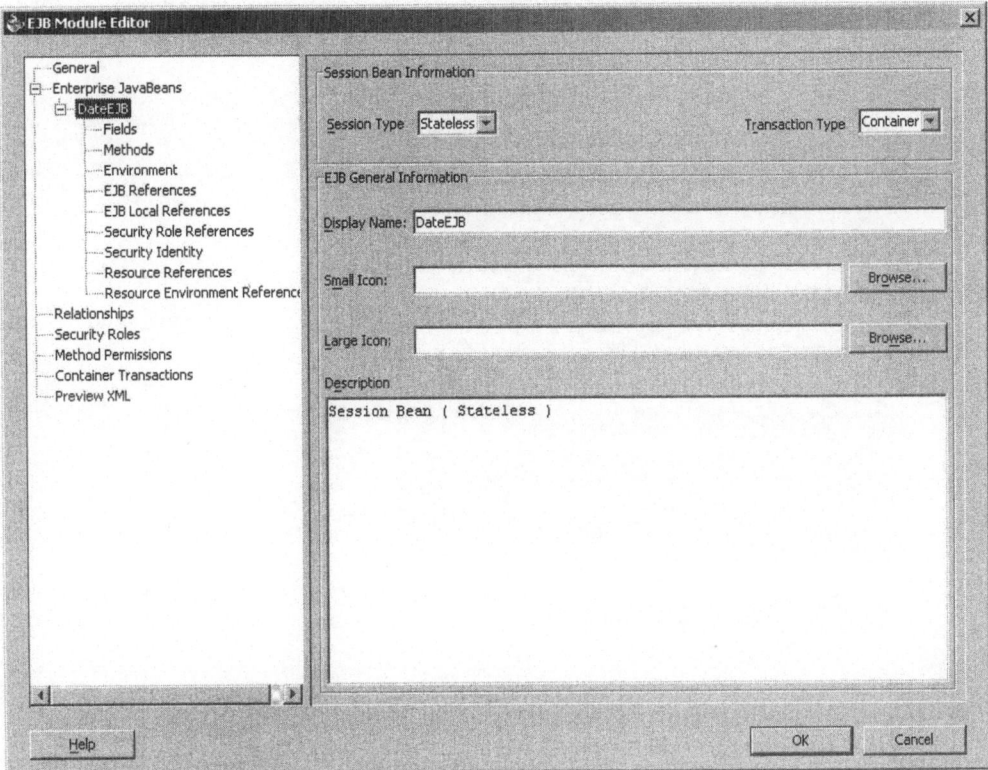

Figure 6-7. EJB Module Editor

In the EJB Module Editor, select Enterprise JavaBeans ➤ DateEJB ➤ Methods. Here select the Business Methods option in the Methods category listing, and click the Add button to get the screen shown in Figure 6-8. Here, state the method name as getCurrentTime and the return type as java.lang.String. You need not change any other settings. Click OK on the Business Method details dialog, and then click OK again on the EJB Module editor dialog. Now move to the Fields section for DateEJB, and you will find that JDeveloper has added a new field named currentTime. This feature came as a surprise to me and although it is useful, you need to be aware of JDeveloper's capability to spring such occasional surprises. Click OK on the EJB Module Editor screen.

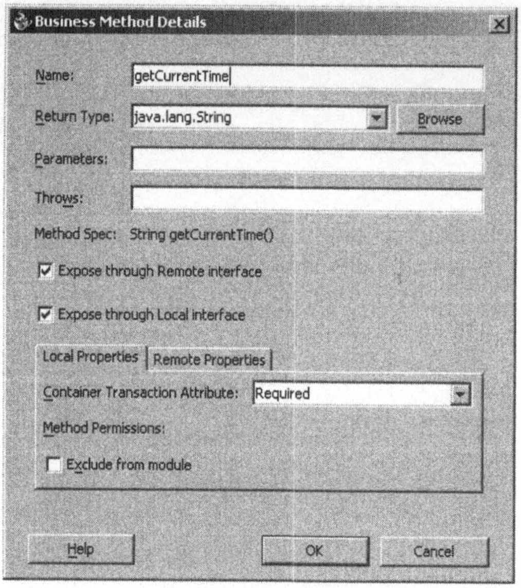

Figure 6-8. Add Business Method

Now that you have all that you need, let's look at all the various files related with DateEJB that have been created.

- **DateEJBBean.java:** This is the only class, because all the others are interfaces. This file contains the business logic. When you use JDeveloper, often this is the only file that you have to manually edit and write Java code for the business logic expected from the various methods. The other files can be managed using wizards and editors that JDeveloper provides.

- **DateEJBLocalHome.java:** The local home interface extends EJBLocalHome and states signatures for the life-cycle methods, such as create.

- **DateEJBHome.java:** The remote home interface extends javax.ejb.EJBHome, and even the signature definitions are similar to the local home interfaces. Note that all methods throw java.rmi.RemoteException.

- **DateEJBLocal.java:** The local interface extends EJBLocalObject, and exposes the getCurrentTime method.

- **DateEJB.java:** This is the remote interface, and also exposes the getCurrentTime method. All methods exposed through the Remote interface must throw java.rmi.RemoteException.

Apart from these java files, a couple of XML files are also important, as these files convey key deployment instructions to the container.

- **ejb-jar.xml**: This file is the standard J2EE EJB JAR deployment descriptor and should be placed in the META-INF directory. As it is defined by the specification, it must be present regardless of the server you are using. The EJB Module Editor takes care of most of the settings that are possible using this file. Ideally, you should not have to edit this file manually.

- **orion-ejb-jar.xml**: This file is the OC4J-specific EJB deployment descriptor. Most application servers have some file of this sort holding information specific to that server. Right-click the file's listing in the Applications Navigator and choose Settings to get to the screen as shown in Figure 6-9. You need not make any changes.

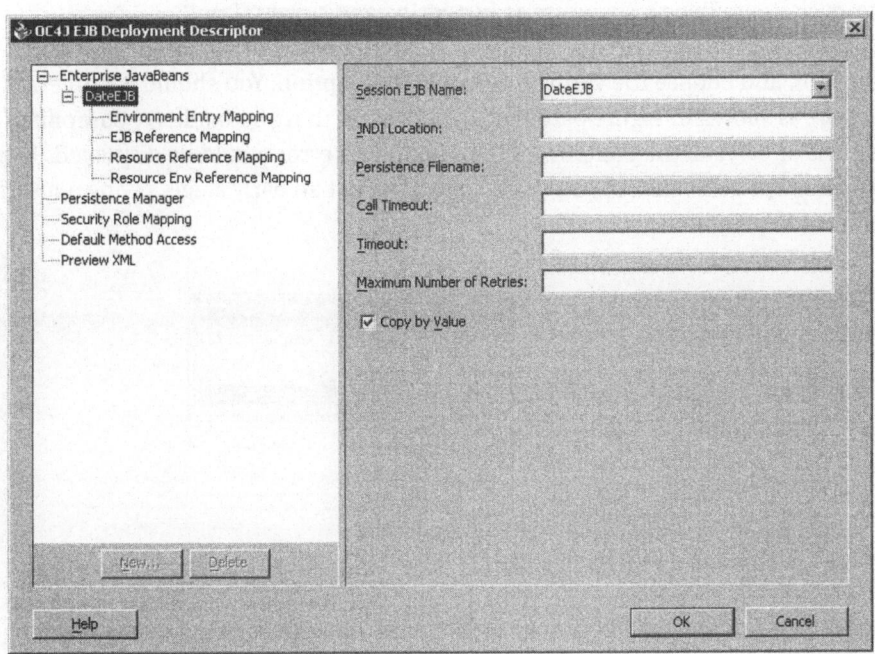

Figure 6-9. OC4J EJB Deployment Descriptor editor

Verifying Enterprise Beans

A problem with working with EJBs is that many errors are such that they do not appear at compile time, but show up at run time. These errors appear after you have gone through the time-consuming task of deploying applications and starting the server. It can be really annoying to then get an error saying that you haven't thrown a RemoteException in a Remote interface method.

> **NOTE** *One important reason why errors do not appear at compile time is that the bean class does not implement the home, remote, or local interfaces. Although the method signature as exposed in the remote or local interface, and that present in the bean class, have to be exactly the same, the compiler isn't capable of picking up this error. The EJBObject or EJBLocalObject that the server creates internally implements the interfaces and the error gets thrown at this stage.*

JDeveloper provides a way to handle this situation. Let's try out the Verify Enterprise Bean tool. In the DateEJB example, the local interface DateEJB.java has a method getCurrentTime that throws RemoteException. Just delete the throws clause to have a signature as just String getCurrentTime();

Now save the file and then right-click DateEJB listed in the Applications Navigator, and choose the Verify Enterprise Bean option. You should get an error message as shown in Figure 6-10. The tricky part is that you could try compiling the class or even all the contents of the EJB and no error would be displayed. The Verify Enterprise Bean tool helps you track errors at an early stage, saving a lot of trouble and irritation.

Figure 6-10. Verify Enterprise Bean

The Bean Lifecycle

Once all the files that you require are in place, you can move on to actually writing the tiny bit of logic that you expect from your bean method. As you saw earlier, the bean class is named DateEJBBean.java. So you can either open DateEJBBean.java directly, or right-click DateEJB in the Applications Navigator and select the option Go to Bean Class. This will also result in the file DateEJBBean.java opening up in the Code Editor.

In this file you will notice a number of empty methods, and also the one business method you added earlier. These methods have a specific purpose to serve in the lifecycle of a stateless session bean. With stateless session beans, instances are locked into a particular client, and so bean instances are continually created and removed from the ready pool. The steps involved in case of DateEJB are as follows.

1. A new instance is created using Class.newInstance(). An empty constructor is required for this call to work.

2. The method SessionBean.setSessionContext is invoked. An object of the EJBContext for the lifetime of the bean is passed to this method.

3. The container invokes the ejbCreate method. This method is important, because you are expected to perform all initialization activities in this method. You do not have the constructor to work with, so this is the method you are to bank on.

4. Now the bean instance is ready to service business method requests, so the call to the method getCurrentTime would take place in this step.

5. The ejbRemove method should be used to free up resources, and is called just before the instance is removed from memory.

NOTE *The methods ejbActiviate and ejbPassivate are not relevant to stateless session beans and are never invoked. The container in cases of stateful session beans, however, does invoke these methods.*

TIP *To check out the lifecycle of the session bean, you can try placing System.outs in the various lifecycle methods discussed earlier and monitor the embedded OC4J log to know exactly in which order the methods were invoked.*

Coming back to your application, the only change you need to make in the DateEJBBean.java file is that instead of returning null, the getCurrentTime method should return the date and time. The statement should be as follows.

```
return "" + new java.util.Date();
```

That's it. You are done creating your stateless session bean. It would be wise to again have a look at the various files before you look at the client code. Also try to think of what would be the steps involved in accessing the bean from standalone Java code as well as a JSP.

Bean Client

You now have a stateless session bean in place that exposes a single business method through a local interface as well as a remote interface. To access the method using the local interface, the client also has to be running in the same JVM, and local interfaces are used primarily for one EJB to access another. We will take up accessing using local interfaces later, when you have multiple EJBs in the example. For the time being, you will stick to accessing using the remote interface.

Right-click DateEJB in the Applications Navigator, and click the New Sample Java Client option. You should get a screen as shown in Figure 6-11. Here select the option Connect to OC4J Embedded in JDeveloper. Click OK.

NOTE *The New Sample Java Client option appears only if you are using the remote interfaces, and does not appear if you are using just local interfaces.*

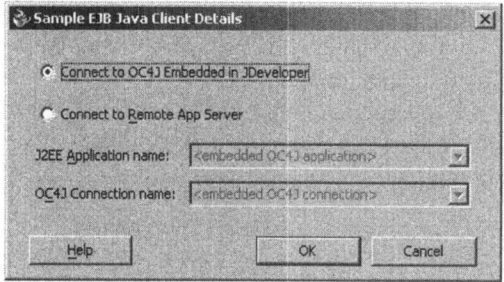

Figure 6-11. Sample EJB Java Client Details

A Java class named DateEJBClient will be automatically created for you. DateEJBClient not only has the code to look up and access the DateEJB, but even the call to the getCurrentTime method is present in a commented form.

Uncomment the call to the getCurrentTime method and place it in a System.out.println to have the following piece of code:

```
System.out.println("Date & Time >>>"+ dateEJB.getCurrentTime(  ));
```

Executing the Bean and Client

The only thing left to do now is to run the bean and the client. This is simple enough. Right-click the DateEJB listing and select the Run DateEJB option. The shortcut key F11 will also do the job.

Once you get the message "Oracle Application Server Containers for J2EE 10*g* (9.0.4.0.0) initialized," OC4J is running fine. You can also check if OC4J is running through the Run Manager. To display the Run Manager, select the View ➤ Run Manager option from the menu. You will get a display similar to that shown in Figure 6-12. Model.jpr would not be listed in your case, as I got this shot while the client code was executing.

Figure 6-12. Run Manager

TIP *Because all executing processes appear in the Run Manager, you can also terminate them from the Run Manager if the process hangs up for some reason.*

To execute the client, just right-click the listing and choose the Run DateEJBClient.java option. For the sample client, JDeveloper uses the JNDI properties as specified in <JDEV_HOME>\jdev\system9.0.5.0.0.1375\ oc4j-config\.client\jndi.properties.

CAUTION *The JDeveloper 10g preview that I am using had a bug here, and the client refused to work as expected. I am assuming that the bug isn't present in your copy of JDeveloper. If required, search Oracle Technology Network's (OTN) JDeveloper forum for the solution. The solution I got on the OTN was to replace the DateApp-jazn-data.xml file with the contents of the jazn-data.xml file that you can find in the <JDEV_HOME>\jdev\sys-tem9.0.5.0.0.1375\oc4j-config directory.*

When you execute the client, you should get an output similar to the following that I got on my machine.

```
Date & Time >>>Tue Sep 16 17:40:49 GMT+05:30 2003
```

The output shows that your stateless session bean is working fine, and dishing out the current date as expected. Although the standalone client is quite useful to try things out, in real-life scenarios you would be accessing the bean through a Servlet, JSP, or maybe a Java class.

JSP Client

For the sake of ease of getting the output, you will access the bean directly from a JSP. Note, however, that sticking to the MVC pattern, or according to accepted best practices, accessing EJBs directly from JSPS is not recommended.

For the ViewController project, add a new JSP Page named DateJSPClient.jsp. This file will be created by default in the public_html directory for the project. You need not change this. Once the JSP is created, add a scriptlet and modify the JSP as shown in Listing 6-1.

Listing 6-1. JSP EJB Client

```
<%@ page contentType="text/html;charset=windows-1252"%>
<%@ page import="javax.naming.*"%>
<%@ page import="javax.rmi.*"%>
<%@ page import="com.jdevbook.chap6.model.*"%>
<html>
<head>
<meta http-equiv="Content-Type" content="text/html; charset=windows-1252">
<title>Date JSP Client </title>
</head>
<body>
The Date and Time is:
<%
      Context context =  new InitialContext();
      DateEJBHome dateEJBHome = (DateEJBHome)
        PortableRemoteObject.narrow(context.lookup("DateEJB"),
DateEJBHome.class);
      DateEJB dateEJB;
      dateEJB = dateEJBHome.create();
      out.println(dateEJB.getCurrentTime());
%>
</body>
</html>
```

Try the Make DateJSPClient.jsp option. You will encounter some errors. The classes you created in the Model project are no longer accessible. You can fix this by going to the Project Properties ➤ Dependencies section for the ViewController project, and then selecting Model.jpr as a dependency. This will solve the problem of the EJB files not being accessible.

Also, because classes from the javax.ejb package need to be used, you need to add J2EE to the selected libraries list in the Project Properties ➤ Profiles ➤ Development ➤ Libraries section. Now run the DateEJB, followed by running the DateJSPCLient.jsp file. Your browser should pop up and display the output of the EJB method call.

Now that you have a feel of Enterprise JavaBeans, and also tried out a session bean example, let's look at the persistence capabilities of Enterprise JavaBeans. To try these out, however, you will have to use a database.

Using a Database

Because JDeveloper is an Oracle product, working with databases seems to come quite naturally to it. Although JDeveloper can work well with all Java Database Connectivity (JDBC)-compliant databases, things get even better if you are working with an Oracle database.

To create a new database connection, get the Connections Navigator to display by selecting View ➤ Connection Navigator. Here you will find that in addition to database connections, connections to SOAP Server, UDDI Server, Application Servers, and more are also listed.

To work with databases, a basic requirement is that you have a database created on your server. You cannot create new databases using JDeveloper. I created a new General Purpose Database on an Oracle 9*i* database and will be using the Username: *scott* and Password: *tiger* to log in to the database. The *scott* login gets created automatically when you create a new database on Oracle.

Right-click Database listed in the Navigator, and select the New Database Connection option. Click Next on the Welcome Screen. In Step 1, name the connection as OracleDBConn and choose Oracle (JDBC) option from the Connection Type. Click Next. On the authentication screen enter username as *scott* and password as *tiger*. The user *scott* with the password of *tiger* is present by default on most if not all Oracle database installations. You can however use any other user that you might have set up in the database.

The Deploy Password option stores the password in plain text in the connection.xml file so that you do not have to enter a password every time you wish to connect to the database. This option is meant to ease development and can be disabled once development is complete. Check the Deploy Password option for this example. On the next screen, as shown in Figure 6-13, enter the connection details. If you are using a database installed on your local machine, you probably will not have to change any details except for the system identifier (SID) to be used. I am using the SID *testnew* for this example. You also have an option to use the *thin* driver or the *oci* driver.

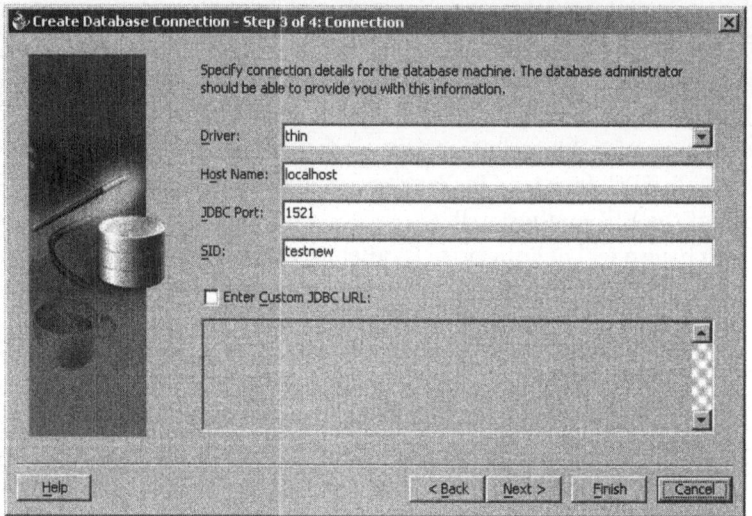

Figure 6-13. New Connection Details

 NOTE *To use the OCI driver for Oracle database, some native settings are also involved. JDeveloper documentation describes what settings are necessary for the OCI driver to work properly.*

In the case of Oracle, you do not have to enter a Custom JDBC URL, but you might have to use that option if you are using any other database, such as MySQL. Click Next. On this screen, click the Test Connection button. If every thing is in place, and your database service is also running, you should get a "Success!" message in the Status box. If you get an error message, the common causes are that all the essential Services aren't running, or if you are using a database other than Oracle, the JDBC driver configuration could be the problem. Click Finish.

In the Connection Manager, expand OracleDBConn to get a display like that shown in Figure 6-14.

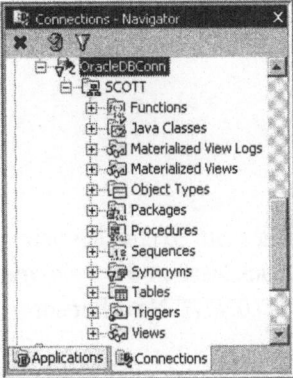

Figure 6-14. Connections Navigator

When you select the connection in the Connections Navigator, the Structure Window will display the details for that connection, as shown in Figure 6-15.

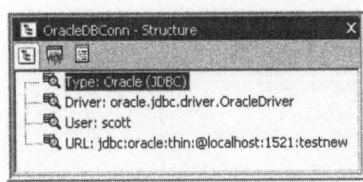

Figure 6-15. Connection Details

Now that you have your database connection working, let's think of an example where you create a couple of tables, and then work with the data in those tables using entity beans.

Student Course Application

In this application, you will create tables that will hold Students data and Courses data. You will create entity beans for both tables, and then have a stateless session bean communicating with both beans. The Sample Java Client will communicate only with the session bean, and not with the entity beans. You will not write any JDBC code. The beauty of entity beans lies in how easily you can work with databases and perform tasks like fetching data, inserting new data, and updating data.

For this example, you will also try out creating a new application template that will cater specifically to the needs of your application. All you require is EJB and Java support. There is no ready-made template provided that uses only these technologies, so you will create one.

Create Tables

Figure 6-14 shows the various elements available to the user *scott*. To create a new table, right-click Tables and select the New Table option. Click Next on the welcome screen. On the screen for Step 1, enter the table name as *STUDENT*. No other settings need to be changed. Click Next.

As shown in Figure 6-16, Step 2 is where you enter details of the columns for the table. Click the + image to add a new column. To keep things simple, you will have just two columns. The table structure is as shown in Table 6-1.

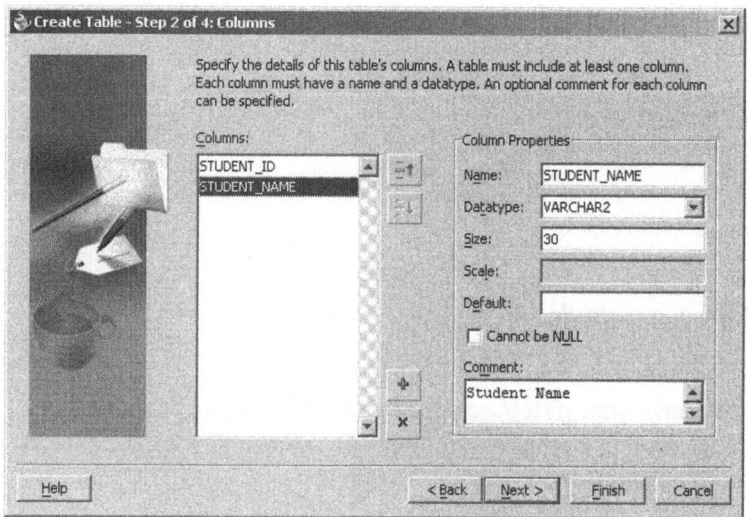

Figure 6-16. Columns

Table 6-1. STUDENT Table

Column Name	Datatype	Size	Comment
STUDENT_ID	NUMBER	5	Student Id
STUDENT_NAME	VARCHAR2	30	Student Name

Click Next. The next screen is where you define constraints. Click the + image, and define the column STUDENT_ID as the primary key, as shown in Figure 6-17.

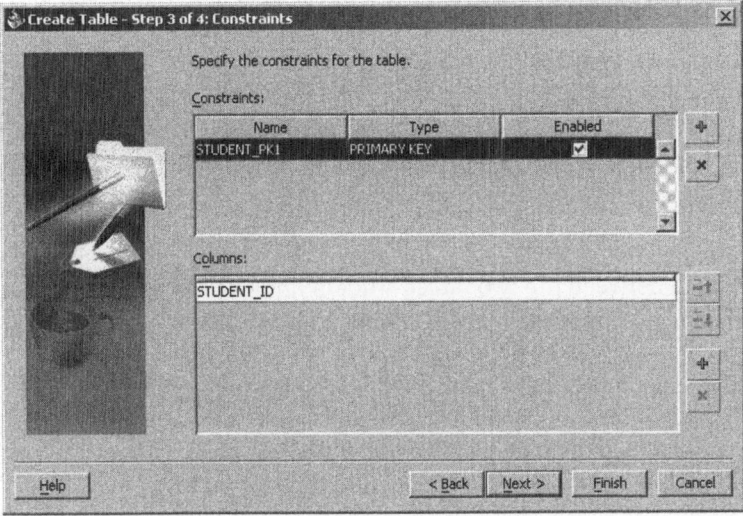

Figure 6-17. Constraints

If you want to configure any storage options, you can click Next to get to a screen, as shown in Figure 6-18. If not, you can click Finish on Step 3 itself. I did not make any changes to the storage options.

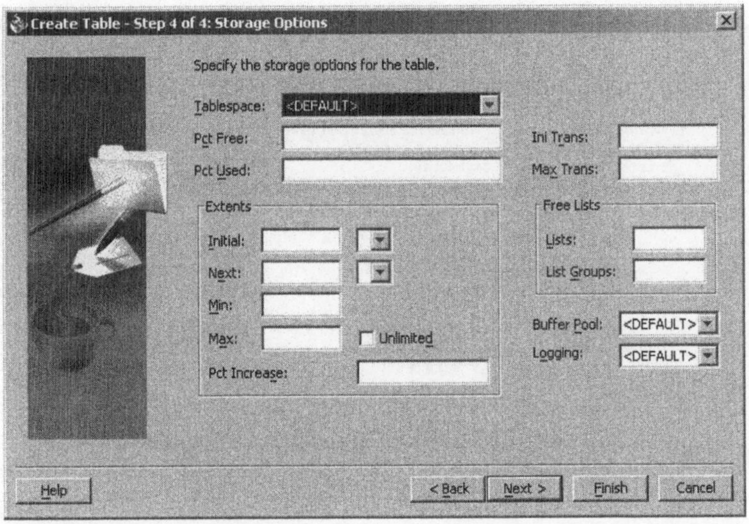

Figure 6-18. Storage options

The Last screen is a useful feature where the exact SQL queries that will be executed are displayed. You can also use the Save option to save the script to a *.sql file. Click Finish. Use the same steps to create a *COURSE* table as shown in Table 6-2. Set the column COURSE_ID as the primary key.

Table 6-2. COURSE Table

Column Name	Datatype	Size	Comment
COURSE_ID	NUMBER	5	Course Id
COURSE_NAME	VARCHAR2	30	Course Name

The relationship between the two tables Student and Course is that one course can have many students, but one student can have only one course. To define this relationship you need to edit the STUDENT table. Right-click the STUDENT table and select the Edit option. Add a new column COURSE_ID of type Number and size 5.

Next you need to define a foreign key constraint so that the column COURSE_ID, which is the primary key for the COURSE table, is defined as the foreign key for the STUDENT table. Move to the Constraints section in the Edit screen. Here, click the + sign to add a new constraint, and for this new constraint choose type as FOREIGN KEY. Next, select the COURSE Table, and because you have named the field as COURSE_ID in both tables, choose COURSE_ID as the Column as well as the Reference Column. Figure 6-19 shows the constraint settings. Click OK, and the new constraint is now in place.

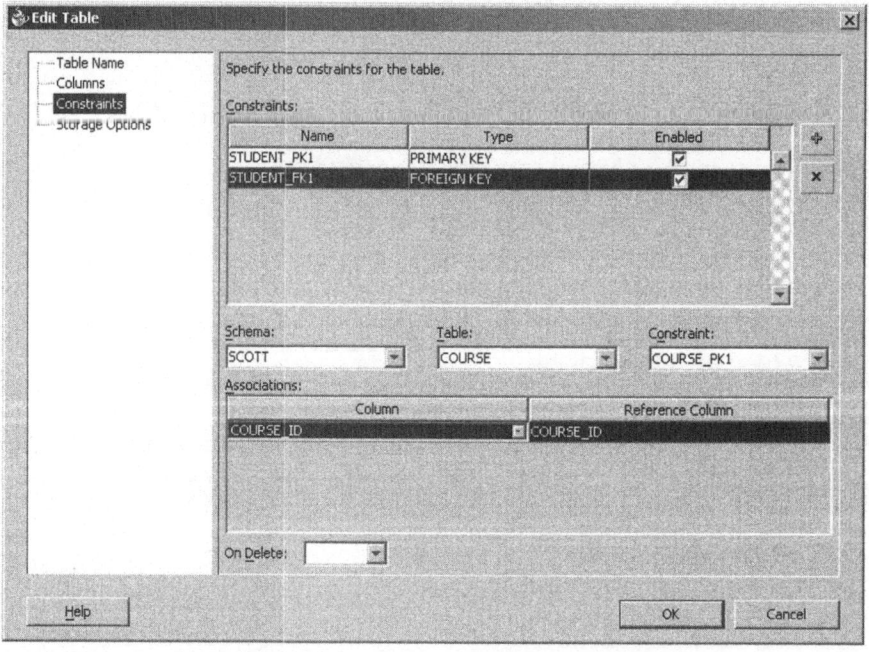

Figure 6-19. Editing Constraints

New Application Workspace

For this application you will be using just EJB and Java. There is no application template that defines just these two technologies, however. Although you can create a new project in an existing workspace, let's instead explore JDeveloper's capability to define application templates. You will create a new application template whose technology scope will be just EJB and Java.

Select New Application Workspace from the New Gallery, and then in the Create Application workspace that pops up, select the Edit Templates option. In the Edit Templates screen, click the New button. In the dialog that pops up, enter EJB-Java as the template name. Once the template is created, select the EJB-Java template in the templates list and then click the New button. You will now get a Create project Template dialog. Here enter the Project template name as EJB Application and the Project name as EJBApp.jpr. You should get a screen similar to Figure 6-20. Move Enterprise JavaBeans and Java to the Selected Technologies list, and change the default package to ejbapp. Click OK.

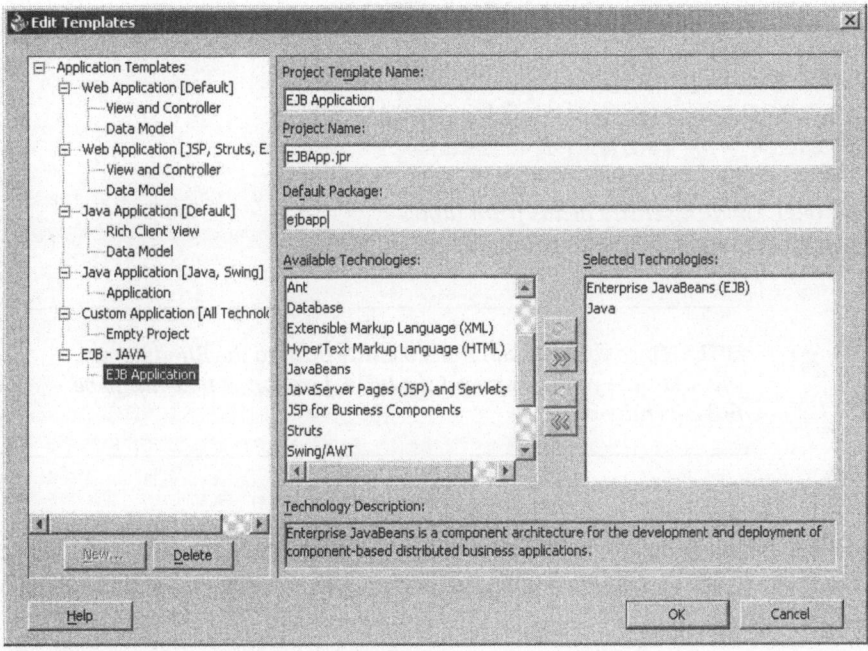

Figure 6-20. New Application Template

You should get back to the Create Application Workspace screen with the new template preselected in the application template list. Here change the application name to EJB_DB_App and the package prefix to com.jdevbook.chap6. A new workspace and a new project named EJBApp will be created for you.

Now right-click the project and select New. In the New gallery, you will find only options specific to the technology scope of EJB and Java. In Business Tier ➤ Enterprise JavaBeans (EJB), select the EJB Diagram option and click OK. You need to change the prepopulated package for the diagram to com.jdevbook.chap6.ejbapp. Change the name to Student Course EJB Diagram.

Now that you have the tables and the diagram canvas in place, next comes the really cool part. Just a few drag and drops and your EJBs will be done. Move to the Connections Navigator and from the Tables listed, drag the tables COURSE and STUDENT and drop them on to the EJB Diagram. You should get a dialog as shown in Figure 6-21. Here select the EJB 2.0 Entity beans option.

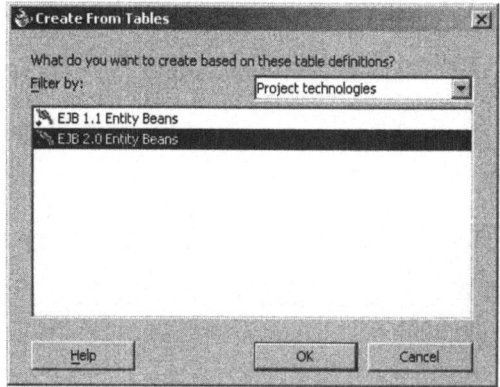

Figure 6-21. Creating entity beans from tables

NOTE   *Once you add one EJB 2.0 entity bean to the EJB diagram, the next time you will not get the EJB 1.1 option. It now has to be EJB 2.0 entity bean.*

Select the two entity beans represented in the diagram. Right-click and choose the Optimize Shape Height option. You should now have a diagram similar to that shown in Figure 6-22.

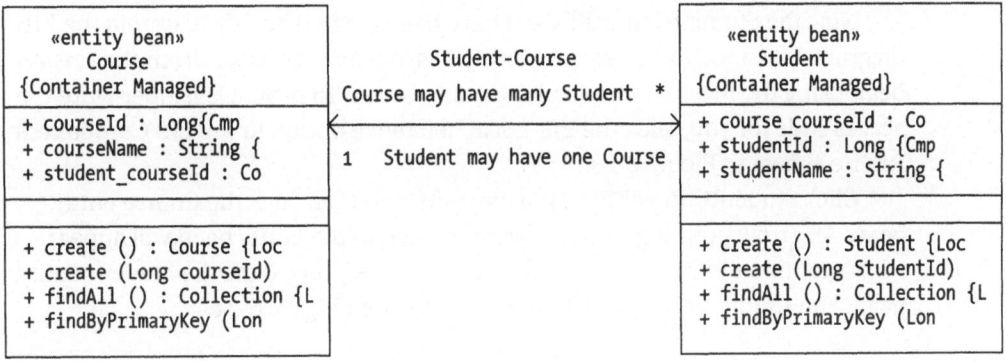

Figure 6-22. *Student and Course entity beans*

The next step is to create a new stateless session bean that will talk to the two entity beans. Although the session bean will expose its methods through a remote interface, the communication between the session bean and the entity beans will be through a local interface. The assumption is that all the three EJBs are running in the same JVM.

To add a new stateless session bean, select the Session Bean option from the EJB Component Palette, as shown in Figure 6-23, and then click anywhere in the EJB diagram. The Create Enterprise JavaBean wizard should start up. You have already seen this wizard in the earlier example. Create a stateless session bean named *StudentCourseEJB* with container-managed transactions. The bean class will be com.jdevbook.chap6.ejbapp.StudentCourseEJBBean. Include only remote interfaces for the bean.

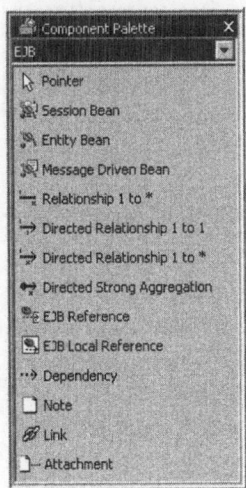

Figure 6-23. *EJB Component Palette*

Now the StudentCourseEJB will have been created and displayed in the EJB diagram. You need to access both entity beans using local calls from the session bean using the local interfaces of the entity beans. To have JDeveloper write the access code for you, click the EJB Local Reference option in the EJB Component Palette shown in Figure 6-23.

Click StudentCourseEJB in the diagram, and then click the Course entity bean. An arrow pointing from the session bean to the entity bean will appear, with a caption ejb/local/Course. Repeat the same process for the Student entity bean. You should now have a diagram as shown in Figure 6-24.

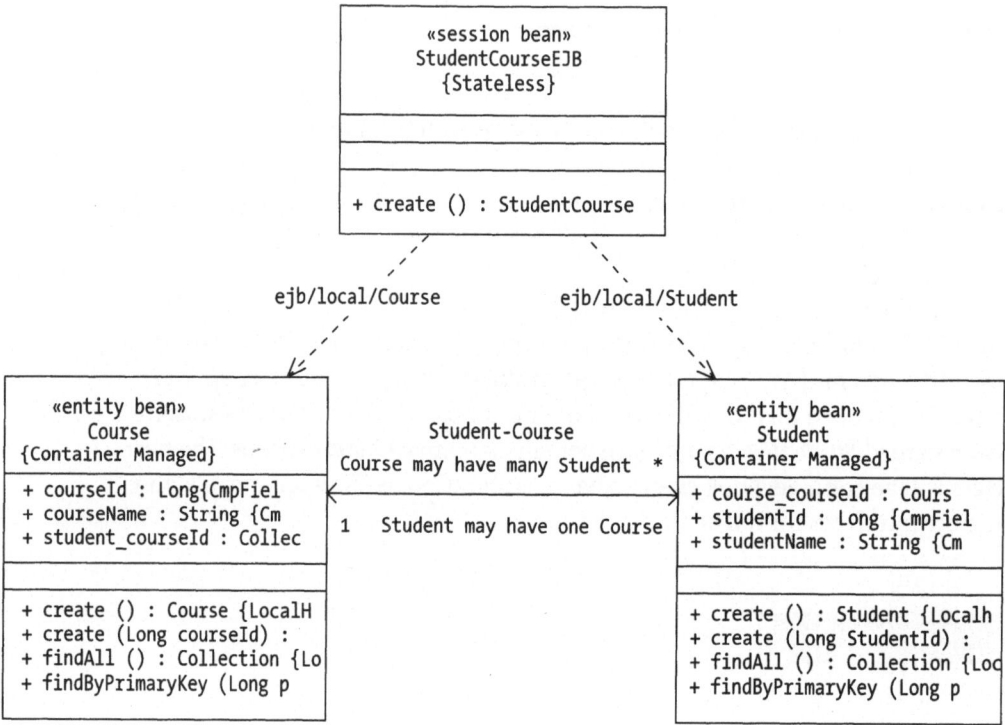

Figure 6-24. EJB diagram

Double-click any of the EJBs and the EJB Module Editor will appear. Here you will find that the two local references that you created are reflected in the Enterprise JavaBeans ➤ StudentCourseEJB ➤ EJB Local References section. Also check out the Preview XML section in the editor to have a look at the EJB Deployment Descriptor. This is the file where the changes you make using the UI actually get reflected. To have a better understanding of EJB deployment, and to be able to deploy on multiple servers, you need to be familiar with the EJB deployment descriptor, that is, the ejb-jar.xml file that appears in the META-INF directory.

Let's now add business methods to the StudentCourseEJB. These methods are the ones that the Java client will use and the contents of these methods will communicate with the entity beans. You will add two methods. One will add a new course, and the other will add a student for a course.

The method to add a new course is shown in Listing 6-2. This code will get a local reference to the entity bean, create a new course, and set the course name.

Listing 6-2. New Course Method

```
public void newCourse(String courseId
  , String courseName)
  throws NamingException, CreateException
{
  //Get Course Local Home Reference
  CourseLocalHome coursLocHome= getCourseLocalHome();
  //Create New Course
  CourseLocal courLoc= coursLocHome.create(new Long(courseId));
  //Set Course Name
  courLoc.setCourseName(courseName);
}
```

The newStudent method is shown in Listing 6-3. The only difference here is that you have to find the Course, on the Course Id provided, and then associate it with the student.

Listing 6-3. New Student Method

```
public void newStudent(String studentId
  , String studentName
  , String courseId)
  throws CreateException, FinderException, NamingException
{
  //Get Local Home reference
  StudentLocalHome stLocHome= getStudentLocalHome();
  //Create new Student
  StudentLocal stLoc= stLocHome.create(new Long(studentId));
  //Set Student Name
  stLoc.setStudentName(studentName);

  //Get Course Local Home Reference
  CourseLocalHome courseLocHome= getCourseLocalHome();
  //Find Course By Id
  CourseLocal courLoc= courseLocHome.findByPrimaryKey(new Long(courseId));
  //Set Course For Student
  stLoc.setCourse_courseId(courLoc);
}
```

Now again go over to the EJB Module Editor and check if the business methods listed in Enterprise JavaBeans ➤ StudentCourseEJB ➤ Methods are correct. If you have compiled the bean class, JDeveloper will have inserted the new methods properly. All you need to do is to select the method and check the Expose through Remote Interface option for both methods. This is important, because unless the method is exposed through the remote interface, it cannot be used by the client.

Now you just need to create a new Sample Java Client and invoke these methods. Just to be sure, use the Verify Enterprise Bean option for all the EJBs. Next create a New Sample Java Client for StudentCourseEJB, choosing the Connect to OC4J Embedded in JDeveloper option.

Please refer to a Caution earlier in the chapter for a fix related to a problem I faced with the Sample Java Client.

In the client code generated, use these three lines of code in place of the commented remote calls that the client would have generated for you.

```
studentCourseEJB.newCourse( "11", "J2EE" );
studentCourseEJB.newStudent( "333", "Boris Becker", "11" );
System.out.println("New Course and Student inserted");
```

Now run StudentCourseEJB followed by running the client. You will get the New Course and Student Inserted message, and the data should be inserted in the appropriate tables. Note that because Student Id and Course Id are the primary keys, for a second invocation you would have to change the values.

This was an example where you used session beans, entity beans, and an EJB diagram. Instead of a Sample Java Client, you could very well have used a JSP or Servlet, or even another EJB as a client for the stateless session bean.

Deploy to jar or ear

Most EJBs and J2EE applications tend to move around as enterprise archive (.ear), Web Archive (.war) or Java Archive (.jar) files, so easy deployment of applications in any of these file formats is a useful feature to have. JDeveloper provides deployment profiles for EJB applications.

For the EJB_DB_App, go to the General ➤ Deployment Profiles section in the New Gallery dialog. Choose the EJB JAR File - J2EE EJB Module option. If you choose the default options, you should have a new file named ejb1.deploy created in the root directory of the project and listed under Resources in the Applications Navigator.

The EJB JAR Deployment Profile Settings, as shown in Figure 6-25, provides various options to customize the archive that will be created. Once the ejb1.deploy file is created appropriately, all you need to deploy the EJB or application to an application server, or an .ear or .jar file, is to right-click the *.deploy file and choose the relevant Deploy to option. To deploy to an application server, a new connection has to be set up in the Application Servers section in the Connections Navigator.

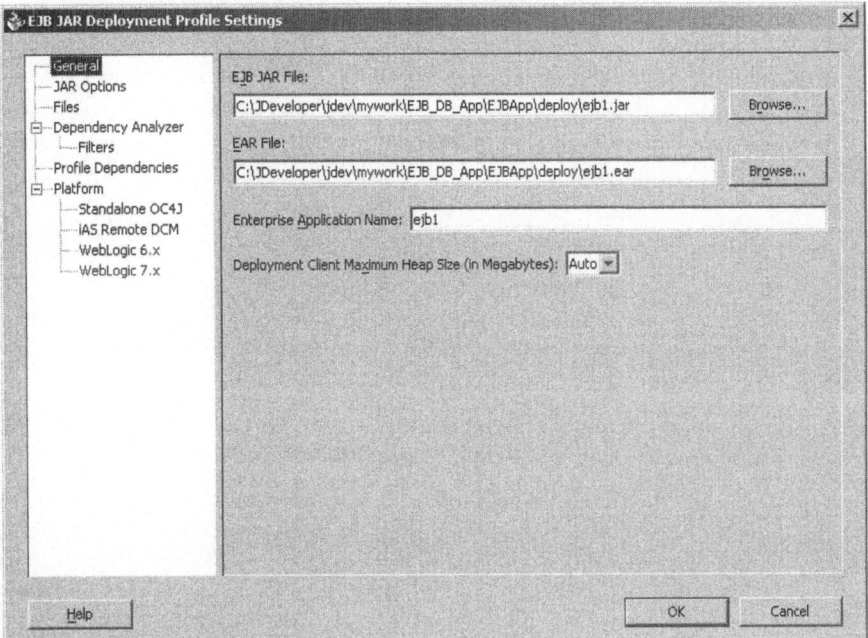

Figure 6-25. EJB JAR Deployment Settings

Summary

In this chapter, I delved into EJB territory and showed you why EJBs are so popular these days and what it is that they offer. You had a look at JDeveloper's capabilities to quickly create an application using EJBs. You also saw how easy it is to work with databases, and how tables can be created, modified, and used to create entity beans.

Most J2EE applications these days use JSP/Servlets along with EJBs, and often use a framework like Struts. This chapter, along with the previous one, should provide you good grounding to start developing your own J2EE applications.

Application Development Framework

IN THE PAST FEW CHAPTERS you saw a standard way of developing a Java 2 Enterprise Edition (J2EE) application using Java Server Pages (JSPs)/Servlets and Enterprise JavaBeans (EJBs). However, there is no denying that J2EE can get quite complex at times, and you need to understand many things to be able to deploy a quality J2EE application. Developing an application and developing a quality application are two very different things in J2EE.

Many attempts at reducing the complexity of J2EE and building frameworks and abstractions that will make the developer's task easier have already been made. The Application Development Framework (ADF) is Oracle's attempt at this. Apart from reducing complexity, raising the overall quality of the application being developed is also something that ADF aims at.

With version 10g, everything that isn't Java (as you know Java independent of JDeveloper) seems to fall into the ADF zone. Many of the features such as the Business Components for Java (BC4J) and JClient were already around in earlier versions; however, with ADF, Oracle has consolidated the existing bits and built on them to provide even more productivity and ease of use.

Answering Key Questions

Whenever you think of any framework, a few questions need to be answered even before you consider ADF as an option:

Do you have to pay for ADF usage? No. ADF is licensed as part of JDeveloper; no separate license is required to deploy applications based on ADF.

Once you develop with ADF, can you deploy only on an Oracle application server? ADF applications will run on any J2EE-compliant application server.

Does ADF only work with Oracle databases? No. ADF will work with other databases such as DB2, SQL Server, and so on.

Can you develop and maintain applications using non-Oracle tools? As yet, no non-Oracle tool provides support for ADF development. However, since ADF depends on XML files for its operation, you do have the option of editing the XML directly using any other tool.

Is the learning curve steep? JDeveloper provides many wizards and tools to simplify development with ADF. However, it does take some time to get used to the tool. The basic tasks are not very difficult, but advanced functions are a little complex.

Can applications developed with earlier JDeveloper versions work with ADF? Yes. Oracle claims to be strongly committed to compatibility between the previous version and 10g.

Do you have to choose between pure J2EE and ADF, or can both work together? ADF components can work well in tandem with normal J2EE components such as EJBs, JSPs, and so on.

Should you opt for ADF-based development on your project? This is a tough question. ADF is certainly a useful offering. However, you need to consider whether you are committed to using JDeveloper and Oracle technologies over the long run. Also, it is unlikely that a job advertisement saying "expertise in ADF expected" would get much response. So individuals skilled in ADF become a vital resource. To build expertise, you will have to incur some training expenses.

What Is ADF?

The ADF frequently asked question (FAQ) Web page says the following:

> *Oracle ADF is a comprehensive productivity layer for J2EE developers. It simplifies building applications as a set of business services with Web, wireless, and rich client interfaces. ADF accelerates development with ready-to-use J2EE Design pattern implementations and metadata-driven components that you'd otherwise have to code, test, and debug by hand.*

I could not find much information about how exactly ADF has evolved and why it was conceptualized in the first place. I would think that the framework was created because developers were trying to simplify working with Java and J2EE and interacting with databases. If you want to achieve this while maintaining high quality and abstracting the complexity of the framework itself from end users, you need a good tool to use. So while ADF implements various design patterns and tries to develop high-quality applications, JDeveloper makes it easier to use ADF itself.

Although ADF emphasizes the Model-View-Controller (MVC) architecture and view options such as JClient and UIX, the best offering is the ease with which interaction with the database is possible using ADF tools. Even the power of the view offerings lies in how easily the view can be bound to data.

Understanding the Components of ADF

The ADF documentation talks a lot about MVC architecture and how ADF fits in place to enable the creation of MVC-based applications. Figure 7-1 shows how the various elements in ADF stack up.

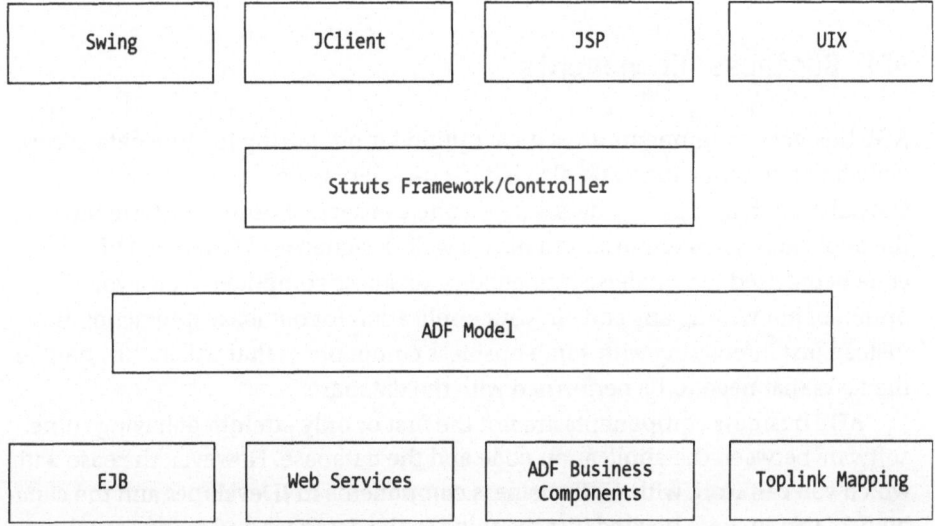

Figure 7-1. ADF component stack

The following are the various ADF components with respect to the MVC architecture:

Model layer: This is the layer where you have your business logic and services. Although it can be in the form of EJBs or Web Services, ADF provides ADF business components that cannot only be bound to data but can also enable easy creation of rules and the application of business logic. The Model layer is where ADF provides the most value because you can quickly get business services up and running.

Controller layer: Because ADF can work well with the Apache Struts framework you learned about in Chapter 5, the Struts controller plays the role of controller in an ADF-based MVC architecture. However, with ADF the action does vary. ADF introduces the idea of a data action.

View layer: As shown in Figure 7-1, you have multiple view options. The view can be a normal JSP, ADF UIX, Swing, or JClient. UIX is a set of Extensible Markup Language (XML)–based UI components for Web applications. For Java client applications, you can work with Swing components, or you can use Oracle ADF JClient. JClient is a set of Java classes that are specifically meant for building data-bound User Interface (UI) applications.

You will now look in some detail at the three key elements of ADF: ADF business components, ADF JClient, and ADF UIX.

ADF Business Components

ADF business components are a great option for not having to write data access code for your application and also have top-quality code doing the job for you. Considering that improper data access code can severely affect performance of the application, it is important to have a well-designed and optimized bit of code being used for database interactions. Business components give you the option of not writing any code in your application for database interaction but instead just interacting with some business components that will in turn handle the tasks that need to be performed with the database.

ADF business components are not the first or only attempt at having some software between the application code and the database. However, the ease with which you can work with ADF business components in JDeveloper and the capability of taking them beyond just mapping to the database and being actual business services with some logic in them is what makes ADF business components special.

You will now see an example where you will create new business components and later use them through options such as UIX and JClient.

Exploring the Business Component Types

ADF business components do a great job of simplifying and optimizing interactions with a data source such as a database. The two key elements of business components that make this possible are entity objects and view objects.

Entity Objects

Entity objects represent objects in the database while also encapsulating some business logic and validation logic. The application's view of the database cannot go beyond the entity object. Although entity objects can be used with data sources other than databases such as spreadsheets or XML files, entity objects are best used with databases.

Entity objects can serve as exact representations of tables where each column stands for an attribute in the entity object. However, it is possible to get rid of attributes that you do not intend to use but are being represented in the entity object. You can also introduce new attributes that are not present in the table.

The JDeveloper documentation lists the following kinds of business rules that can be implemented using entity objects:

- **Validation logic**: Validates data based on various rules to ensure that only valid data gets entered into the database.

- **Security logic**: Ensures that only authorized users can access data.

- **Creation logic**: Performs actions on the creation of new rows.

- **Deletion logic**: Performs actions on the deletion of rows.

- **Other logic**: Has events being triggered when certain data is modified. When these events are triggered, specific actions can be taken.

View Objects

View objects are meant for clients. These are the objects that clients in an ADF application will generally interact with. So view objects fetch data from a data source, mostly a database. The view object then customizes this data for client use.

View objects can work like entity objects where the view object maps to a database table. However, that is not how you have to use them. View objects are meant to provide data that the client wants so that data can very well come from more than one table or be just a specific chunk of data in a one table.

With view objects you can add complex SQL queries and test them using the JDeveloper tools. It is also possible to parameterize the queries and provide the parameters at run time. View objects provide some tuning options that can be used to get them to perform even better.

Another important capability of view objects is that you can add new methods that can process the data and return results that the client expects. So although a lot of logic is being provided and processed by the framework, you also have the option to introduce your own snippets of logic.

You will now look at an example where you create and use entity objects and view objects.

Developing an Example Application

In the example in Chapter 6, you created and used two tables, namely STUDENT and COURSE. You will now use the same tables, but you will now use business components for all the interactions with the tables.

You will first create a new application workspace named *StudentCourseADF* where the package prefix is named *com.jdevbook.chap7* and the application template is named *Web Application [Default]*. This will create a Model project where the business components will reside and a view project where the Struts components, ADF UIX, and JSPs will be created.

Your next step is to create the entity objects that will map with the two tables COURSE and STUDENT. To create entity objects, you have multiple options to choose from:

- You can choose Business Tier ➤ Business Components ➤ Entity Object from the New Gallery. This can be used to create a single entity object.

- You can choose Business Tier ➤ Business Components ➤ Business Components from Tables option in the New Gallery, which lets you create multiple entity objects at once. Based on the relationships between the tables, the associations in the entity objects will also be created automatically.

JDeveloper has a good way of providing diagrammatic ways to represent things. So apart from the Unified Modeling Language (UML), Struts, and database diagrams, you also have a business components diagram. This diagram can represent application modules, entity objects, view objects, and the associations between the objects.

To create a business components diagram, in the New Gallery for the Model project, select the option Business Tier ➤ Business Components ➤ Business Components Diagram and then click OK. Name the diagram *StudentCourse Components Diagram*. The package will be named *com.jdevbook.chap7.model*.

You should now have a blank diagram, and the Component Palette will display the Java and Business Components options. You can choose components in the palette, as shown in Figure 7-2, to create new business components. However, an even easier way is to just use the tables COURSE and STUDENT and drag and drop them on the diagram.

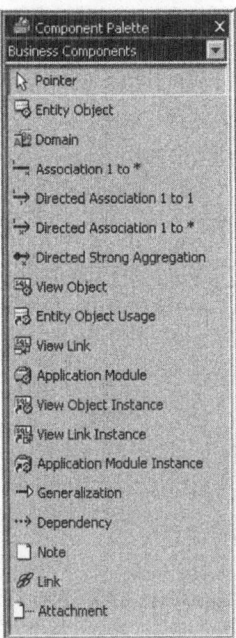

Figure 7-2. Business Components Component Palette

Expand the database connection you created in Chapter 6, and drag the tables STUDENT and COURSE to the diagram. You should get the Create from Tables dialog box, as shown in Figure 7-3. Click OK.

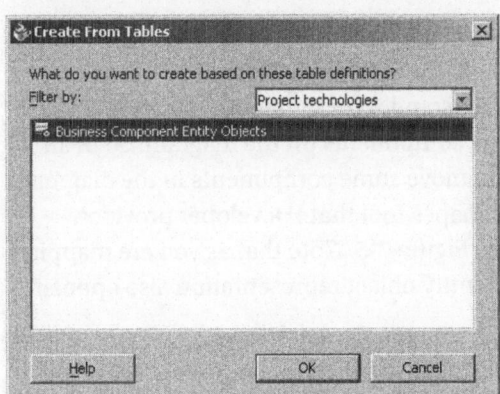

Figure 7-3. The Create from Tables dialog box

As shown in Figure 7-4, not only will the two entity objects representing the tables be created, but the association between the two entities will also be created.

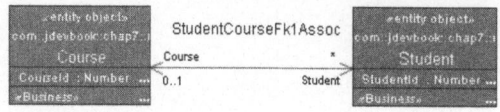

Figure 7-4. Student and Course entity objects

Before you start exploring the entity objects created, you will use another useful tool provided by JDeveloper to generate default data model components associated with the entity objects. Just select both entity objects in the diagram, and either right-click and select Generate ➤ Default Data Model Components option or select the same from the Model menu.

This will introduce a few new listings to the project in the Applications Navigator:

- **AppModule**: The application module is an implementation of a business service and aggregates view objects and links required for the task. You can also introduce new client methods for the task.

- **CourseView and StudentView**: The CourseView and StudentView generated will be a similar representation to the entity object you created earlier. However, you can customize it to your needs.

- **StudentCourseFK1Assoc and StudentCourseFK1Link**: These are used to reflect the one-to-many relationship that exists between the tables COURSE and STUDENT.

You will now drag these elements to the business components diagram to get a diagrammatic and easier-to-understand representation. JDeveloper isn't particularly good at sizing and placing components on the diagram. So in all probability you will have to resize and move some components in the diagram. You could also try using the Lay Out Shapes tool that JDeveloper provides.

Your view objects should look like Figure 7-5. Note that as you are mapping view objects to the entity objects, an entity object representation also appears for each view object.

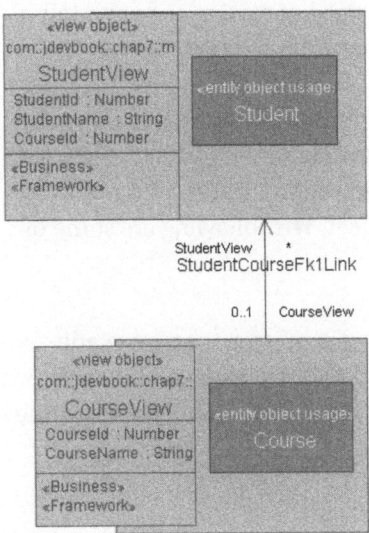

Figure 7-5. Student and Course view objects

The application module shows the view object instances it is working with as well as a master-detail relationship between CourseView1 and StudentView2. As shown in Figure 7-6, two StudentView instances are used, one for direct interaction with the Student entity object and the other with respect to the foreign key link StudentCourseFK1Link.

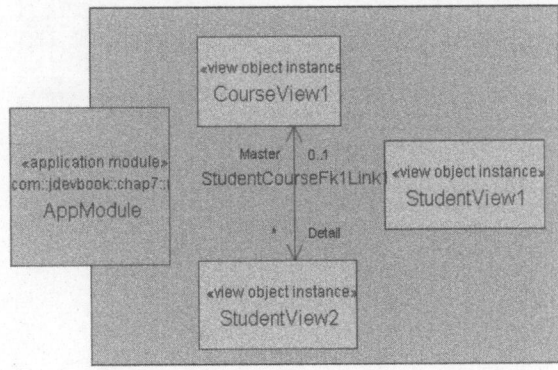

Figure 7-6. The application module

You will now explore these objects you have created to understand what they are capable of doing. For this example, you will check that the CourseId entered is in the specified range of 10–1,000. Instead of writing code and implementing this in the application, you can easily introduce this validation rule through the entity object UI.

Open the Entity Object Editor either by double-clicking the Course entity object as displayed in the business components diagram or by double-clicking it in the Applications Navigator. The Entity Object Editor offers a simple UI for manipulating various settings for the entity object. The following are some of the important tasks possible:

- Not only can you add and remove attributes, but you can even edit the attribute details that were set based on database table values. As shown in Figure 7-7, you can even hide, format, or provide tooltip text for the attributes.

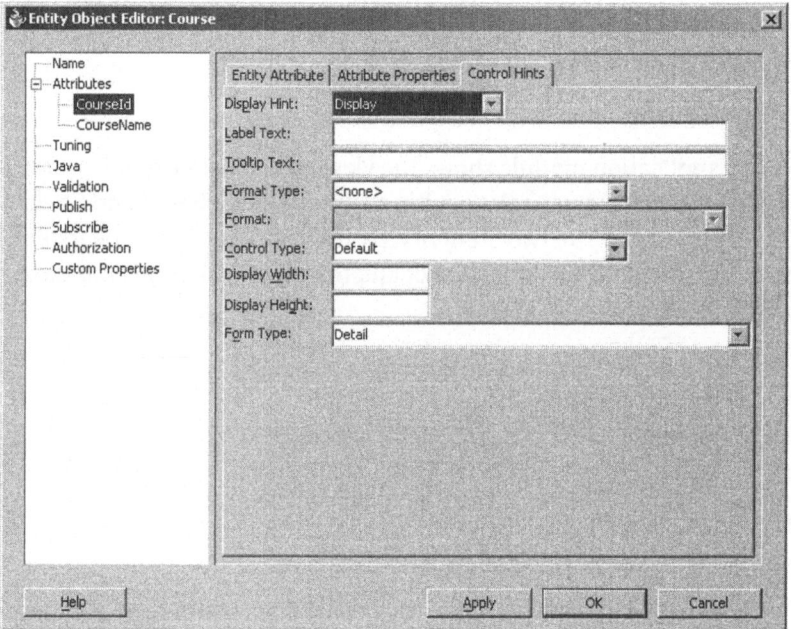

Figure 7-7. CourseId control hints

- In the Java section in the Entity Object Editor, you can define which Java files you want generated as well as the methods that should be generated. Just generating methods does not change how the entity object works but gives you the option to edit these methods and customize the implementation.

- You can publish events and also subscribe to events so that a specific method is invoked when a certain event occurs.

- You can specify permissions at an attribute level. Double-click the attributes listed in the Authorization section to get a screen similar to the one shown in Figure 7-8.

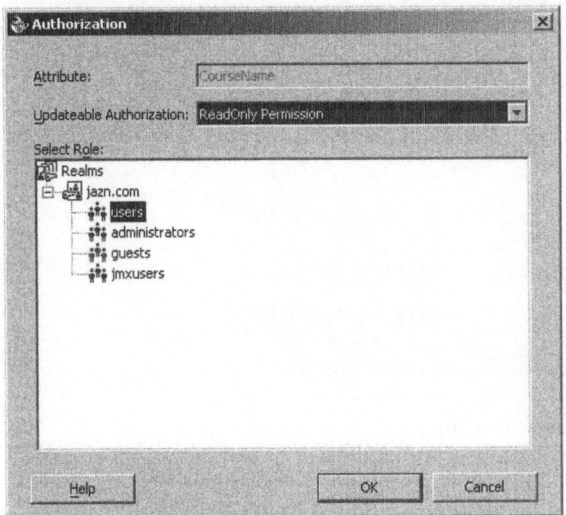

Figure 7-8. The Authorization dialog box

- You can specify validation rules for individual attributes.

You will now add a new validation rule for CourseId such that only values between 10 and 1,000 will be accepted as valid input.

Open the Entity Object Editor for the Course entity object and move to the Validation section. Here select Course, and click the New button to get the screen shown in Figure 7-9.

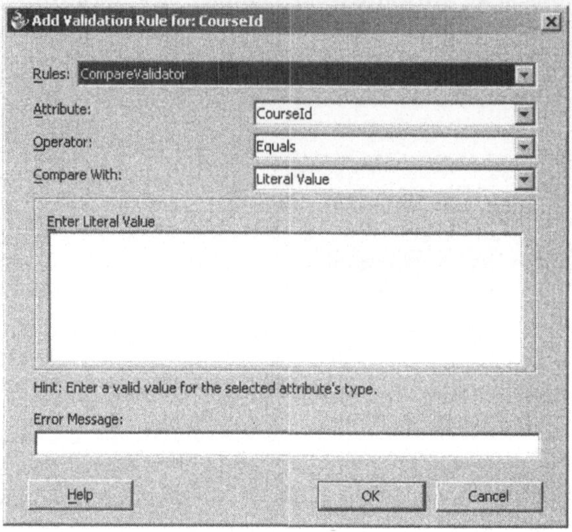

Figure 7-9. Adding a validation rule

The Rules drop-down list will have four kinds of validators:

- **CompareValidator**: You can define the value to which the attribute value should be compared. The Compare With drop-down list gives you the option to not only compare with a literal value but also to compare with query results or view object attributes.

- **ListValidator**: The ListValidator can compare the value with a list of values either specified or returned by a SQL query or provided as a view object attribute.

- **RangeValidator**: You define the range that the attribute should be in. Note the use of the Between or Not Between attribute. Incorrect usage can get you the opposite effect from what you want.

- **MethodValidator**: You can use this rule to define the method that will do the validation. You have to provide a method that matches the signature stated in the hint. Because you have not defined any new method, you will not get any methods listed here.

You will use the RangeValidator and define the operator as *Between*, the minimum value as *10*, and the maximum value as *1000*. The error message you will use is *The CourseId has to be between 10 and 1000*.

Another type of predefined validator is UniqueKeyValidator. Select the UniqueKeyValidator, and state the error message as *CourseId not unique*. The Validation section in the Entity Object Editor for the Course entity object will now be as shown in Figure 7-10. Click OK.

TIP *The UniqueKeyValidator is not available at the attribute level and is available for the entire entity object. So this rule is not displayed in the Rules drop-down list if you selected an attribute and then clicked the New button.*

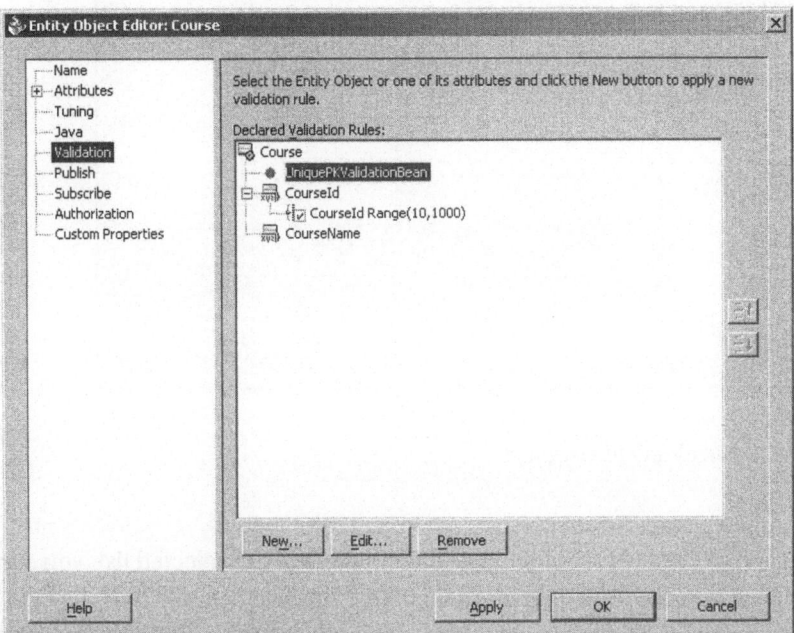

Figure 7-10. Course validations

You will now look at the Student and Course view objects. Because you created the view objects based on the entity objects, the view objects look very similar to the entity objects at the beginning. Double-click the CourseView view object listed in the Applications Navigator or displayed in the diagram to get the screen shown in Figure 7-11.

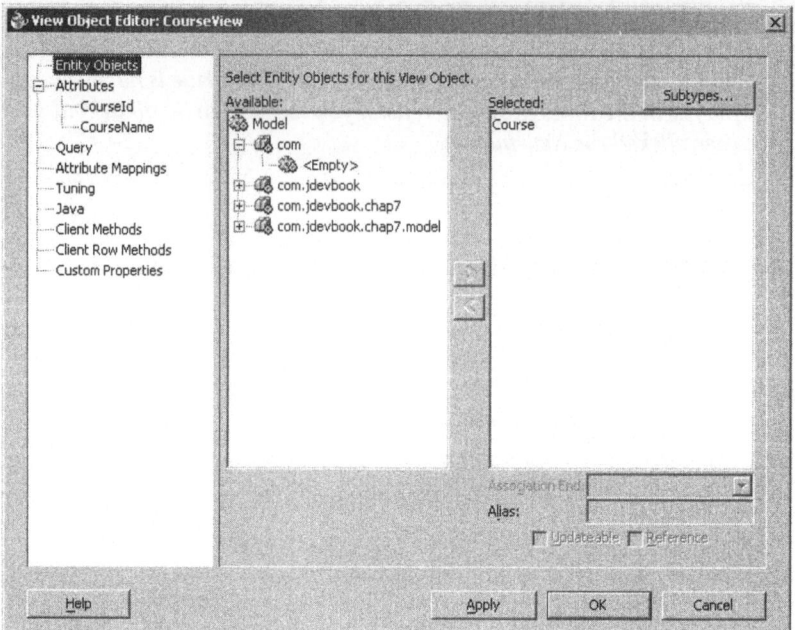

Figure 7-11. CourseView view object

Although the Course entity object is the only one in the selected list, you can add more. A view object is certainly not restricted to a single entity object view. Unlike entity objects, with view objects you can state the query that will be used to fetch data from the data source. You can also add new methods and expose them to the client.

You will now create a new view object and have it fetch and represent only a specific chunk of data such as all Java courses only. You will just pick up all students who have taken Java courses. Any course that has *Java* as the first word in the name will be considered as a Java course.

To create a new view object, right-click com.jdevbook.chap7.model as displayed in the Applications Navigator and select the New View Object option. Click Next on the welcome screen, and on the next screen (step 1), change the name of the view to *JavaCourseView*. In step 2, select the Course entity object as well as the Student entity object, and click Next.

In Step 3, as shown in Figure 7-12, select the attributes CourseId and CourseName from the COURSE table and StudentId and StudentName from the STUDENT table. Click Next.

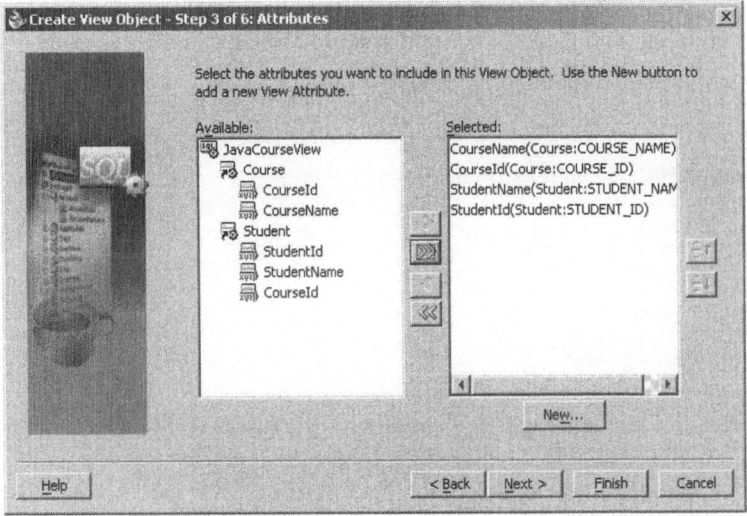

Figure 7-12. Creating view object attributes

You do not need to make any changes to the attribute settings in step 4. Click Next. Step 5 is important, because you have to customize the query. You will find that a table join has been written for you; you just need to add *AND Course.COURSE_NAME LIKE 'Java%'* to the Where field, as shown in Figure 7-13. The query will then fetch the students' data for the Java course.

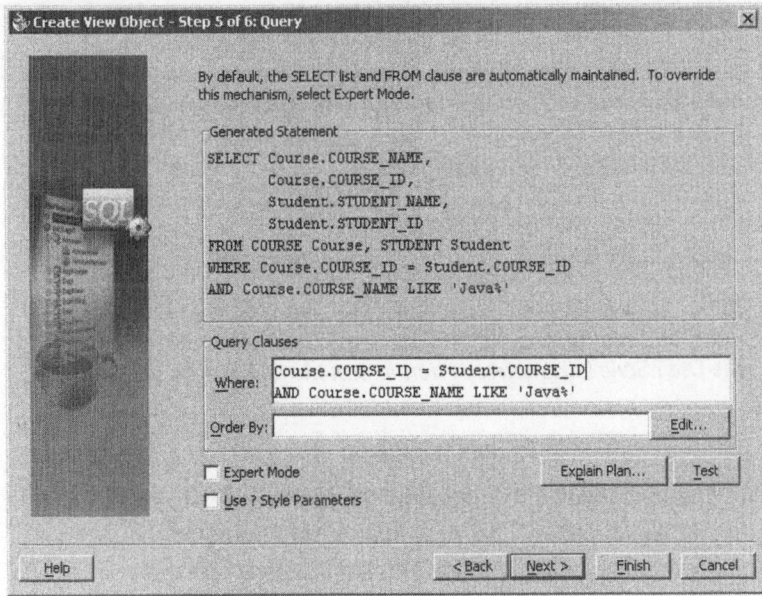

Figure 7-13. Creating the view object query

Click the Test button to check if the query is valid. If it isn't, you should get a proper error message pointing out the cause for the error. Click the Explain Plan button to get the display shown in Figure 7-14.

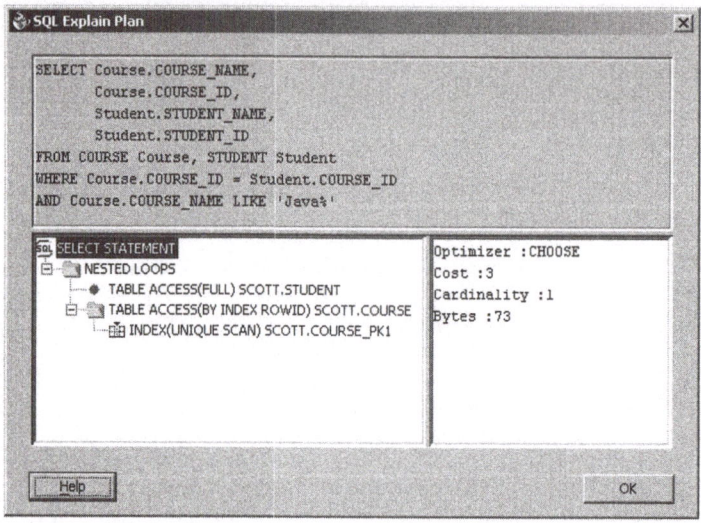

Figure 7-14. The SQL Explain Plan dialog box

 NOTE *The SQL Explain Plan dialog box displays the execution plan chosen by the Oracle optimizer for the query. An execution plan is the sequence of operations that will be performed to execute the SQL. For the SQL Explain Plan dialog box to work, a new PLAN table has to be created. Click OK when you get a pop-up message asking if the table should be created.*

 TIP *You can use the Expert Mode if you want to edit the entire query and not just the WHERE and ORDER BY clauses. You can use the Use ? Style Parameters option to provide parameters at run time.*

Click Next. You do not need to make any changes to step 6. The final screen will now display details of the view object being created. Click Finish. The JavaCourseView will now be listed in the Applications Navigator.

Next, you need to associate the new view object you just created with the application module you created earlier. This is important because only after the view object is part of the data model that the application module represents can it be easily tested and used.

To add the JavaCourseView view object to the application module AppModule, double-click AppModule as listed in the Applications Navigator or right-click and select the Edit AppModule option to get the screen shown in Figure 7-15. Now move JavaCourseView to the AppModule data model. A new instance of JavaCourseView named *JavaCourseView1* will be displayed in the AppModule data model. Click OK. The JavaCourseView view object is now part of the AppModule data model, and the business components are now done. You will now test this module.

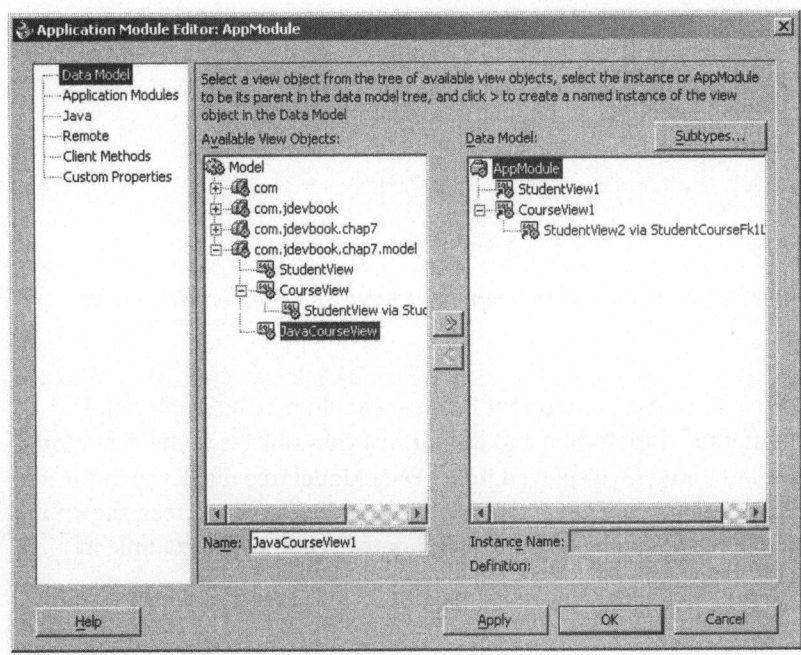

Figure 7-15. AppModule data model

Testing the Application Module

Once the application module is done, before you integrate the business components with a UI, it is recommended that you first test if the components are actually performing as expected. Testing business components without a UI could be rather difficult; however, fortunately JDeveloper provides a cool testing environment where you can quickly and easily test the business components.

Right-click AppModule, and choose the Test option to get the screen shown in Figure 7-16. Not only can you change the settings to use a Java database connectivity (JDBC) data source instead of a URL, but you can use many other configurations if you switch to the Properties tab. You do not need to make any changes here. Click Connect.

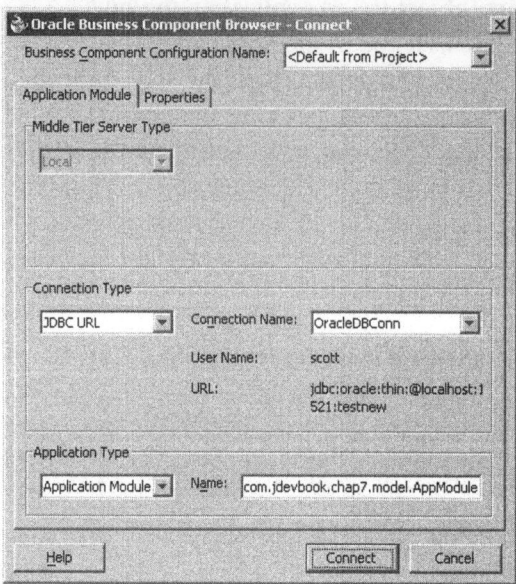

Figure 7-16. The Oracle Business Component Browser—Connect dialog box

The Oracle Business Component Browser should now be displayed. The application module AppModule and the various view objects in the data model for AppModule should be displayed in the Data Model tree displayed in the left pane. Double-click CourseView1 and StudentView1 to get the screen shown in Figure 7-17. The data displayed is the data I entered in the EJB example in Chapter 6.

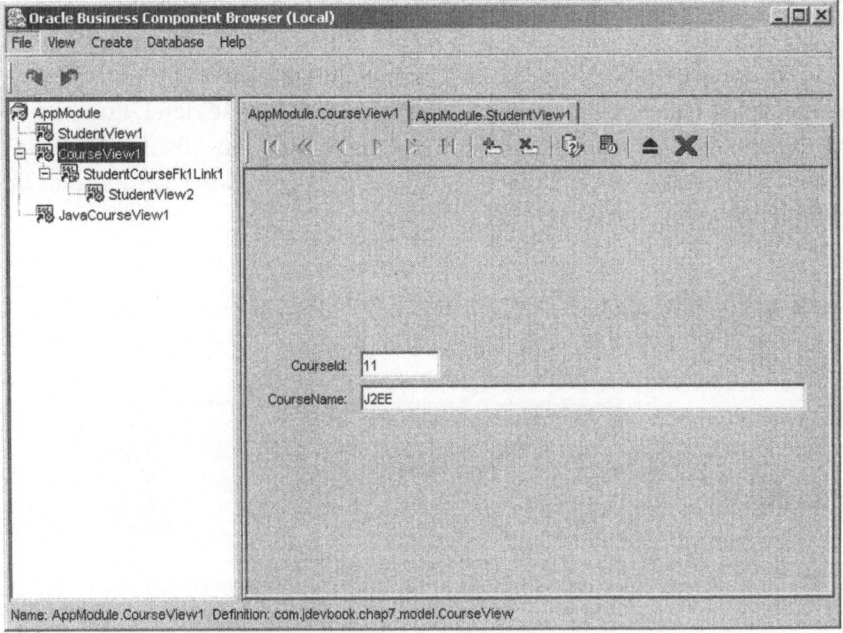

Figure 7-17. The business component browser

To try your business components, first enter a course and then add students for that course. Double-click CourseView1, or right-click and select the Show option. Now click the plus (+) sign to insert a new record. Insert *6* in the CourseId field, and either use the Tab button or click the CourseName field. You should immediately get the screen shown in Figure 7-18. This means that the validation on the field CourseId that you defined earlier is working fine. Click OK. Now change the CourseId to *12*, and enter the course name as *Java with JDeveloper.*

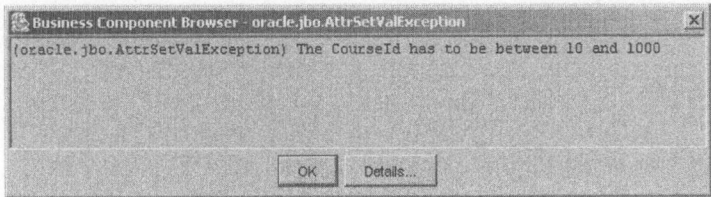

Figure 7-18. Validation display

Now commit the change by either using the Commit icon in the toolbar or using the Database ➤ Commit command. Now use the StudentView instance to insert two new students. The first student has StudentId *444*, StudentName

Pete Sampras, and CourseId *12.* The second student has StudentId *555,* StudentName *Andre Agassi,* and CourseId as *11.* Then commit the changes.

Now you have Pete Sampras learning Java with JDeveloper and Boris Becker and Andre Agassi learning J2EE. Now double-click JavaCourseView1, and you will get the screen shown in Figure 7-19. JavaCourseView1 only fetches the Pete Sampras record because he is the only student studying a course with *Java* as the first word in the course name.

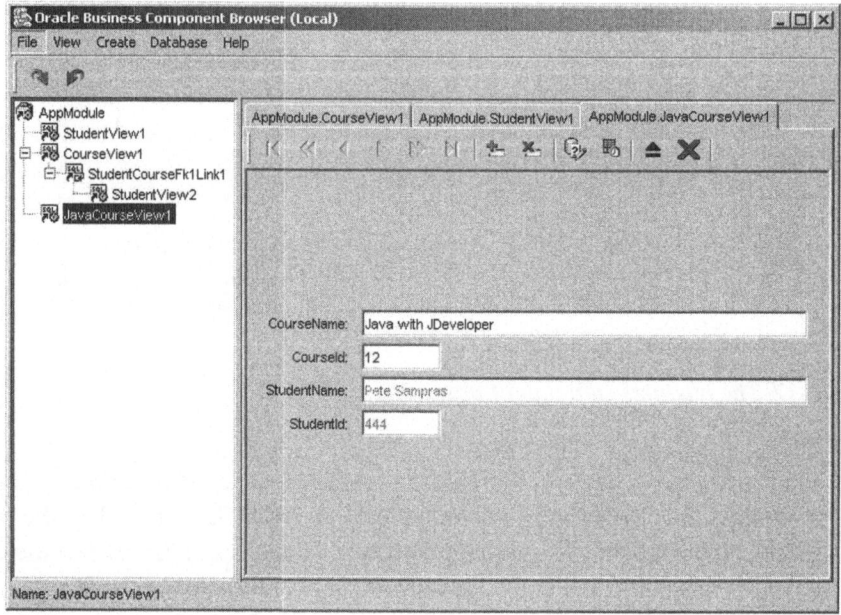

Figure 7-19. JavaCourseView1

You now know that all your business components are working as expected and can move on to creating a UI that uses these components.

Introducing UIX

UIX is a J2EE-based framework for building Web applications. UIX pages can serve as an alternative to using JSPs. UIX in tandem with business components can get a dynamic and data-centric application up quickly.

> **CAUTION** *While interacting with business components through a UIX interface and having your server running, do not use the business component browser you saw earlier to make changes in the background. I did do that and faced error messages saying that another user has modified a certain record.*

UIX fits into the View layer of ADF's MVC scheme of things. UIX pages are XML pages that use a set of tags that convey the "how" and "what" of the page. UIX pages have a hierarchy of XML elements based on the display expected. If you are already worrying about having to study a new set of tags, fret not. Ideally, using all the tools that JDeveloper provides, you do not need to manually edit the XML at all.

My first impression of UIX was that it felt a lot like developing a Swing or Abstract Window Toolkit (AWT) client. There were various layouts, components, events, and so on already defined, and all I had to do was to drag and drop components. Because UIX is most useful when used along with ADF business components, in this section you will develop a UIX-based Web application that interacts with the business components you developed earlier in the chapter.

UIX applications also use the Struts controller you saw in Chapter 6 to manage the flow of the application. So the easiest way to work with UIX is by using the Struts flow diagram. In the ViewController project that is part of the StudentCourseADF workspace, right-click the file struts-config.xml that you will find in the WEB-INF directory and select the option Edit Struts Page Flow. A blank diagram will be created, and the Struts flow components will appear in the Component Palette.

Add the Page Forward component to the diagram, and then double-click it to get the screen shown in Figure 7-20.

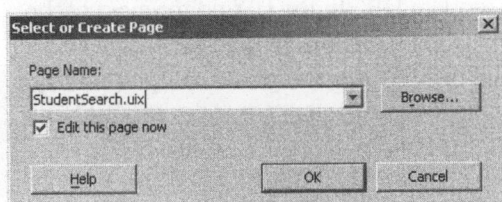

Figure 7-20. Creating a UIX page

Here name the page *StudentSearch.uix*, and keep the Edit This Page Now option checked. The StudentSearch.uix page will now be available for editing in the Design view, as shown in Figure 7-21. The layout is already defined, as are the locations of various components present on a regular Web page. If you move to the XML view of the page, you will find that there are actually tags named *corporateBranding* and *productBranding*.

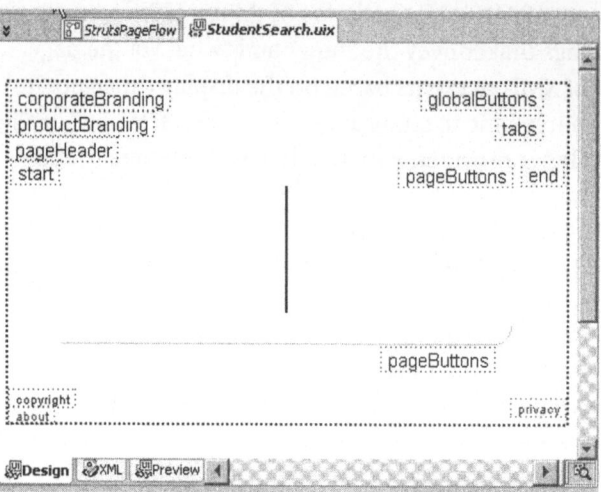

Figure 7-21. StudentSearch.uix in the Design view

If you tried adding text directly in the Design view and failed, you have company. Coming from how JDeveloper handles HTML and JSP editing in a What You See Is What You Get (WYSIWYG) mode, even I tried to add text directly in the Design view. However, that does not work in UIX. In the UIX editor most of the editing happens in the form of editing property values in the Property Inspector.

To add any new content, you need to add the appropriate component from the Component Palette. The Component Palette available is quite comprehensive with many components for forms, navigation, layout, and so on.

 NOTE *The Structure window displays the structure of the UIX page, and you can even drag and move elements within the Structure window.*

For this example, you will now look at the Data Control Palette and use it to add data controls to your UIX page. The Data Control Palette window, as show in Figure 7-22, plays an important role in creating data-driven pages. The application module and the view objects that are part of the data model for the application module are available through the Data Control Palette. The Drop As drop-down list is particularly useful because that is where you specify how the data control should be displayed. Click various elements listed in the Data Control Palette, and notice how the options in the Drop As list change accordingly.

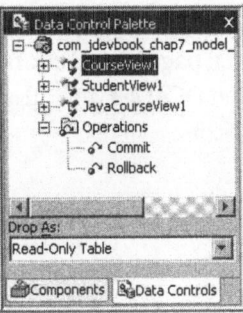

Figure 7-22. Data Control Palette

For this example, you will select StudentView1 and choose the Search Form option in the Drop As drop-down list. Next you simply drag StudentView1 to the center of StudentSearch.uix. Because you do not intend to use any of the other elements such as branding, you can easily get rid of those from the display by clicking the Show Empty Named Children image at the bottom right of the StudentSearch.uix page, as shown in Figure 7-23.

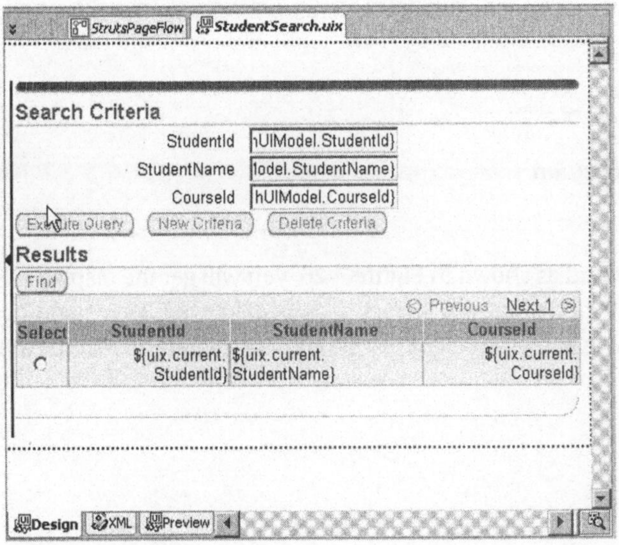

Figure 7-23. Student search

Guess what? That's all you have to do to create a search page. Go back to the Struts page flow diagram, and as shown in Figure 7-24, you will find that a new data action named *page1DataAction* has already been generated for you. A data action class is an ADF-specific thing and is required to be able to fetch the data you display on StudentSearch.uix. All data action classes extend `oracle.adf.controller.struts.actions.DataAction`. Right-click page1DataAction, and select the option Run /page1DataAction. The Embedded OC4J server will start, and your browser should display as shown in Figure 7-25.

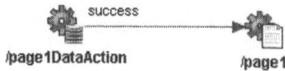

Figure 7-24. Struts flow diagram

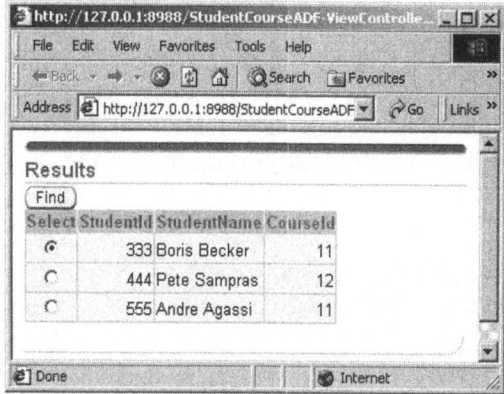

Figure 7-25. Display on execution

Click the Find button, and as shown in Figure 7-26, you will get the display that you see in the preview mode that you expected to be displayed. This might be a bug in 10g preview, or, who knows, it might just be a feature where all records are displayed by default.

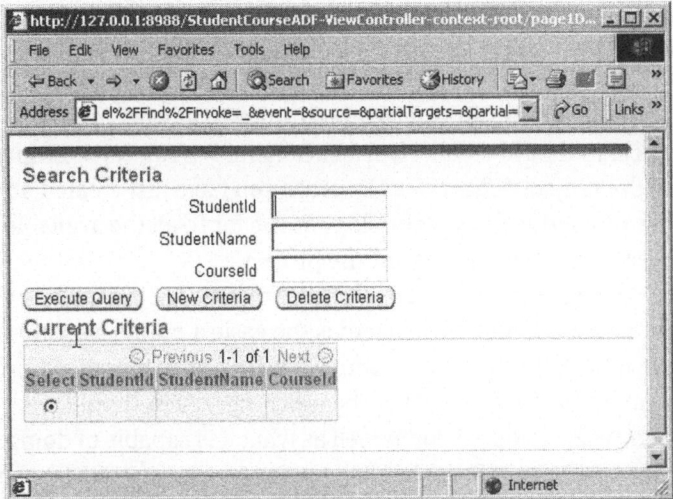

Figure 7-26. Expected search display

Along similar lines to the search form you created, you could also drag and drop other data controls onto the page. Click the button Show Empty Named Children at the bottom right to again display all the tags in the UIX page. You have as yet not utilized most of these tags and their capabilities to include and lay out content and images. Because real applications will have corporate branding, copyrights, and so on, these tags are very relevant. The easiest way to use tags such as corporatebranding and productbranding is to simply drag and drop any image from Windows Explorer or similar file manager, and JDeveloper will do the rest.

Although using these UIX capabilities is fairly simple, coming to terms with the dozens of UIX components and knowing which one does what can be quite a task. After this quick look at UIX, you will now move to another component of ADF, JClient.

Introducing JClient

JClient provides a view alternative in the ADF scheme of things. Although UIX was meant for Web applications, JClient is meant for Swing-based client applications. JClient provides a set of classes that can use business components to quickly create data-bound Java UI applications. Apart from JClient's data-binding capabilities, developing a JClient application is not very different from a standard Swing application.

You will now look at an example that will make it quite obvious that JClient is perhaps the fastest and easiest way to build data-bound Swing applications.

You will use the business components you developed earlier in the chapter to create an application that will display the courses available and the students in each course.

First, create a new empty project in your StudentCourseADF workspace that you already have in place. In the New Gallery, select General ➤ Projects ➤ Empty Project. Second, name the project *JClientView*. Because you have just created an empty project and have not defined any technology scope for it, all the available options will be displayed in the New Gallery for the project.

In the Client Tier ➤ Swing/JClient for ADF section, you will see the various JClient options you have. The JClient Form Wizard is the easiest option available, and by the time you are done with the wizard, you will have a proper application running. Select the Form option, and click OK. The welcome screen should tell you what information the wizard will ask for as well as what it is capable of doing. Note that the JClient forms rely on existing business components projects for the data model. Click Next.

In step 1, select the option Master-Detail and select Form as the way to implement the form. You can also create an applet by choosing that option. Click Next. Here, select Table as the master template as well as the detail template. Click Next. In step 3, the wizard asks for the data model to be used. Because you have nothing defined for the JClientView project, the drop-down lists will be empty. Click the New button. As shown in Figure 7-27, the BC4J Client Data Model Definition Wizard should pop up. Using this wizard you will just define a client data model using an existing business component project. You will not create any new business components. Click Next.

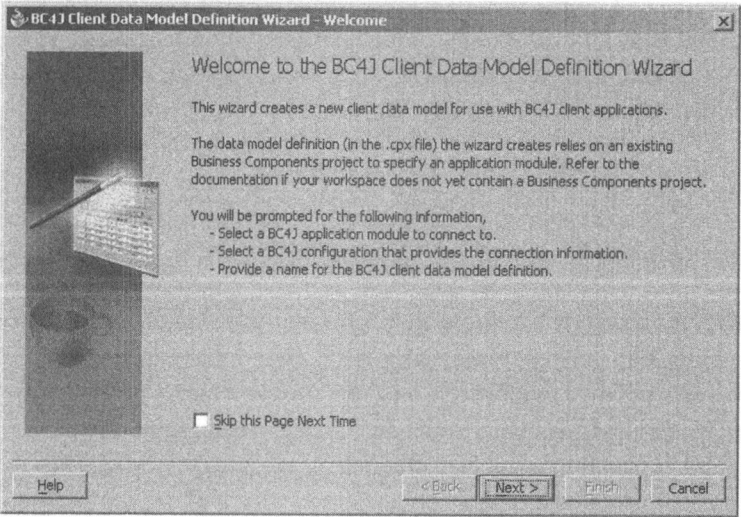

Figure 7-27. BC4J Client Data Model Definition Wizard

Because Model.jpr is the only business component project in the current workspace, the details of that project and the application module in that project will be prepopulated, as shown in Figure 7-28. If there were other projects or application modules available, those would have been displayed in the drop-down lists. Click Next and then Finish on the following screen. You will automatically be taken back to the JClient Form Wizard, and the data model definition field should have been populated. Click Next. In the Panel View screen, because the COURSE table is the master table and the STUDENT table is the detail one, CourseView1 will be displayed as the master and StudentView1 will be displayed as the Detail. Click Next.

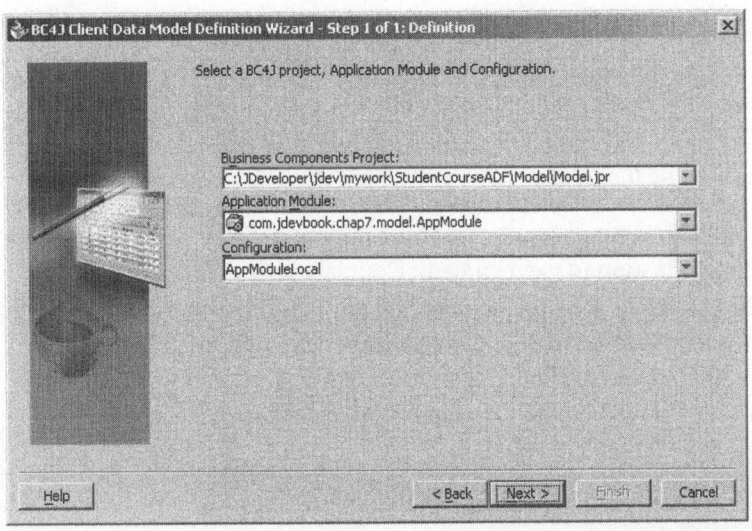

Figure 7-28. Data model definition

The CourseId and CourseName attributes should be selected on the Master View Object Attributes selection screen. Click Next. On the Detail View Object Attributes selection screen, select StudentId, StudentName, and CourseId. Click Next. For step 7, as shown in Figure 7-29, change the package name to *com.jdevbook.chap7*. Click Next. On the Finish screen, have a look at what components are being created by the wizard. Click Finish.

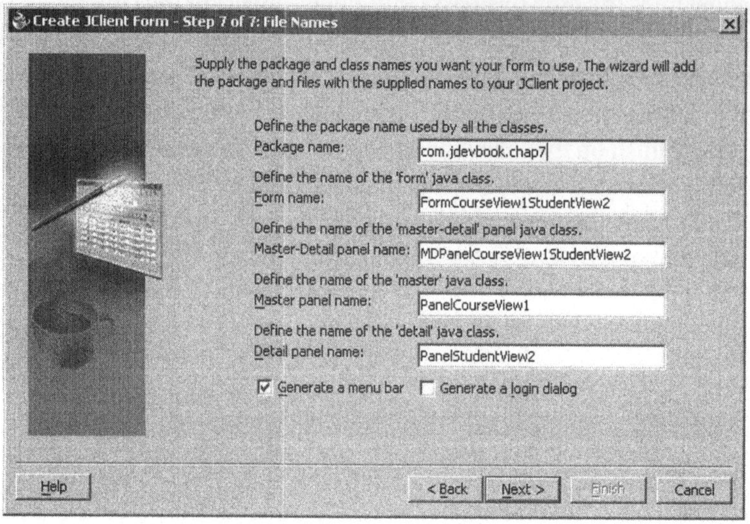

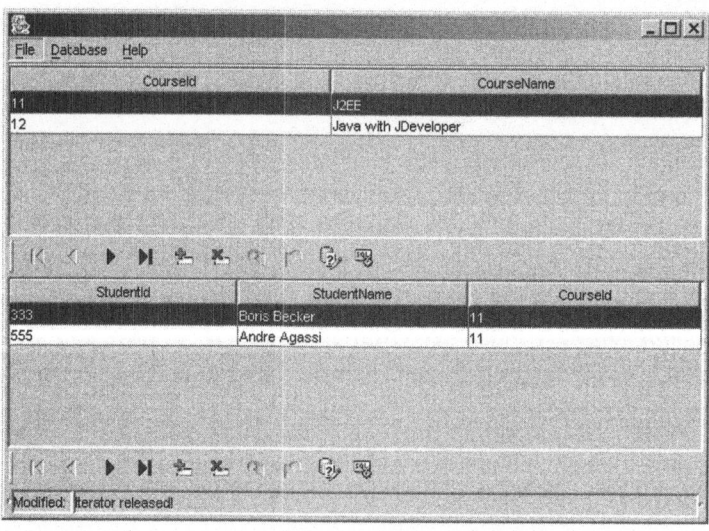

Figure 7-29. Setting the filenames

A complete application to view and edit Course and Student details is now ready. You need to modify nothing. Just run the project JClientView, and you will get a display as shown in Figure 7-30. The functions that are possible using this application are View, Insert, Delete, Commit, Rollback, Sort, and so on. In less than five minutes of work, you have a proper application in place. Cool!

Figure 7-30. The course/student JClient application

In this example all you did was to click Next buttons and a couple of options. You will now create a JClient example where you have to do a little more, but the example will portray how you can develop customized applications with JClient. You will develop a similar application to the one you just created but with more customization.

For the project JClientView, select the Client Tier ➤ Swing/JClient for ADF ➤ Empty Panel option and click OK. Click Next on the welcome screen. In step 1, name the package *com.jdevbook.chap7* and name the panel *CourseStudentPanel*. Keep the Generate a Runnable Panel option checked, and click Next followed by Finish on the last screen.

A blank panel should now be displayed. You will first add the label that you want to use. From the Swing Component Palette, choose the JLabel option and then draw a JLabel onto the panel. A grid appears once you click the panel. Use this grid to get the positioning right. Select the label and edit the text property that is displayed in the Property Inspector. Change it to *Course – Student JClient App*. Also change the font property to Arial, size 13, bold. Change the horizontal alignment to CENTER and the foreground to Color.blue.

Now you want to insert the data controls for Course and Student, so you will insert two JScrollPanes to hold the data controls. Select JScrollPane from the Swing Containers Component Palette, and draw two JScrollPanes on to the Panel. You should now have a display as shown in Figure 7-31.

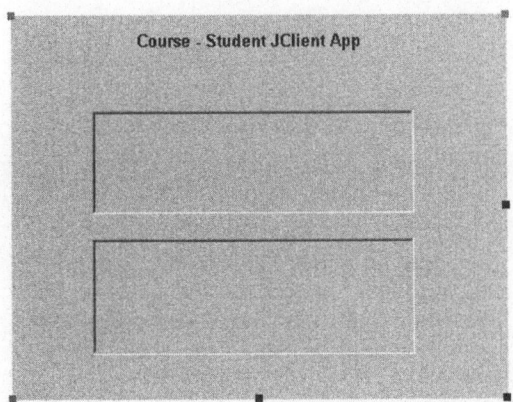

Figure 7-31. Course/student JClient application—incomplete panel

Now move to the Data Control Palette. Select CourseView1 and Drop As Table. Now drag and drop CourseView1 on to the top of the JScrollPane named *jScrollPane1*. Next drag StudentView2 as a table, and drop it onto the bottom of the JScrollPane named *jScrollPane2*. The reason why you are using StudentView2 and not StudentView1 is that you want the Students listing to be displayed with reference to the Course display.

Now you will place a few buttons that will make navigating through the course easier. From the Operations list for CourseView1, as shown in Figure 7-32, select First and choose Button as the Drop As option. Now drag First and drop it above the Course table. Similarly drag and drop the Next, Previous, and Last operations onto the panel. Resize the buttons as appropriate, and change the text property for each button to reflect their functionality. That's it. You have another data-bound application ready to roll. Run CourseStudentPanel.java to get the display shown in Figure 7-33. You will now learn how you can easily package your JClient application into a Java archive (JAR) file.

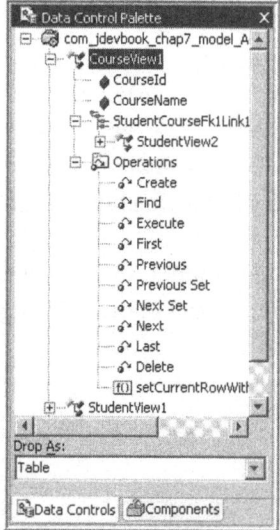

Figure 7-32. Data Control Palette

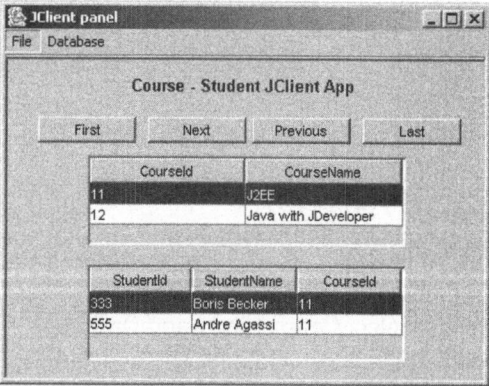

Figure 7-33. Course/student JClient application

Deploying to JAR

JClient's projects can be deployed to JAR files, which can be executed completely independent of JDeveloper. To deploy your JClientView project to a JAR file, go to the New Gallery for the JClientView project, select General ➤ Deployment Profiles ➤ JAR File–Simple Archive, and click OK.

Save the deployment profile as a file named *archive1.deploy*. The archive1.deploy file should now be listed in the Resources section of the project. Right-click the file, and select the Settings option to get to the JAR Deployment Profile Settings screen. If you are not sure whether the required libraries will be available to run any JClient project, it makes sense to select all the libraries displayed in the Dependency Analyzer. Because you intend to run this JAR file independent of all other packages and without having to edit the classpath, check all libraries displayed in the Dependency Analyzer. These libraries should also give you some idea of what a JClient application internally uses and depends on.

One last change you need to make is in the JAR Options section of the JAR Deployment Profile Settings screen; check the box for Include Manifest File and name the Main Class option *com.jdevbook.chap7.CourseStudentPanel*. This is the class that has the main method that needs to be executed. You do not have to change any of the other settings. Click OK.

To actually generate the JAR file, right-click archive1.deploy and select the option Deploy to JAR file. This process will take a fair amount of time, and the file archive1.jar should be generated in the deploy directory within the project JClientView. This file has all the dependent libraries packaged into it and will be more than 30 megabytes (MB) in size.

The next step is to just run the application using the command java -jar archive1.jar. Remember to have your necessary Oracle database services running. Use the Java development kit (JDK) that is part of JDeveloper to execute the JAR file because I did get some errors when trying to execute the JAR file using the Sun version.

Summary

In this chapter, you learned about the ADF that has been introduced in JDeveloper 10g. You also tried out the components of ADF such as the UIX, JClient, and ADF business components. You also developed a few applications using ADF and JClient and packaged a JClient application into a JAR file.

There's no denying that, with ADF, Oracle has come up with a neat way to quickly create data-bound applications. The thing to consider before adopting ADF is the long-term commitment that is required to make an ADF adoption really successful. ADF can only get better with time, as more tools are developed and as the user community drives more innovation and content on the subject.

Web Services

THE FIRST THING THAT comes to mind when one thinks of Web Services is the hype surrounding it for the past few years. No discussion on anything in software or even computing is complete without a direct or indirect reference to Web Services.

Lots of excitement and tons of jargon make Web Services appear as if it were something right out of the movies; a mysterious new invention that would change the world forever. Web Services is certainly quite far off from doing anything of that sort. The core idea underlying Web Services is fairly simple. I would put it down as a technology to get diverse systems talking to each other using a straightforward communication technique, adhering to definite rules, and based on XML.

That might not be the best definition of Web Services that you will come across, but it does convey the things about Web Services that really matter to me. In this chapter, I will spend some time discussing the scope and need for Web Services. I will then look at how JDeveloper can help you develop Web Services–enabled applications.

The Need for Web Services

There isn't anything new about distributed computing, and systems based on distributed computing technologies, such as Remote Method Invocation (RMI), Distributed Component Object Model (DCOM), and Common Object Request Broker Architecture (CORBA), have been around for a long time. These provide ways to remotely invoke a piece of code across a network. Therefore, if I know of a program that is capable of providing some specialized service, but it resides on a different machine on the network, I can invoke that piece of code remotely using the appropriate distributed technology.

You may wonder, if this capability of having distributed architectures has been around for some time, what is so special about Web Services? The strength of Web Services lies in the flaws of earlier technologies like RMI and DCOM.

RMI is very much a Java thing. It can be used to invoke remote Java methods from another piece of Java code, and does a good job of it. DCOM, on the other hand, comes from the Microsoft stable, which means that it is very much Windows-specific. CORBA came in to bridge the gap and enable easy communication between distributed computing environments regardless of the underlying technology. CORBA has been found lacking in some areas, however, and has faded over the past few years.

Pre-Web Services technologies are restrictive, not only in terms of the programming languages that could be used, but also in terms of the platform. So as long as you were working in an all-Windows world, things were fine with DCOM. Similarly as long as it was Java all over, RMI did fine. Think of a scenario, however, where you need a complex functionality written that you intend to use in your Java application. Your friend, Mr. X, in a different department in the company, tells you that he is already running and using exactly that same functionality, and that you could also use it. The only flaw is that while you are on Java, the functionality that you want to reuse is in a Microsoft environment. This is a scenario where Web Services can make your day, making it easily possible for your Java application to use the service already implemented in a Microsoft technology. Enter diversity, enter Web Services.

The application of Web Services is far reaching. It isn't something meant only for big applications and companies, but can also be used for smaller and user level applications. Just the other day I was looking at Web site promotion and registration to search engine tools available and found that many of these providers have simply exposed the functionality as a paid Web service. Makes sense, doesn't it? Why ship software or an application programming interface (API)? Expose a paid Web service that can be used by any kind of application. Both Microsoft- and Java-based Web sites can use the Web promotion Web service.

The advantages of Web Services can be described as:

- **Reusability**: Web Services provide an opportunity for extensive reuse of code and functionality. Once the functionality is developed and exposed as a Web service, you do not have to develop anything similar again.

- **Open standards and XML-based**: Web Services revolve around XML, making them straightforward and fairly simple to understand. Also, Web Services standards are decided upon by a standards body and not by a single vendor. All the major players have a say in any Web service standard being developed. Because Web Services communicate over HTTP using XML, unlike other distributed computing technologies, Web Services are firewall-friendly.

- **Interoperability and flexibility**: Web Services make it possible for diverse systems to talk to each other. This is a big advantage, especially when it comes to integrating with legacy systems that have been around for a long time. Web Services-based applications tend to be flexible with a minimum of tight coupling between elements.

The next section looks at a popular concept in the Web Services space, service-oriented architecture (SOA).

Service-Oriented Architecture (SOA)

As the name suggests, the SOA is focused on finding a service and getting things done using that service. The service-oriented architecture is particularly useful when it comes to projecting the advantages of Web Services to management types who have a minimal understanding of technology. SOA is the "in" thing these days, so make it a point to talk of SOA whenever you discuss Web Services. It is a simple concept and something that you probably use anyway while using Web Services.

Now you'll take a look at the three elements of SOA and how they work in tandem. As shown in Figure 8-1, find-bind-publish is what SOA deals with.

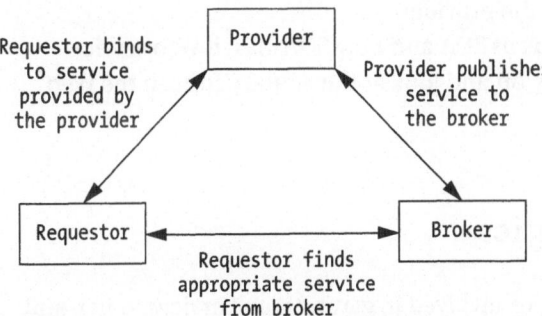

Figure 8-1. Service Oriented Architecture

Provider

The Provider is the owner of the Web service, and provides that service for use by other parties. The provider is expected to expose a description of the service and have an implementation of the service. The SOA does not discuss any specific technology that the implementation should be in, or the way in which the service should be exposed.

In Figure 8-1, the provider is the one who publishes the service to the broker.

Broker

The Broker is a registry of data about providers and the various services they provide. For example, when an employer goes to a placement agency and tells them that he wants a J2EE person with 3 years of XYZ experience, the agency looks up the information of candidates they maintain and returns a list of appropriate candidates. Similarly, a broker in SOA is like a middleman that is meant to hold information and make it available for search and lookup. The broker should be able to provide all the information that would be required to use any service provided by a provider.

In Figure 8-1, the broker is the one to whom the service is published by the provider. The requestor finds an appropriate service by querying the broker.

Requestor

A Requestor is the end user for the service. The requestor talks to the broker and finds a service that suits the need. Based on the service details, the requestor then uses the service offered by the provider.

In Figure 8-1, the requestor talks to the broker to find the service, and then binds to the service provided by the provider.

Now that you have had a look at SOA and how SOA-based Web service applications work, you can move on and look at the actual actors in the Web Services story.

Web Services Technologies

There are a number of technologies involved in getting Web Services to tick and do something useful. Each of these plays an important role in making web services a reality. Some of these might seem simple and obvious, but don't forget that it took many decades of computing development to devise and use Web Services.

Simple Object Access Protocol (SOAP)

Simple Object Access Protocol (SOAP) has been the flag-bearer of the Web Services team. The hype surrounding web services began with SOAP. A catchy name certainly helped in making it popular, and articles about SOAP were flying around even when hardly anybody knew what animal Web Services was.

The first thing about SOAP is that it is XML. SOAP is a way of sending and receiving data using XML in a proper predefined manner. So can you term any XML document that you send over the network as a SOAP message? No. A SOAP message has to be in a form as specified by the SOAP specification. The application-specific XML has to be placed within XML tags that are specified by the specification. The components of a SOAP message are as follows:

- **SOAP Envelope**: As shown in Figure 8-2, the SOAP envelope is the outermost element of the SOAP message XML structure. It defines the namespaces to prevent conflict between tag names used in the XML.

- **SOAP Header**: The SOAP header does not contain application-specific XML, but contains instructions and directives for the SOAP server that processes the message.

- **SOAP Body**: The SOAP body is where you place the application-level XML.

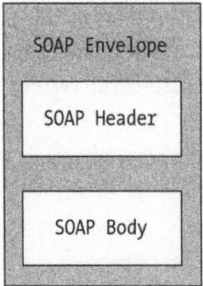

Figure 8-2. SOAP Message

To have a SOAP message, create a proper SOAP envelope and provide the additional information required for communication over the protocol that it is bound to. This protocol in most cases is HTTP, and so you need to provide HTTP-specific information.

Web Services Description Language (WSDL)

Earlier in this chapter, I discussed the Service Oriented Architecture (SOA). You saw that the find-bind-publish mechanism was key to the working of SOA. For example, suppose you have just managed to develop a new program to say calculate the distance of the moon from the earth at a particular time and place. You decide to expose it as a web service. This would be the *publish* part of SOA. Now you need to know what information to convey and how to convey it. You may wonder if there isn't a standard for this as well.

Enter Web Services Description Language (WSDL).WSDL is XML that describes a web service. The provider of the service creates the WSDL file for the service. WSDL is meant to provide all the information that a requestor of the service will require. The WSDL file provides information about the location, functionality provided, and usage instructions for a service. You will see some actual examples of WSDL later in this chapter. The WSDL specification can be found at http://www.w3.org/TR/wsdl.

Universal Description, Discovery, and Integration (UDDI)

Universal Description, Discovery, and Integration (UDDI) is primarily used to refer to UDDI registries. The UDDI registries are the brokers in the SOA story. UDDI is a standard for interaction with these registries, which hold information about services and serve as the broker. The UDDI specification can be found at http://www.uddi.org. UDDI is a standard for publishing and discovering information about Web Services. UDDI information is again categorized into three types:

- **White Pages**: These store information about companies and not about Web Services.

- **Yellow Pages**: This is where information is stored based on category, similar to how telephone yellow pages behave.

- **Green Pages**: This provides the actual technical information about Web Services, their functions, and so on.

JDeveloper provides a UDDI browser that enables discovery of Web Services using UDDI.

Now that you have had a quick look at the three key standards for Web Services, it's time to look at JDeveloper's capabilities for creating and using Web Services.

A Simple Java Web Service

For your first example, you will create a simple Java class and expose its methods as Web Services, with nothing special about the Java class. Create a new Application Workspace named WebServApp using the application template as Custom Application and package prefix as com.jdevbook.chap8.

In the New Gallery, choose General ➤ Simple Files ➤ Java Class and create a new class named *ServiceClass* in the package com.jdevbook.chap8. In this new class, you will add a simple method named *numberSquare* that takes an integer as input and returns a String message stating the number square. The code for ServiceClass is shown in Listing 8-1.

Listing 8-1. ServiceClass

```
package com.jdevbook.chap8;
public class ServiceClass
{
```

```
    public String numberSquare(int number)
    {
      return "The square of the number "+ number +" is "+ number * number;
    }
}
```

The next step is to convert this Java class into a Web service. You have
two options here: You can either go to the New Gallery and choose General ➤
Web Services ➤ Java Web Service, or just right-click the ServiceClass listing in
Applications Navigator and choose the option Generate Web Service from
Class. Use the Generate Web Service from Class option, and without any fur-
ther input from you, JDeveloper automatically creates a new web service
named MyWebService1, a web.xml file, and a WebServices.deploy file. The
Applications Navigator will display listings as shown in Figure 8-3.

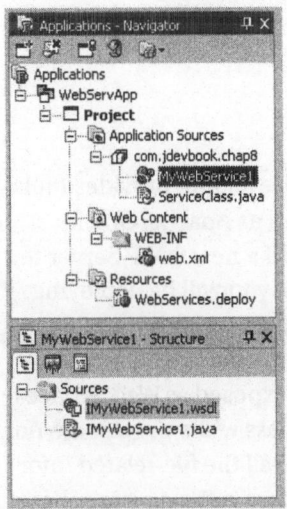

Figure 8-3. Applications Navigator and Structure Window

Note that when you select MyWebService1, the Structure Window lists two files,
IMyWebService1.wsdl and IMyWebService1.java. Now take a look at some detail of
the web service that was created by JDeveloper. Double-click MyWebService1 in the
Applications Navigator to get a screen, as shown in Figure 8-4.

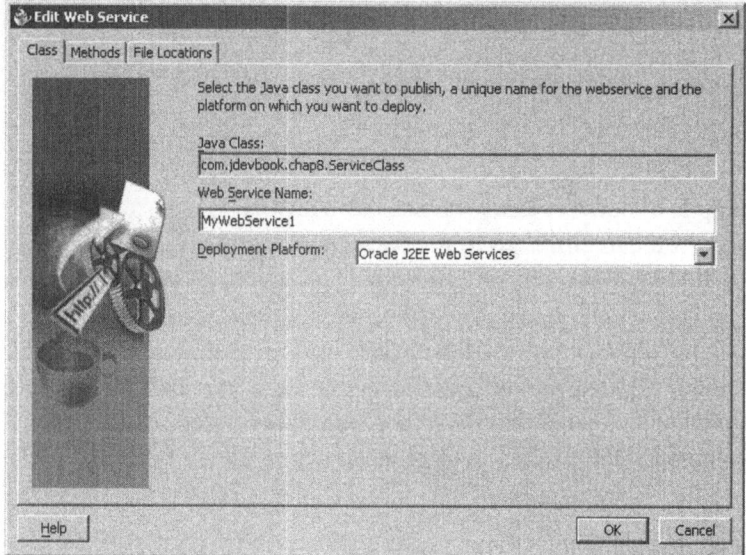

Figure 8-4. Edit Web Service, Class tab

Note the Deployment Platforms option provided. JDeveloper provides tools to deploy on OracleAS Containers for J2EE (OC4J) as well as Apache/Oracle SOAP Server. To deploy to a SOAP server, you have to add a new SOAP Server to the list displayed in the Connections Navigator. Because you will be deploying on the Embedded OC4J server, select Oracle J2EE Web Services.

Select the Methods tab. The only available method in the class ServiceClass should appear checked. Only the checked methods are exposed as Web Services, so you have an option to expose some methods in the class while the rest are not.

The File Locations tab, shown in Figure 8-5, is where all the file-related information is displayed. The only thing you should change here is the port number from 8888 to 8988, because Embedded OC4J's HTTP port is 8988 by default. The Application Server Endpoint field lists the application servers configured to deploy on an installed application server instead of the embedded server. Because you haven't configured an application server yet, this drop-down will appear empty. You can also click the New button to create a new application server connection.

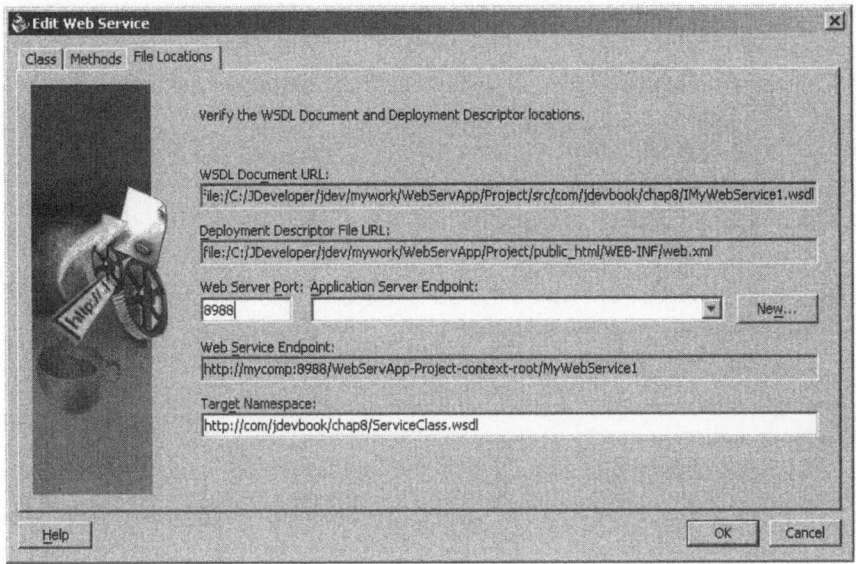

Figure 8-5. Edit Web Service, File Locations

Click OK. You should get a message saying that WSDL changes will be lost.
Click OK. Now have a look at the WSDL file for the Web service. You can open the
WSDL file by double-clicking the WSDL file listed in the Structure window, or by
right-clicking the web service listing and selecting the option Go to WSDL.

As I mentioned earlier, the WSDL file is meant to provide information about
the web service and its usage. Take a look the file to see how this information is
actually conveyed.

Listing 8-2. ImyWebService1.wsdl

```
<?xml version = '1.0' encoding = 'UTF-8'?>
<!--Generated by the Oracle9i JDeveloper Web Services WSDL Generator-->
<!--Date Created: Tue Oct 07 16:57:41 GMT+05:30 2003-->
<definitions
    name="MyWebService1"
    targetNamespace="http://com/jdevbook/chap8/ServiceClass.wsdl"
    xmlns="http://schemas.xmlsoap.org/wsdl/"
    xmlns:xsd="http://www.w3.org/2001/XMLSchema"
    xmlns:soap="http://schemas.xmlsoap.org/wsdl/soap/"
    xmlns:tns="http://com/jdevbook/chap8/ServiceClass.wsdl"
    xmlns:ns1="http://com.jdevbook.chap8/IMyWebService1.xsd">
```

```
<types>
  <schema
      targetNamespace="http://com.jdevbook.chap8/IMyWebService1.xsd"
      xmlns="http://www.w3.org/2001/XMLSchema"
      xmlns:SOAP-ENC="http://schemas.xmlsoap.org/soap/encoding/"/>
</types>
<message name="numberSquare0Request">
  <part name="number" type="xsd:int"/>
</message>
<message name="numberSquare0Response">
  <part name="return" type="xsd:string"/>
</message>
<portType name="ServiceClassPortType">
  <operation name="numberSquare">
    <input name="numberSquare0Request" message="tns:numberSquare0Request"/>
    <output name="numberSquare0Response" message="tns:numberSquare0Response"/>
  </operation>
</portType>
<binding name="ServiceClassBinding" type="tns:ServiceClassPortType">
  <soap:binding style="rpc" transport="http://schemas.xmlsoap.org/soap/http"/>
  <operation name="numberSquare">
    <soap:operation soapAction="" style="rpc"/>
    <input name="numberSquare0Request">
      <soap:body use="encoded" namespace="MyWebService1"
      encodingStyle="http://schemas.xmlsoap.org/soap/encoding/"/>
    </input>
    <output name="numberSquare0Response">
      <soap:body use="encoded" namespace="MyWebService1"
      encodingStyle="http://schemas.xmlsoap.org/soap/encoding/"/>
    </output>
  </operation>
</binding>
<service name="MyWebService1">
  <port name="ServiceClassPort" binding="tns:ServiceClassBinding">
    <soap:address location="http://mycomp:8988/WebServApp-Project-context-root/
    MyWebService1"/>
  </port>
</service>
</definitions>
```

The definitions tag states the name of the Web service and the namespaces for the tags to avoid tag name conflicts. The types tag comes into play when you use complex data types in the WSDL. Because this service is straightforward and accepts an integer and returns a String, however, there isn't any need for complex data types.

The message tags describe the message that is sent as request to the service and the message that is sent back as response. The xsd:int and xsd:string are XML Schema-defined usages. The porttype tag holds operation tags that state the basic input and output for the operations supported by the service. The porttype tag maps a set of operations to one or more endpoints.

The binding tag is where the protocol and data format information is specified. The protocol is commonly HTTP, and the data format is SOAP. The service tag holds a collection of ports and specifies the address for binding. In this example, the address on my machine is http://mycomp:8988/WebServApp-Project-context-root/MyWebService1. The *mycomp* bit can change based on what name you have assigned to your machine.

Now that you have your Web service in place, try to use it. Right-click MyWebService1 and click Run MyWebService1. Once the service is running, the following lines should be displayed on the embedded server console:

```
The application can be accessed at location:
http://127.0.0.1:8988/WebServApp-Project-context-root/MyWebService1
```

This is the endpoint for the web service, as you saw in Figure 8-5. Access this URL using your web browser, and you should get a page like the one shown in Figure 8-6. Click the Service Description link and the WSDL file will be displayed.

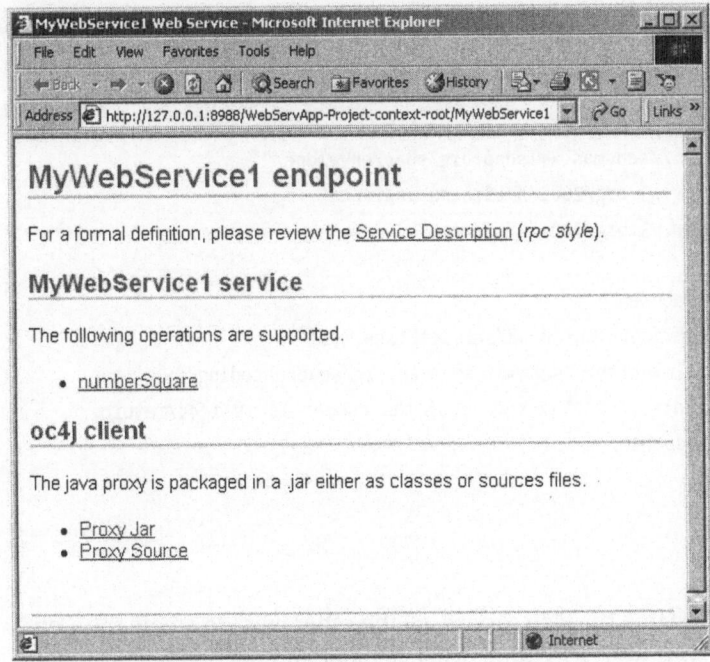

Figure 8-6. MyWebService1 endpoint

Click the *numberSquare* link and you will get the page shown in Figure 8-7, asking for input for MyWebService1. I entered the value 12 and clicked invoke to get the SOAP message shown in Listing 8-3.

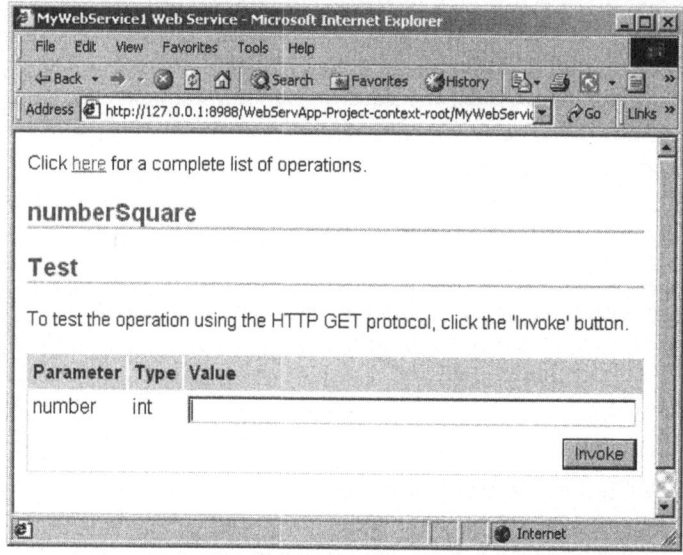

Figure 8-7. Test numberSquare Operation

Listing 8-3. Test numberSquare SOAP Response

```
<?xml version='1.0' encoding='UTF-8'?>
<SOAP-ENV:Envelope
xmlns:SOAP-ENV="http://schemas.xmlsoap.org/soap/envelope/"
xmlns:xsi="http://www.w3.org/2001/XMLSchema-instance"
xmlns:xsd="http://www.w3.org/2001/XMLSchema">
<SOAP-ENV:Body>
<ns1:numberSquareResponse
xmlns:ns1="http://com/jdevbook/chap8/ServiceClass.wsdl"
SOAP-ENV:encodingStyle="http://schemas.xmlsoap.org/soap/encoding/">
<return xsi:type="xsd:string">The square of the number 12 is 144</return>
</ns1:numberSquareResponse>

</SOAP-ENV:Body>
</SOAP-ENV:Envelope>
```

Although you created the web service, all the other work to create the Web front-end that you just used was done by JDeveloper and the embedded server. Open up the web.xml file and you will find the piece of code shown in Listing 8-4.

Listing 8-4. Servlet Definition in web.xml

```
<servlet>
  <servlet-name>MyWebService1</servlet-name>
  <servlet-class>oracle.j2ee.ws.StatelessJavaRpcWebService</servlet-class>
  <init-param>
    <param-name>class-name</param-name>
    <param-value>com.jdevbook.chap8.ServiceClass</param-value>
  </init-param>
  <init-param>
    <param-name>interface-name</param-name>
    <param-value>com.jdevbook.chap8.IMyWebService1</param-value>
  </init-param>
</servlet>
<servlet-mapping>
  <servlet-name>MyWebService1</servlet-name>
  <url-pattern>/MyWebService1</url-pattern>
</servlet-mapping>
```

So the Servlet oracle.j2ee.ws.StatelessJavaRpcWebService was the one that was doing the job every time you fired a request to get the screens shown in Figures 8-6 and 8-7.

Just having a Web interface to check the service details and invoking the service isn't enough. You need to try using a proper Java client to use the service through Java code. Fortunately, the creators of JDeveloper have thought of this requirement and provided a quick way to create a Java client for the service. Right-click the service in the Applications Navigator and select the Generate Sample Java Client option. Without further ado, JDeveloper will create a new file named *EmbeddedMyWebService1Stub.java*. This class is the stub for our service and the important method in this class is the method numberSquare. The method numberSquare, as shown in Listing 8-5, uses classes that are part of the package org.apache.soap to invoke the method numberSquare as exposed by MyWebService1.

Listing 8-5. EmbeddedMyWebService1Stub

```
package com.jdevbook.chap8;
import oracle.soap.transport.http.OracleSOAPHTTPConnection;
import org.apache.soap.encoding.soapenc.BeanSerializer;
import org.apache.soap.encoding.SOAPMappingRegistry;
import org.apache.soap.util.xml.QName;
import java.net.URL;
import org.apache.soap.Constants;
```

```
import org.apache.soap.Fault;
import org.apache.soap.SOAPException;
import org.apache.soap.rpc.Call;
import org.apache.soap.rpc.Parameter;
import org.apache.soap.rpc.Response;
import java.util.Vector;
import java.util.Properties;

public class EmbeddedMyWebService1Stub
{
  public EmbeddedMyWebService1Stub()
  {
    m_httpConnection = new OracleSOAPHTTPConnection();
    m_smr = new SOAPMappingRegistry();
  }

  public static void main(String[] args)
  {
    try
    {
      EmbeddedMyWebService1Stub stub = new EmbeddedMyWebService1Stub();
      // Add your own code here.
      System.out.println(stub.numberSquare(new Integer(12)));
    }
    catch(Exception ex)
    {
      ex.printStackTrace();
    }
  }

  private String _endpoint =
    "http://127.0.0.1:8988/WebServApp-Project-context-root/MyWebService1";

  public String getEndpoint()
  {
    return _endpoint;
  }

  public void setEndpoint(String endpoint)
  {
    _endpoint = endpoint;
  }
```

```
private OracleSOAPHTTPConnection m_httpConnection = null;
private SOAPMappingRegistry m_smr = null;

public String numberSquare(Integer number) throws Exception
{
  String returnVal = null;

  URL endpointURL = new URL(_endpoint);
  Call call = new Call();
  call.setSOAPTransport(m_httpConnection);
  call.setTargetObjectURI("MyWebService1");
  call.setMethodName("numberSquare");
  call.setEncodingStyleURI(Constants.NS_URI_SOAP_ENC);

  Vector params = new Vector();
  params.addElement(new Parameter("number"
    , java.lang.Integer.class, number, null));
  call.setParams(params);

  call.setSOAPMappingRegistry(m_smr);

  Response response = call.invoke(endpointURL, "");

  if (!response.generatedFault())
  {
    Parameter result = response.getReturnValue();
    returnVal = (String)result.getValue();
  }
  else
  {
    Fault fault = response.getFault();
    throw new SOAPException(fault.getFaultCode(), fault.getFaultString());
  }

  return returnVal;
}

public void setMaintainSession(boolean maintainSession)
{
  m_httpConnection.setMaintainSession(maintainSession);
}
```

```
    public boolean getMaintainSession()
    {
      return m_httpConnection.getMaintainSession();
    }

    public void setTransportProperties(Properties props)
    {
      m_httpConnection.setProperties(props);
    }

    public Properties getTransportProperties()
    {
      return m_httpConnection.getProperties();
    }
}
```

The endpoint is http://127.0.0.1:8988/WebServApp-Project-context-root/
MyWebService1. You next create a Call object and set all the transport and service details required for the call to the service to be possible. We next pass the
parameters that are required by the service. Note that although the method in
your service takes an int primitive, while invoking the service you use the Integer
wrapper class, because you cannot store primitives in the params vector.

Next you invoke the service and get a Response object that provides the
value returned by the service. The only thing you have to change, as shown in
Listing 8-5, is to actually add a call to the numberSquare method in the Stub
from the main method provided.

Now run the Web service MyWebService1, followed by running
EmbeddedMyWebService1Stub. You should get the following line on the
Project.jpr message console:

```
The square of the number 12 is 144.
```

The way to access the Web service through a stand-alone Java application or
through a JSP or Servlet would be almost the same. If you just instantiate the
stub class and call the numberSquare method from within your Servlet, you will
have the Web service output for use in your Servlet.

You just saw how JDeveloper can generate a sample Java client to access the
Web service. Now have a look at the other stub-skeleton creation options that
you have.

Stubs and Skeletons

JDeveloper provides a Web Service Stub/Skeleton wizard that can be started either through New Gallery General ➤ Web Services ➤ Web Services Stub/Skeleton, or by right-clicking the web service and selecting the Generate Web Service Stub option. This time, take the second option to start the wizard. Click Next on the Welcome screen to get the screen shown in Figure 8-8.

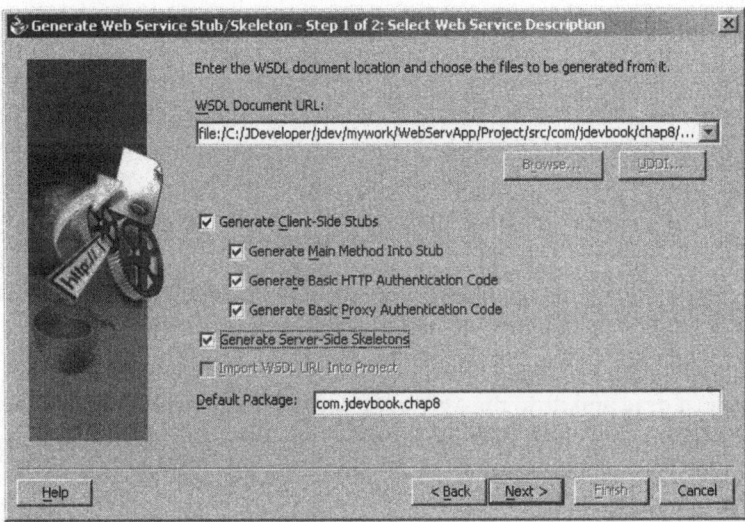

Figure 8-8. Generate Web Service Stub/Skeleton: Step 1

Here, check all the boxes provided so that JDeveloper generates a main method, Basic HTTP Authentication Code if the web server requires authentication, as well as Proxy Authentication Code, if that is required. Click Next. Step 2 displays details of what JDeveloper will create. Note that unlike the EmbeddedMyWebService1Stub code you saw in Listing 8-5, the MyWebService1Stub constructor has lots of properties being set, to provide for basic and proxy authentication.

Executing this stub by changing the main method provided, as you did with EmbeddedMyWebService1Stub, would get you the same result as earlier.

Web Services Diagram

The diagramming capability of JDeveloper is one of its important features. JDeveloper provides the option to represent the web service and related files diagrammatically. To create a new web service diagram, select the General ➤ Web Services ➤ Web Service Diagram option in the New Gallery. In the Create New

Web Service Diagram dialog, specify the package as com.jdevbook.chap8 and the name as My Web Service Diagram.

A blank Web service diagram should be created and the Web service palette should be displayed in the component palette, as shown in Figure 8-9. You can use the components of the Web service palette to create new Java/JMS or PLSQL Web Services, as well as show dependencies and add notes and attachments.

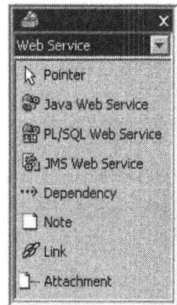

Figure 8-9. Web Service Palette

In this case, just drag and drop the MyWebService1 and the stubs and skeletons you created earlier to get a diagram as shown in Figure 8-10. The Web service diagramming capability is decent and can be useful to get a quick feel of the system and the services being used.

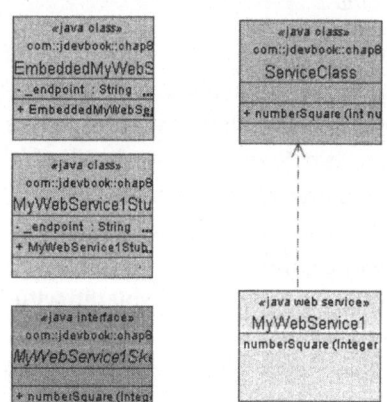

Figure 8-10. My Web Service Diagram

UDDI Browser

In the discussion about SOA and UDDI earlier in the chapter, I mentioned that the broker plays an important part in the SOA architecture. The UDDI registry plays that role, and is the place to search for Web Services that would do a particular task. JDeveloper comes with a built-in UDDI browser that can make this task easier. You can use this UDDI browser from right within JDeveloper to search for services, check out the service descriptions, and even get stubs for the services generated by JDeveloper.

As shown in Figure 8-11, IBM, Microsoft, and the Oracle UDDI registry connections come preconfigured in JDeveloper by default. You can also add new UDDI registry connections using the New UDDI Registry Connection option available through the New Gallery or by right-clicking UDDI Registry listing.

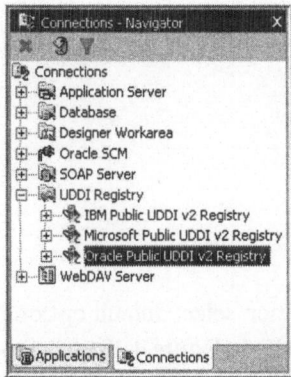

Figure 8-11. UDDI browser

 TIP   *To test if a registry is working, right-click the registry listing, select the Edit option and then use the Test feature provided.*

Take an example where you find a Web service and then get JDeveloper to display details of the service, and also generate a stub for using the service. To find a new Web service, right-click the registry listing and select the option Find Web Services. You are provided a search based on category as well as name. The categorization is based on four taxonomies, namely UDDI Types, NAICS, ISO 3166 and UNSPSC. For this example, just stick with name search. I tried searching with various values to get a good example. The word *test* got lots of non-working registry entries, while some other common words surprisingly got no results. On searching for the name *zip* on the IBM UDDI registry I got the screen shown in Figure 8-12. Because the registry is constantly changing, you might get different results.

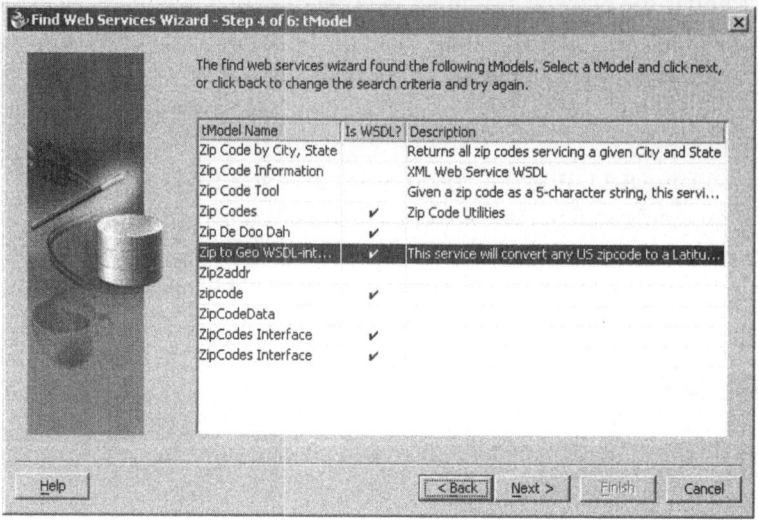

Figure 8-12. Finding Web Services

Choose the Zip to Geo WSDL interface service, and then select default options on the screens that follow. You should get the screen shown in Figure 8-13 after finishing the wizard. Select the last option in the UDDI registry, and then drill down into the UDDI display in Connections Navigator to get a display as shown in Figure 8-14.

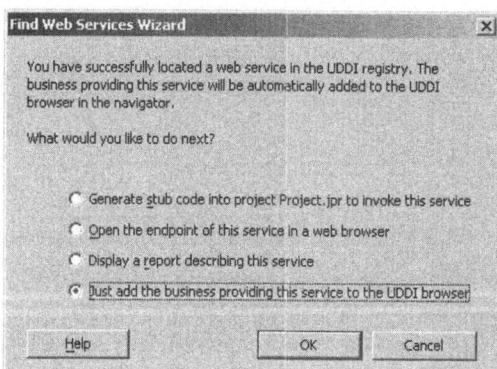

Figure 8-13. Web service options

CAUTION *When you try out the Find Web Service feature, select services that provide a WSDL interface. Some of JDeveloper's features work only if the WSDL is present. Also, when you ask JDeveloper to generate the stub for the service, the project that is being used is where the stub file gets created, so ensure that you are using the right project before you generate the stub, or the stub file may be created in the wrong project.*

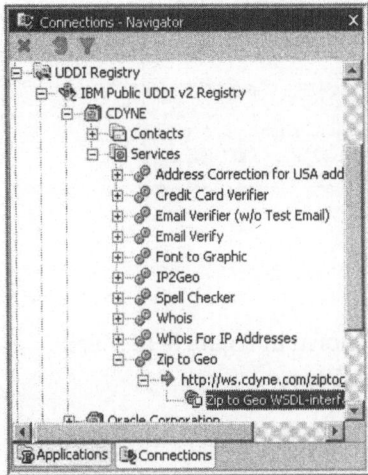

Figure 8-14. UDDI Registry

Now select Zip to Geo, right-click, and select the option View Report. This option generates a well-formatted report based on service details provided in the WSDL. Select the last level of the service, after drilling down in the listing, and then right-click to get an option to generate a stub and skeleton for the service. You will get the screen shown in Figure 8-15.

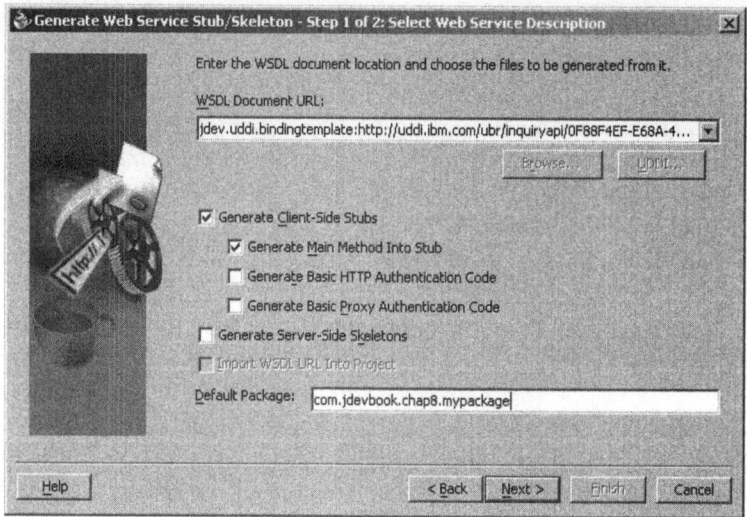

Figure 8-15. Generate Stub/Skeleton Step 1

Step 2 of the wizard will get you the screen shown in Figure 8-16. Click Finish to accept the default options for stub creation.

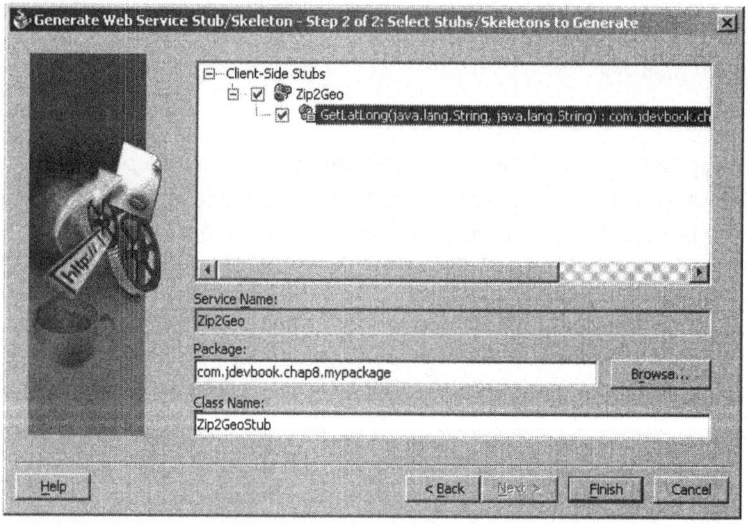

Figure 8-16. Generate Stub/Skeleton Step 2

After you complete the stub creation, what is particularly impressive is that JDeveloper goes beyond just creating a stub like the stub classes you saw earlier in the chapter. Although the service in question is not returning a simple type like a String or an Integer but a complex type named LatLongReturn, even that class was automatically generated based on the details provided in the WSDL. You can now use the stub to invoke and use the service.

Summary

In this chapter, you looked at JDeveloper's Web service capabilities. When you work with web services, IDE help is essential to make your task easy and fun. JDeveloper certainly does a good job of abstracting a lot of complexity from the developer and providing tools and wizards to do most tasks.

In the next chapter, you will look at the various debugging, code improvement, and code monitoring tools that make JDeveloper go beyond what most other IDEs offer.

Debugging and Code Improvement

THE CODE ENHANCEMENTS and monitoring tools that JDeveloper provides are what set it apart from the crowd. Of the number of integrated development environments (IDEs) available on the market, JDeveloper is right at the top because it offers a great mix of all the things that a Java developer requires.

After spending thousands of dollars on a commercial IDE, it does not make sense if you again have to hunt for good debugging, code optimizing, and performance monitoring tools. Even if you do manage to find one, integrating that tool with the IDE and application server you are using is another tough task to accomplish. In this chapter, you will see how JDeveloper provides a neat suite of applications that will more or less eliminate the need for using any other tools during development.

Introducing the Tools

This chapter will focus on a set of tools that are well integrated into JDeveloper and do not require any separate installation. These tools are as follows:

- **Debugger:** You can use the debugger to locate and fix errors in the code.

- **UI Debugger:** This is a debugger meant specifically for locating and fixing errors in Java graphical user interfaces (GUIs).

- **CodeCoach:** This points out mistakes in code and assists in writing better code.

- **Memory Profiler:** This shows details of how memory is being utilized.

- **Events Profiler:** The Events Profiler displays details about various events that occur during processing.

- **Execution Profiler:** This tool is meant to analyze application performance based on samples.

- **TCP Packet Monitor:** You can monitor Transmission Control Protocol (TCP) request/response package using this tool.

In this chapter, you will avoid writing new code and creating new projects/ workspaces. You will instead try these tools on code you have already developed in earlier chapters. So keep earlier code on hand before you commence trying the examples in this chapter.

Using the Debugger

Webster's dictionary defines a *debugger* as a program that helps in locating and correcting programming errors. The important word here is *helps* because however good a debugger is, a lot still depends on programmer expertise. The debugger cannot go beyond helping the programmer in finding the error. A debugger cannot fix errors. It is the programmer who can fix errors based on the information provided by the debugger.

When do you use a debugger? Java is a compiled language, so the compiler reveals at the time of code compilation any syntax blunders that you might have committed in your code. The debugger has a role to play when it comes to fixing run-time errors as well as logical errors. Logical errors that the debugger can help with are of the kind where some logic code appears correct to the developer, but it does not perform as expected. In such cases, the debugger can be the best way to quickly isolate the erroneous piece of code.

You will try out the debugger using the program you developed in Chapter 3— an addition class that takes two numbers from the user and prints their addition. You will not be using this example to fix any bug but instead you will use it to check the flow of the application, to check how values change along the way, and to see how and what the debugger is capable of displaying.

NOTE *The number of things that are displayed by the debugger can be somewhat overwhelming. Try to focus on just what is useful for the kind of applications you are developing.*

Open the file AdditionClass.java in the project SimpleApp1 in the workspace MyJavaApps. The Code Editor should display the Java code for the class. The class has a method named *doAddition* and a main method. An important concept that is inherent to using debuggers is that of breakpoints. *Breakpoints* are breaks in the code execution that you introduce to examine the state of the program at that specific stage in program execution. Breakpoints are important because if you do not tell the debugger where to pause execution, it is of no good using the debugger for the class or project. I say this because even with the debugger, the execution will complete in a fraction of a second, and you will not be able to analyze anything.

NOTE *Breakpoints need to be set on lines of code that will actually execute. JDeveloper will not stop you from setting breakpoints on nonexecutable bits of the code such as blank and commented lines. However, such breakpoints will simply be ignored and execution will not pause.*

To set a break point anywhere in the code, you need to click in the line gutter to display a red button. The line gutter is the vertical strip on the Code Editor's extreme left. Click the lines as shown in Figure 9-1 to set these three breakpoints.

```
AdditionClass.java
12    public static void main(String[] args)
13    {
14        AdditionClass additionClass = new AdditionClass();
15
16        if (args.length != 2 )
17        {
18            System.out.println("Usage: AdditionClass <argument 1> <argument 2>");
19            return;
20        }
21        else
22        {
23            System.out.println(args[0] + " " +args[1]);
24            int iResult = additionClass.doAddition(Integer.parseInt(args[0])
25               , Integer.parseInt(args[1]));
26            System.out.println("Result of addition = "+ iResult);
27        }
28    }
29
30    int doAddition(int val1, int val2)
31    {
32        return val1 + val2;
33    }
34 }
Code  Class  UI
```

Figure 9-1. AdditionClass with breakpoints

Once the breakpoints are set, select View ➤ Debugger ➤ Breakpoints to get a listing of the breakpoints for the class. To have more details about breakpoints be displayed, check the details you want displayed by selecting Debugger ➤ Breakpoints in the Preferences dialog. Checking all the options here should get you the display shown in Figure 9-2. You can also right-click the column names displayed in the Breakpoints window and choose the columns to be displayed.

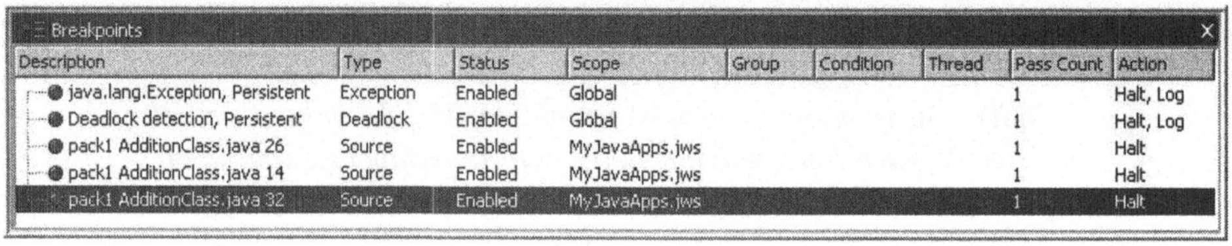

Breakpoints									X
Description	Type	Status	Scope	Group	Condition	Thread	Pass Count	Action
● java.lang.Exception, Persistent	Exception	Enabled	Global				1	Halt, Log
● Deadlock detection, Persistent	Deadlock	Enabled	Global				1	Halt, Log
● pack1 AdditionClass.java 26	Source	Enabled	MyJavaApps.jws				1	Halt
● pack1 AdditionClass.java 14	Source	Enabled	MyJavaApps.jws				1	Halt
● pack1 AdditionClass.java 32	Source	Enabled	MyJavaApps.jws				1	Halt

Figure 9-2. Breakpoints listing

The two breakpoints with global scope are there to halt and log messages when encountering deadlocks and exceptions. You can also use the options in Debugger ➤ Breakpoints ➤ Default Actions in the Preferences dialog to have JDeveloper do more than just stop execution when encountering a breakpoint.

To disable or toggle a breakpoint, you can right-click the breakpoint and select that option or right-click that breakpoint's listing in the Breakpoints window.

To debug the class, you can either choose Debug AdditionClass.java or Debug SimpleApp1.jpr from the Debug menu. In this particular case, either option will work as the default run target for the project SimpleApp1 is AdditionClass.java. The default run target is defined in Project Properties ➤ Profiles ➤ Development ➤ Runner. On this screen, enter *22 78* in the Program Arguments field.

Debug SimpleApp1.jpr by clicking the Debug icon in the toolbar or selecting the Debug SimpleApp1.jpr menu command. You should now get the screen shown in Figure 9-3. If you do not see all the tabs and windows shown in the figure, select View ➤ Debugger from the menu, and you will get a list of all windows that can be displayed while debugging an application. Except Breakpoints, all the other options are grayed out if you are not running the debugger.

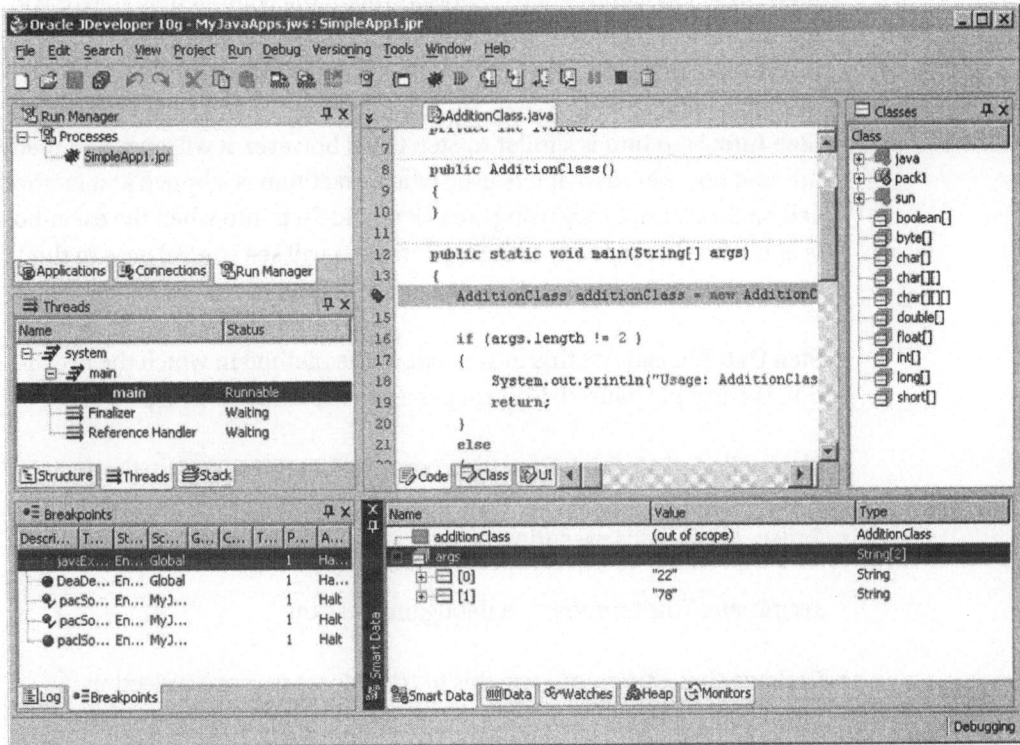

Figure 9-3. Debugger windows

To use the debugger, you also need to be aware of some debugging options that help you move through the code and debug it in a step-by-step fashion. Being aware of these options will help you get more from the debugger. The options are listed in the Debug menu as well as in the toolbar, as shown in Figure 9-4.

Figure 9-4. Debugging tools

The following is a listing of tools shown in Figure 9-4 from left to right. Point your mouse over any of the tools, and you will get a tooltip for that tool:

- **Debug**: This debugs the selected project and uses the default run target for the project.

- **Resume**: You can resume code execution that has been stopped either manually or on encountering a breakpoint using this tool.

- **Step Over:** You can use this to move through the code step by step. If you use Step Over when executing a method call, the method gets executed, but you will not see control pass to that method as the next step.

- **Step Into:** Step Into is similar to Step Over; however, it will step into methods and not over them if it is used when execution is stopped at a method call. In the example, try using Step Over and Step Into when the execution is at the first breakpoint; with Step Into, you will see control pass to the constructor, but with Step Over this will not happen.

- **Step Out:** You can use this to step out of the method in which the execution is currently paused. Control passes to the calling method.

- **Step to End of Method:** Execution continues to the end of method.

- **Pause:** This pauses execution of code.

- **Terminate:** This terminates a debugging session.

- **Garbage Collect:** You can use this to try to force garbage collection.

 NOTE *The stepping mechanism to move through code gets affected if there are breakpoints set. If you try to step over a method in which a breakpoint has been set, execution will still pause at the breakpoint.*

You will now quickly look at what information each of the windows displayed in Figure 9-3 provides. I have already covered breakpoints, so I will now cover the role that the Classes window plays with respect to the SimpleApp1 example.

Classes

The Classes window lists all the classes that have been loaded. You can use the Debugger ➤ Classes option in the Preferences dialog to display the memory consumption of a class, the number of instances created, and the source file for that class. You need to select View ➤ Debugger ➤ Classes to display the Classes window.

After getting to the first breakpoint when running the project SimpleApp1.jpr, the Classes window should appear as shown in Figure 9-5. In Figure 9-5, the instance count for AdditionClass class is at zero because I stopped execution just before execution of the code that creates a new instance of AdditionClass.

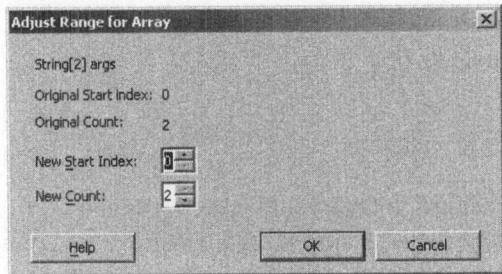

Class	Count	Memory	File
⊞ 🖳 java			
🖳 pack1			
🗀 AdditionClass	0	0	AdditionClass.java
⊞ 🖳 sun			
🗐 boolean[]	0	0	
🗐 byte[]	64	112913	
🗐 char[]	3536	198364	
🗐 char[][]	102	1224	
🗐 char[][][]	1	412	
🗐 double[]	0	0	
🗐 float[]	0	0	
🗐 int[]	4	2904	
🗐 long[]	1	36	
🗐 short[]	2	8232	

Figure 9-5. Classes window

Data

The Data window displays arguments, local variables, and static variables. By
default, it just displays the name, value, and type of the variable; however, you
can get to the Preferences dialog box either by selecting Debugger ➤ Data in
the preferences dialog or by right-clicking in the Data window and selecting the
Preferences option.

The right-click menu provides some useful options. Inspect opens a new
window for that particular element in the listing. Watch adds that element to the
Watches list displayed in the Watches window. I will discuss the Watches window
in a later section. You can use the Export option to export the data to a file.

A neat feature that JDeveloper provides is that of adjusting array range. While
debugging AdditionClass, right-click the args array displayed in the Data window
and select the option Adjust Range to get the dialog box shown in Figure 9-6.
Adjust the new start index, and specify the count of elements after the start index
you want displayed.

Figure 9-6. The Adjust Range for Array dialog box

Heap

The Heap window displays information about the objects and arrays in the heap. The Java heap is where Java maintains objects that are currently being used. Objects stay in the heap only as long as they are being used. The garbage collector regularly clears the heap of unused objects.

You need to select View ➤ Debugger ➤ Heap to display the Heap window. The Heap window by default will appear blank. You need to add classes that you want to track in the heap. Once this is specified, the Heap window displays the details of instances of these classes that currently exist in the heap. These entries are referred to as *class folders*.

To add class folders, you have three options:

- Right-click, and choose the option Add Class Folder.

- Drag and drop a class from the Classes window, as shown in Figure 9-5.

- Drag and drop an object or array from the Data, Smart Data, or Watches window.

When moving to the second breakpoint—in other words, after the AdditionClass instance gets created—drag and drop AdditionClass from the Classes window to the Heap window. You should get the screen shown in Figure 9-7.

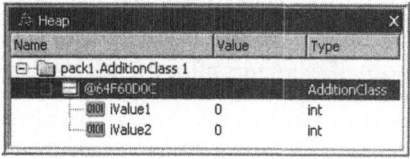

Figure 9-7. Heap window

Monitors

The Monitors window can be useful if you are writing multithreaded Java programs and want to detect and fix bugs that might arise because of the multithreaded nature of the program. This window can display details of the owning thread, the waiting thread, and the blocked threads. In this particular example, you do not have much use of this window; however, when encountering the first breakpoint, the Monitors window should be similar to the window shown in Figure 9-8.

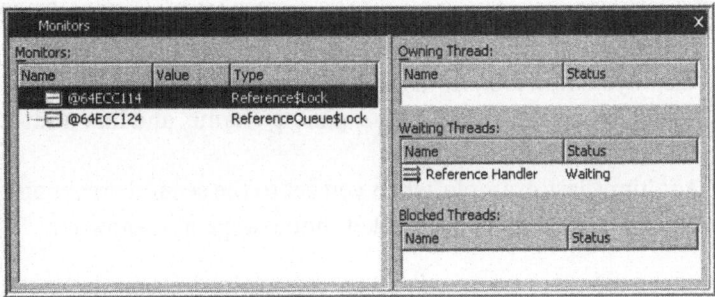

Figure 9-8. Monitors window

Smart Data

The Smart Data window is similar to the Data window and works like the Data window. The big difference is that unlike the Data window that displays information about every object and variable being created, the Smart Data window only takes up data directly relevant to the code you are currently executing.

A useful feature that is present in the Smart Data window as well as the Data window is to modify field values at run time. If you want to change args[0] value from 22 to 33, all you have to do is right-click args[0] listed in Smart Data and select the option Modify Value. On the screen similar to Figure 9-9, enter *33* for the new value. The Interpret New Value As Object Address option is another interesting feature; you can have args[0] point to a different object by changing the object address. Checking this option and specifying the value as 0 will set the reference to *null*.

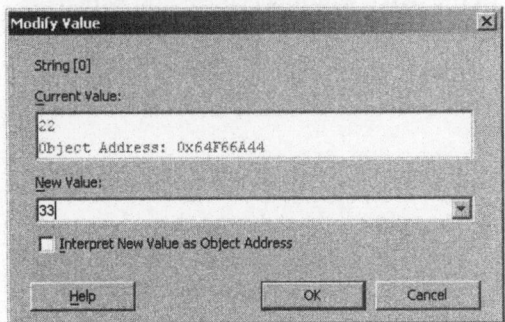

Figure 9-9. Modifying the value

Stack

The Stack window displays methods that have begun execution but have not been completed. So if from within the main method you call method X and from method X you call method Y, when execution gets to method Y, the call stack will display the main method, method X, and method Y. By default only the method name and class is displayed; however, from the Preferences dialog box for the Stack window, you can also display the filename, package name, and line number displayed.

In case of the AdditionClass example, when you get to the second breakpoint, the Stack window with all display options enabled should appear as shown in Figure 9-10.

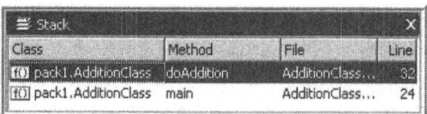

Figure 9-10. Stack window

A really cool feature of the Stack window is that you can trace back to earlier steps in execution. So even after the doAddition method has been executed, you can pop the doAddition method of the stack and get execution back to before the call to doAddition.

Now you can change values and then again proceed to the doAddition method. To pop back to an earlier execution state, right-click the main method as displayed in Figure 9-10 and choose the option Pop Back to Here. You will find that the method doAddition is wiped off the stack, and the execution pointer moves back to the line where you call the doAddition method. The Stack window and the Threads window that I will cover next work in conjunction with each other. So the display in the Stack window is based on which thread is selected in the Threads window.

Threads

The Threads window displays details of the various threads and thread groups involved in the execution of the code. In the Threads window, the current thread name appears in bold. In this example, when execution pauses at any of the breakpoints, the current thread will be main. By default the name and status of each thread is displayed; however, you can display more information using the Preferences dialog box.

The Threads window provides an Export Full Thread Dump option that can export to a file the stack traces for all the threads in the program. You can make any other thread that has not completed yet into the current thread by right-clicking and selecting the Select Thread option.

Watches

The Watches window comes into play when you want to track something specific displayed in some other window such as Data, Smart Data, or Threads, without having to worry about any clutter associated. The Watches window as such does not display anything that cannot be found in any of the other windows. But with the Watches window, it is a lot easier to monitor and track.

You can add a new watch in any of the following ways:

- Using the Add Watch option available when right-clicking

- Using the Watch option available in any of the other debugger windows

- Dragging and dropping elements from other debugger windows into the Watches window

Now that you have looked at the various windows and capabilities of the debugger, you will use the debugger to debug Web applications—the kind of applications that are normally not very debugger friendly.

Debugging Web Applications

Debuggers traditionally have not worked well with Web applications. Debuggers that can be useful with stand-alone applications are nowhere as useful when it comes to Web applications. The number of elements involved in Web applications and the idea of a server waiting for requests and code executing based on that request is something that needs specialized debuggers.

 TIP *The debugger can be useful even when you are learning to use something new such as a framework. Get a sample application, and in one application flow, set breakpoints in the Java Server Pages (JSPs) and classes involved. Then choose the Debug Project option. You can now easily track and understand how the application and framework functions by looking at what data is present at a certain breakpoint as well as in what order the code executes. Try this out with the Struts framework example you created in Chapter 5. You should be able to understand exactly how Struts works.*

JDeveloper is accomplished at debugging Web applications, and you can just as easily debug Web applications as you can debug stand-alone applications. For the Web application debugging, you will use the BasicWebApp project you created in Chapter 5. In this project, you created a JSP that took a first name and last name as input and passed it to a Servlet that generated a welcome message using the first name and last name.

Open the file Welcome.jsp in the Code Editor, and set a breakpoint on the line <%= new java.util.Date() %>. This is the only line in the JSP that you can set a breakpoint on; the rest is just Hypertext Markup Language (HTML), and breakpoints work only with lines of code that execute. Actually, you can set breakpoints on the HTML lines, but these breakpoints will be meaningless because those HTML lines will never execute.

Once the breakpoint in the JSP is set on the JSP expression that prints the current date and time, choose the Debug Welcome.jsp option in the right-click menu. Your default browser should start up, but the JSP will not be displayed because execution stops at the breakpoint. Now that the breakpoint in the JSP has been reached, look at the Data window discussed earlier in the chapter. It should look like Figure 9-11. The thing to note here is that all the JSP implicit objects are being displayed, and so using the debugger, you can see what information each of these objects holds. While working with JSPs, most tasks revolve around these implicit objects. So if you can view exactly what data these hold, this information can go a long way in helping you to find and fix errors.

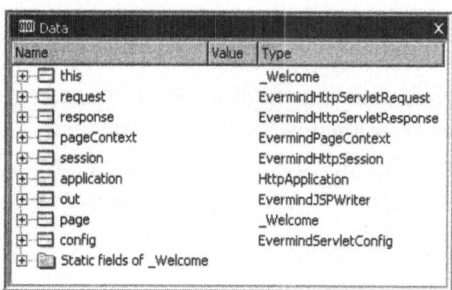

Figure 9-11. Data window for Welcome.jsp

Now click the Resume option from the Debug menu, and Welcome.jsp will be displayed in the browser. A form with two input fields for the first name and last name should be displayed. On submission of this form, a Hypertext Transfer Protocol (HTTP) GET request will be sent that will invoke the WelcomeServlet based on the mapping configured. To debug the WelcomeServlet, you will now set a breakpoint in the WelcomeServlet code. Set a breakpoint on the strLname = request.getParameter("lname"); line of code. Note that the debugger has not been stopped and is running in the background.

Now input values into the HTML form displayed in the JSP and submit it. I entered the first name *Boris* and the last name *Becker*. You will find that execution of the Servlet code stops at the line where you set the breakpoint. Look at the Data window, and you will notice that the request, response, and other objects being used are displayed in the list. The request parameters are stored as a HashMap named *parameters*. As shown in Figure 9-12, the fname request parameter is present in the HashMap where the key is *fname* and the value is *Boris*.

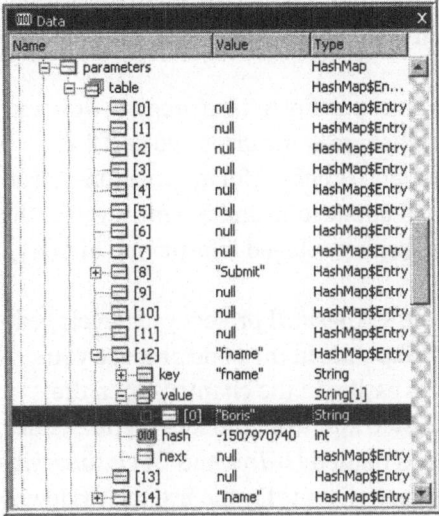

Figure 9-12. Data window: request parameters

As you step through the code in the Servlet, pay attention to the Classes and the Stack windows. The Classes window will show that a lot of classes you are unaware of are being loaded, and this display can help if you are getting unexpected NoClassDefFoundError or ClassNotFoundException exceptions. If a class is being loaded but is not performing as expected, it might also be because a wrong version of the class is being used.

The Stack window will show the stack of methods that are involved in the execution. You can also pop back to earlier methods using the Pop Back to Here option discussed earlier in the chapter. Resume execution, and the welcome message should display in the browser.

 NOTE *Even after a request is processed, the debugger continues to run. So if you change parameter values in the uniform resource locator (URL) displayed in the browser and fire a fresh request, the debugger will still pause execution at the breakpoint and display all the expected information.*

Now that you have seen how the debugger tool can help you quickly and easily debug stand-alone and Web applications, you will move on to a variant of the debugger that is meant solely for debugging Java User Interfaces (UIs).

UI Debugger

The UI debugger is meant for debugging AWT and Swing-based Java applications and applets. The UI debugger has the capabilities of the debugger discussed earlier, so you can very well set breakpoints in the code and get details of the objects, threads, classes, and so on. This functionality and usage is similar to the debugger already discussed.

What makes the UI debugger special is its capability to take program flow and examine the tree structure, the components that are being displayed and their hierarchy, the events that are being triggered, and other useful information—all at runtime. So although you are running your UI application and interacting with the components in the UI, the UI debugger can display detailed information of everything happening with the UI.

To try out the UI debugger, you will use the ABasicUI project you developed in Chapter 3. You do not need to set any breakpoints in the code because you have already experimented with breakpoints earlier in the chapter. Open the project, and select the option UI Debug ABasicUI.jpr from the Run menu. While the application starts up, two empty windows named *UI Tree* and *UI Outline* will display. Select the option View ➤ UI Debugger ➤ Events for the Events window to also be displayed. These three windows are the key to the UI Debugger features:

- **UI Tree:** The UI Tree window displays a hierarchical structure of all the components involved in the application.

- **UI Outline:** The UI Outline window displays an image of the application's GUI. The UI Outline and the UI Tree work in conjunction. If you select a component in the UI Tree, that component automatically gets selected in the UI Outline and vice versa.

- **Events:** The Events window displays information about events as they happen.

Even after you have the application running, you will notice that all three windows are empty. Only after you take a snapshot of the UI will these windows come into action. You can take a snapshot by either using snapshot button or pressing F5. Click F5 and your UI Tree should now appear as shown in Figure 9-13, and the UI Outline window should appear as shown in Figure 9-14.

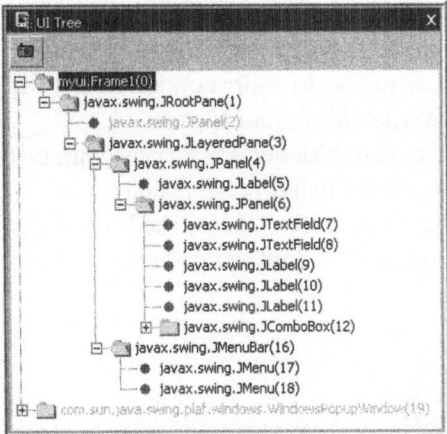

Figure 9-13. UI Tree window

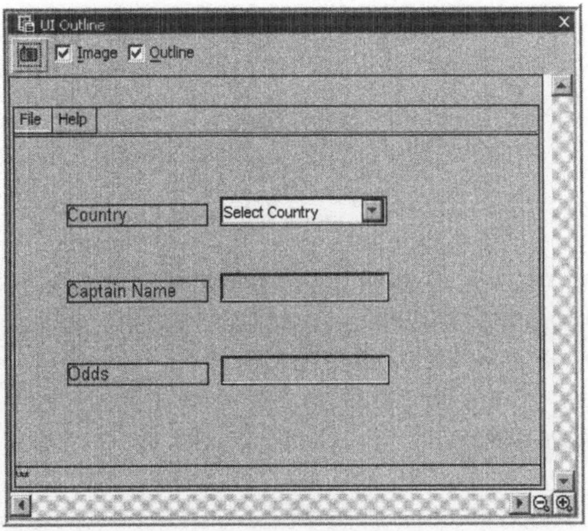

Figure 9-14. UI Outline window

Using the UI Tree and the UI Outline windows, you can see exactly which components are being displayed and the hierarchy of the components. The menu available when right-clicking any component is also quite useful. You can watch components, go to the source code, highlight a component in the actual user interface, or hide it. However, with respect to event handling, the options Trace Events and Show Listeners are the most useful.

In this particular application, you had defined an ActionListener for the Country combo box. To check what are the listeners associated with a component, select the component and then choose the option Show Listeners from the right-click menu. When selecting the JComboBox that lists countries and then clicking the Show Listeners option, the window that appears displays the exact listener associated with the JComboBox. Use the Go to Source option in this window to view the Java code that will execute when that event triggers.

Now that you know that a java.awt.event.ActionListener is associated with that particular combo box, you will trace those events so that every time that event occurs, the Events window will display details of the event. Choose the Trace Events option for the JComboBox, select the java.awt.event.ActionListener listing as shown in Figure 9-15, and click OK.

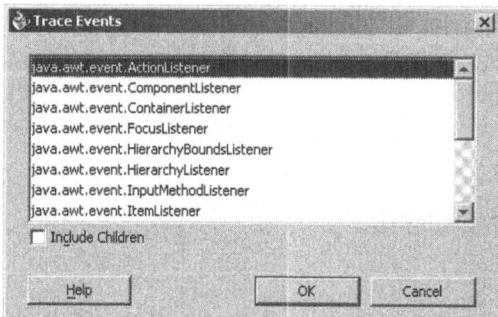

Figure 9-15. Trace events

Now in the application that is running, change the selected value in the Countries combo box to India. The Events window will now get into the action and display details of the event that just happened, as shown in Figure 9-16.

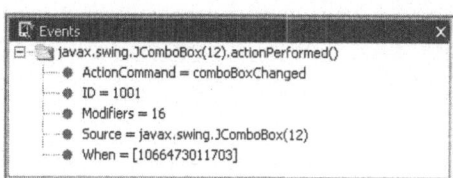

Figure 9-16. Events window

Now that you have looked at the debugging capabilities of JDeveloper, you will move to another useful tool—one that features in a lot of JDeveloper promos, the CodeCoach.

Introducing CodeCoach

The CodeCoach name suggests what the tool does, and I have seen a Web ad where a coach was blowing the whistle on improper code. The catchy name

CodeCoach is for the tool that points to errors in Java code and suggests possible solutions and optimizations. CodeCoach is very much a part of JDeveloper and is not available as an independent tool.

 NOTE *CodeCoach depends on the Oracle Java Virtual Machine (OJVM). So only if you are using OJVM will CodeCoach work. For details on installing the OJVM, refer to Chapter 2.*

 NOTE *With the 10g production release, CodeCoach and the profilers are expected to work on non-Windows platforms as well. Check the documentation for your specific JDeveloper version or the Oracle Technology Network at http://otn.oracle.com to confirm.*

Try and use CodeCoach right from the early stages in the project because keeping all optimization and code improvements until the end of development never seems to get the desired results. If you use CodeCoach after all the code is in place, it just might throw up hundreds of suggestions for all your classes, and you might end up implementing none of those. Instead, if you use CodeCoach regularly, you will keep optimizing and improving your code regularly.

When you run CodeCoach, try out all execution flows to ensure that all the code actually gets executed. This is important because the suggestions CodeCoach generates are based on the code that was executed and the classes that were loaded. There is a possibility of getting improper suggestions from CodeCoach if all the code has not been executed.

 NOTE *To use CodeCoach on Java files, the files also must have been compiled with the Oracle Java Compiler, including debug information. So if you try to run CodeCoach on Java code that was compiled with any other compiler, you will get error messages stating that in the CodeCoach log.*

You will first use CodeCoach on the SimpleApp1 project you created in Chapter 3. You need to configure the CodeCoach properties in the Project Properties dialog box. In the properties for the project SimpleApp1, select Profiles ➤ Development ➤ CodeCoach to get the screen shown in Figure 9-17.

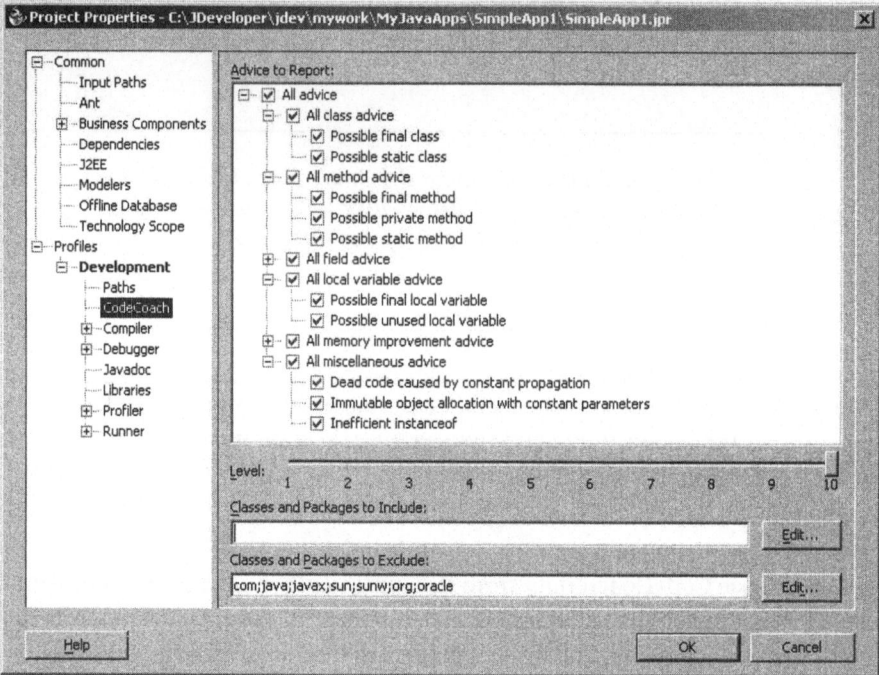

Figure 9-17. CodeCoach properties

In the Project Properties dialog box, the kind of advice CodeCoach offers is listed as are the packages that will be included and excluded. Move the Level slider to 10 so that all advice possible and not just the most important bits are offered.

> **NOTE** *Because the package name for SimpleApp1 project is* pack1, *you did not have to make any changes to the excluded list of packages. However, for other examples in the book where the package name is* com.jdevbook.xxx, *you do have to remove the com package from the excluded list. The com package is part of the excluded list by default. If not removed, the classes in com.* would also be excluded.*

To run CodeCoach on the project SimpleApp1, just select the option CodeCoach SimpleApp1.jpr from the Run menu, and you should get CodeCoach Results as shown in Figure 9-18. The codes CFIN, FUNU, and so on represent certain types of advice. Select any of the advice and right-click to apply a fix, ignore the message, or hide messages of this type. You can even save the results to a file.

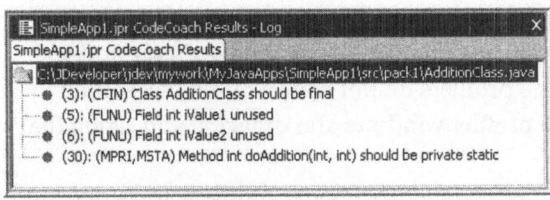

Figure 9-18. CodeCoach results

NOTE *CodeCoach results are displayed only after execution completes. So, in the case of stand-alone applications such as SimpleApp1, the results are displayed immediately after execution completes; however, for Web applications, the results are displayed on stopping the OracleAS Containers for J2EE (OC4J) server.*

You will now try CodeCoach on the StrutsApp project that you developed in Chapter 5. In this case, you do have to change the classes and packages specified in the excluded list. Remove the com package from the excluded list. Next from the Run menu, select the option CodeCoach StrutsApp.jpr. On the application startup, take it through the two application flows discussed in Chapter 5 and then stop the server using the Run Manager that can be displayed from View ➤ Run Manager. On stopping the server, you will find that the CodeCoach results appear under a tab named *Embedded OC4J Server CodeCoach Results* and not under the StrutsApp CodeCoach Results tab.

Because you removed com from the list of excluded packages, you will find a lot of warnings in the CodeCoach results because CodeCoach tried to check packages such as com.sun, com.evermind, and so on. However, these classes have not been compiled using the Oracle Java Compiler with the debug option. So CodeCoach is unable to check these classes. After the warnings, you will find the results for the classes in the com.jdevbook package that you actually wanted to check with CodeCoach.

To avoid getting the warnings for the various com.* packages, add those packages to the excluded list, and CodeCoach will not consider them. You can also state the com.jdevbook package in the included list, and only that package will be considered.

Introducing the Profilers

JDeveloper provides three kinds of profilers: Memory, Events, and Execution. These profilers are meant to provide information about the application that is not obvious otherwise. You have to spend some time with the profilers before you can actually put them to good use. The JDeveloper profilers' look and feel does need some work because the profilers do not have a refined feel about them as yet. Interacting with the profiler windows and dragging and sizing the windows is not much fun.

On the functionality front, however, the JDeveloper profilers are very good and can provide most information that any other commercial profiler does. I am personally not a great believer in optimization exercises undertaken at the end of application development. If performance is a critical issue for the application, you should be monitoring it from the early stages of development. Profiling and trying to fix applications after development might not be a worthwhile exercise in terms of the time and effort you will have to invest in the exercise.

You should use profilers to find areas in your application that need special attention. It is not worth the effort to try and optimize every bit of code that exists. Isolate code that is hitting your application's performance and try to optimize this bit. It is important to be sure of what code is affecting application performance because Java Virtual Machines (JVMs) keep getting faster and smarter, and the optimization tricks that might have worked wonders with older JVMs might just be unnecessary today.

Like CodeCoach, the profilers also work only with the OJVM.

Memory Profiler

The Memory Profiler shows detailed information about how exactly the application is using memory. It can be a useful tool to isolate the cause of excessive memory utilization or memory leaks in the application.

You will use the Memory Profiler on the StrutsApp project to get a feel of what it is capable of doing. Because there are hundreds of classes involved either directly or indirectly, it is better to specify the classes that you want profiled. These are the classes that you can do something about if you find improper memory usage. To configure the Memory Profiler for the project, in the project properties navigate to Profiles ➤ Development ➤ Profiler ➤ Memory. As shown in Figure 9-19, on this screen you can define the columns that should be displayed and the instances to include/exclude. The Update Intervals field is the duration in seconds after which memory sampling is done. The Slider Depth option is the number of memory samples that the profiler will maintain in memory. The default of 20 means that you can refer to 20 previous samples. If you want to see the memory profile of the classes you have created, you could add com.jdevbook to the included instances field, and only the data for classes in that package will be displayed.

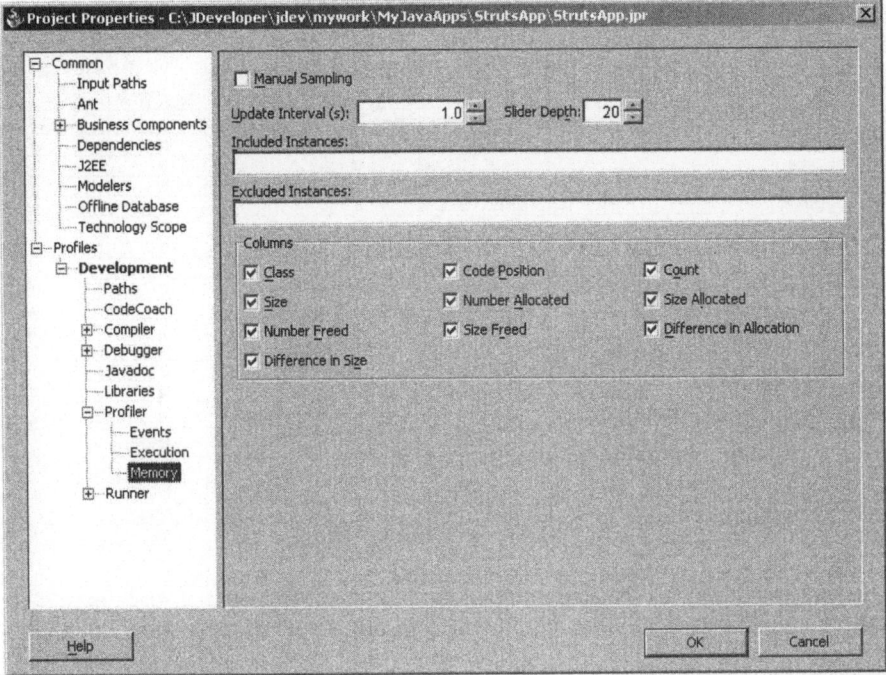

Figure 9-19. Memory Profiler's Project Properties dialog box

You will not make any changes to the Memory Profiler configuration and then run the Memory Profiler for the project using the Run ➤ Memory Profile StrutsApp.jpr menu command. The Web browser will display the welcome page for the project, and a new Memory Profiler window, as shown in Figure 9-20, will pop up.

Memory Sample Table: Profiling: Run 6 Embedded OC4J Server

47/47

Class	Count	Size	No. Alloc	Sz Alloc	No. Fr...	Sz Freed	Diff Alloc	Diff Sz
Totals:	173148	7,138,...	1	32	0	0	1	32
char[]	39283	2,779,532	0	0	0	0	0	0
java.lang.String	38550	925,200	0	0	0	0	0	0
byte[]	567	796,284	0	0	0	0	0	0
java.util.HashMap$Entry	26759	642,216	0	0	0	0	0	0
java.util.jar.Attributes$Name	18061	289,012	0	0	0	0	0	0
java.util.HashMap$Entry[]	7178	287,856	0	0	0	0	0	0
java.util.HashMap	7169	286,760	0	0	0	0	0	0
java.lang.Object[]	1721	101,364	0	0	0	0	0	0
int[]	941	90,728	0	0	0	0	0	0
java.util.jar.Attributes	6655	79,900	0	0	0	0	0	0
java.util.Hashtable$Entry[]	637	61,244	0	0	0	0	0	0
java.util.Hashtable$Entry	2523	60,552	0	0	0	0	0	0
java.lang.reflect.Method	936	52,416	0	0	0	0	0	0
java.lang.String[]	1033	30,976	0	0	0	0	0	0
java.lang.Class[]	1823	26,748	0	0	0	0	0	0
long[]	1263	25,756	0	0	0	0	0	0
java.util.Vector	1057	25,368	0	0	0	0	0	0
java.util.Hashtable	595	23,800	0	0	0	0	0	0
java.net.URL	363	20,324	0	0	0	0	0	0
java.util.BitSet	1260	20,196	0	0	0	0	0	0
java.lang.Object[][]	506	18,564	0	0	0	0	0	0
oracle.xml.parser.v2.CMLeaf	555	17,780	0	0	0	0	0	0
oracle.xml.parser.v2.CMNodeSeq	365	13,156	0	0	0	0	0	0
java.lang.reflect.Constructor	287	12,628	0	0	0	0	0	0
java.lang.StringBuffer	689	11,713	0	0	0	0	0	0
oracle.xml.parser.v2.AttrDecl	176	9,852	0	0	0	0	0	0
oracle.xml.parser.v2.ElementDecl	187	9,724	0	0	0	0	0	0
com.sun.corba.ee.internal.orbutil.Element	385	9,652	0	0	0	0	0	0

Figure 9-20. Memory profile for StrutsApp

Each of the columns provides an explanatory tooltip that appears when moving the mouse over the column names. You have the options to pause, resume, and restart profiling or to take a snapshot. The snapshot option is useful if you have enabled manual sampling in the Memory Profiler's Project Properties dialog box.

Events Profiler

The Events Profiler tracks the time taken for individual events in the program. To use the Events Profiler, you need to spend some time with the profiler application programming interface (API) that is part of the package oracle.jdeveloper.profiler. This API provides for creating new events, starting them, and stopping those events from within your Java code. When you use the Events Profiler on Java code that uses the profiler API, the events defined and used in the code get tracked, and the time taken and other details are displayed.

The best usage of the Events Profiler is with Application Development Framework (ADF) applications because the creators of the ADF have defined events that you can track using the Events Profiler. For this example, you will use the JClient project you developed in Chapter 7. In this project, you used JClient to create a UI for student/course details. Before you use events profiling for this project, you need to make a minor change by selecting Profiles ➤ Development ➤ Profiler ➤ Events in the project properties. As shown in Figure 9-21, uncheck the VM Events check box because you just want to track the Business Component for Java (BC4J) events. BC4J was what the business components for Java were known prior to ADF and version 10*g*.

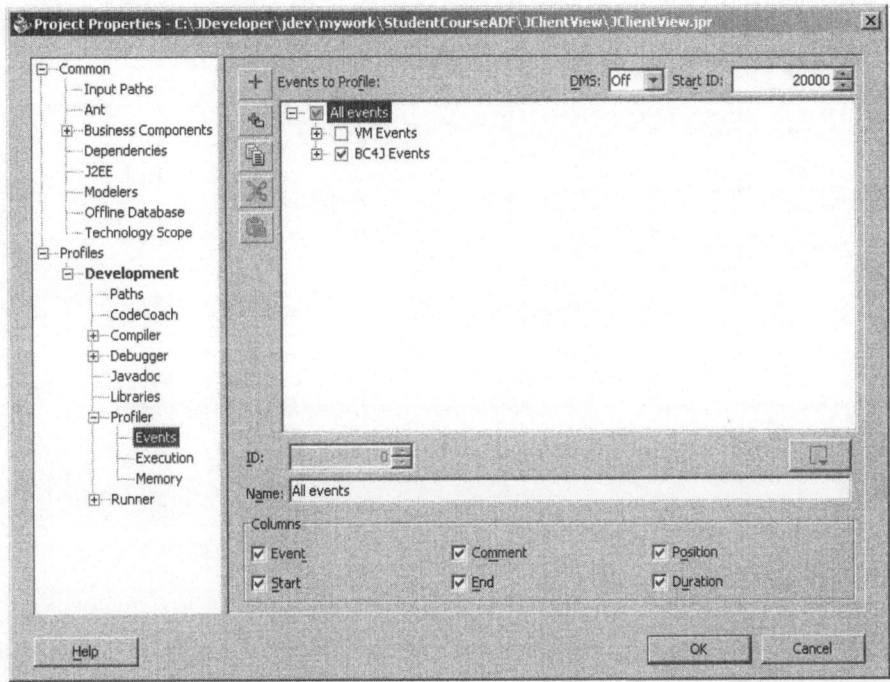

Figure 9-21. Project properties: event profiling

Now from the Run menu, select the option Event Profile JClientView.jpr. A profiler screen will pop up. Here, take a snapshot by clicking the snapshot button provided or by pressing the Ctrl+A combination. You should get the screen shown in Figure 9-22, displaying the various BC4J events that occurred during the execution of the application. The comments for each event are displayed at the bottom of the screen, and the graph on the right maps the events on a timeline.

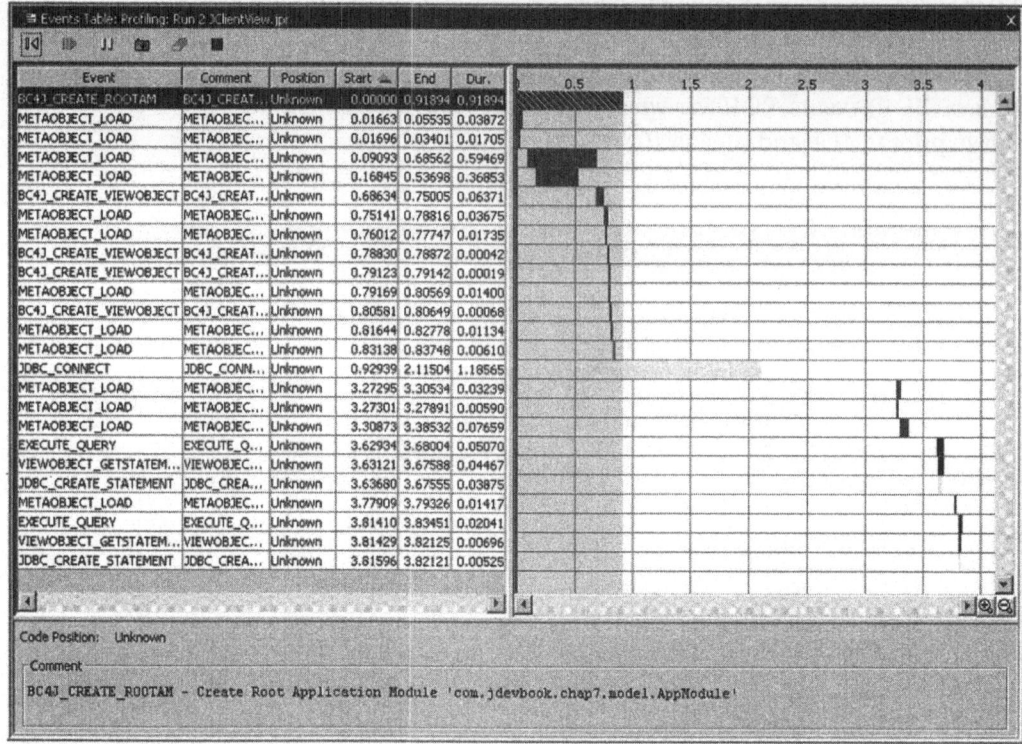

Figure 9-22. JClientView.jpr events profile

The Events Profiler is best used with ADF applications and can provide some useful information about these applications. You will now move to the last kind of profiler, the Execution Profiler.

Execution Profiler

The Execution Profiler is a tool meant to monitor the performance of the application and the time taken by methods involved in the processing. The profiler samples data at regular intervals and based on this data generates reports.

You can change Execution Profiler settings for a project through Profiles ➤ Development ➤ Profiler ➤ Execution in the project properties. The configuration for the Execution Profiler only involves setting the columns to be displayed and the interval after which a sample is taken. The minimum acceptable value is five milliseconds. Do not change this value because taking the maximum samples will get you the most accurate reports. Even five milliseconds is quite a lot of time in Java terms, and it is possible that some methods might take even less than five milliseconds. The UI for the profiler is very cramped, so if you find any columns unnecessary, get rid of them.

To try out the Execution Profiler, you will use the Web Services project Project.jpr that you created in Chapter 8. In this project, run the Web Service MyWebService1. Next open the file EmbeddedMyWebService1Stub, and then select the option Execution Profile Project.jpr from the Run menu. The Execution Profile window will pop up, as shown in Figure 9-23. Click any of the column names to sort data on that basis. In Figure 9-23, I have sorted data based on the time taken in milliseconds. The section on the top right shows the method that called the selected method, and the section at bottom right shows the methods that are called from the selected method.

Call Sample Table: Profiling: Run 14 Project .jpr — Execution time: 1443

Class	Method	Signature	Hit%	Time	On Stack%	Stack time
[Thread]	main		34.65%	500	100.69%	1453
org.apache.soap.util.xm...	getXMLDocBu...	()	10.81%	156	10.81%	156
org.apache.soap.encodi...	<init>	()	9.70%	140	9.70%	140
org.apache.soap.rpc.Call	invoke	(URL,String)	8.66%	125	48.72%	703
HTTPClient.HTTPConnec...	<clinit>	()	5.41%	78	5.41%	78
org.apache.soap.rpc.S...	addBodyPart	(MimeBodyP...	5.41%	78	5.41%	78
org.apache.soap.encodi...	<clinit>	()	4.30%	62	15.11%	218
org.apache.soap.util.mi...	getUniqueValue	()	4.30%	62	4.30%	62
org.apache.soap.util.xm...	refreshDocu...	(String,boole...	2.15%	31	2.15%	31
HTTPClient.Authorizatio...	<clinit>	()	2.15%	31	2.15%	31
org.apache.soap.rpc.S...	setRootPart	(byte[],String)	1.04%	15	10.81%	156
HTTPClient.HTTPConnec...	doConnect	(Timeouts,R...	1.04%	15	2.15%	31
HTTPClient.StreamDemu...	init	(Socket)	1.04%	15	1.04%	15
HTTPClient.HTTPResponse	<init>	(HTTPClient...	1.04%	15	1.04%	15
HTTPClient.Util	getList	(WeakHash...	1.04%	15	1.04%	15
HTTPClient.Util	parseHeader	(String,boole...	1.04%	15	1.04%	15
org.apache.soap.transp...	read		1.04%	15	1.04%	15
org.apache.soap.encodi...	generateStru...	(String,QNa...	1.04%	15	1.04%	15
org.apache.soap.Envelope	<init>	()	1.04%	15	1.04%	15
org.apache.soap.rpc.Call	<init>	(String,Strin...	1.04%	15	1.04%	15
org.apache.soap.encodi...	initializeRegistry	(String)	1.04%	15	1.04%	15
org.apache.soap.encodi...	class$	(String)	1.04%	15	1.04%	15
[Root]	[Root]		0.00%	0	100.00%	1443
org.apache.soap.transp...	save	()	0.00%	0	10.81%	156
org.apache.soap.rpc.S...	setRootPart	(String,String)	0.00%	0	10.81%	156
org.apache.soap.rpc.S...	setRootPart	(MimeBodyP...	0.00%	0	9.70%	140
HTTPClient.HTTPConnec...	Post	(String,byte[...	0.00%	0	7.55%	109
HTTPClient.HTTPConnec...	setupRequest	(String,Strin...	0.00%	0	7.55%	109
HTTPClient.HTTPConnec...	handleRequest	(Request,HT...	0.00%	0	6.44%	93
HTTPClient.HTTPConnec...	sendRequest	(Request,Ti...	0.00%	0	3.19%	46

Called from:

Class	Method	Signature	Hit%	Time
[Thread]	main		10...	703

org.apache.soap.rpc.Call.invoke(URL,String)
Global stats, in method: 125 ms 8.66% On stack: 703 ms 48.72%
Calls: Called from code: 125 ms 17.86%

Class	Method	Signature	Hit%	Time
org.apache.soap.util....	getXMLDocBuilder	()	22...	156
org.apache.soap.tra...	save	()	22...	156
HTTPClient.HTTPCon...	Post	(String,byte...	15...	109
HTTPClient.HTTPCon...	<clinit>	()	11...	78
org.apache.soap.util...	<clinit>	()	4....	31
org.apache.soap.tra...	read	()	2....	15
org.apache.soap.Env...	marshall	(Writer,XML...	2....	15
org.apache.soap.rpc....	buildEnvelope	()	2....	15

Figure 9-23. Execution Profiler

I did not find the Execution Profiler interface that easy to use, and I wasted a lot of time just dragging and sizing columns to get a proper display. Exporting the details to an HTML file is a better option. Use the option Save to HTML that appears when right-clicking the UI. The HTML file generated is well formatted and has proper linking to ease navigation. Figure 9-24 shows how method details are displayed in the HTML file.

Method org.apache.soap.rpc.Call.invoke(URL,String)

Top of the stack 8.66%

On stack 48.72%

Called from :

Class	Method	Hit%	Time
[Thread]	main	100.00%	703

Calls :

Class	Method	Hit%	Time
Inside method		17.86%	125
org.apache.soap.util.xml.XMLParserUtils	getXMLDocBuilder()	22.29%	156
org.apache.soap.transport.TransportMessage	save()	22.29%	156
HTTPClient.HTTPConnection	Post(String,byte[],NVPair[])	15.57%	109
HTTPClient.HTTPConnection	<clinit>()	11.14%	78
org.apache.soap.util.xml.XMLParserUtils	<clinit>()	4.43%	31
org.apache.soap.transport.TransportMessage	read()	2.14%	15
org.apache.soap.Envelope	marshall (Writer,XMLJavaMappingRegistry,SOAPContext)	2.14%	15
org.apache.soap.rpc.Call	buildEnvelope()	2.14%	15

Figure 9-24. Method details in HTML

Now that you have looked at CodeCoach and the profilers, you will look at another useful tool, the TCP Packet Monitor.

Introducing the TCP Packet Monitor

The TCP Packet Monitor makes it possible to view the content of HTTP request and response packets. Using the TCP Packet Monitor, you can even modify and resend the request package and check if the response generated is as expected.

For the TCP Packet Monitor to work, JDeveloper sets up a local proxy and changes the Web Browser/Proxy setting in the Preferences dialog box, defining the proxy host as localhost and the port as 8099. Select the View ➤ TCP Packet Monitor menu command to display the TCP Packet Monitor.

To try the TCP Packet Monitor, you will again use the Web Service example from Chapter 8. The TCP Packet Monitor is particularly useful while working with Web Services because Web Services involve sending requests and responses over HTTP using Extensible Markup Language (XML). The TCP Packet Monitor helps you to see the exact request and response that are being sent and received.

Run MyWebService1 in Project.jpr in the workspace WebServApp. In the TCP Packet Monitor, start monitoring request/response packets using the green arrow button provided. Next run the file EmbeddedMyWebService1Stub that is a client to the Web Service. A request will be sent to the service to which the service will send back a response. The TCP Packet Monitor should have caught this request/response exchange and, as shown in Figure 9-25, will display a summary of the packets. Note that the packet type is http-post (soap). The Data tab, as shown in Figure 9-26, shows the actual SOAP message that was sent as a request and the response to that request.

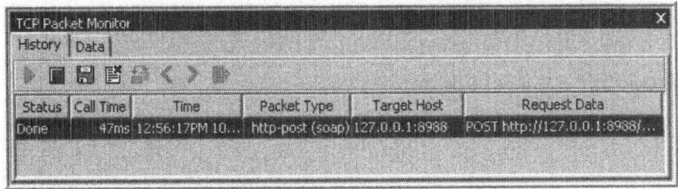

Figure 9-25. TCP Packet Monitor: History tab

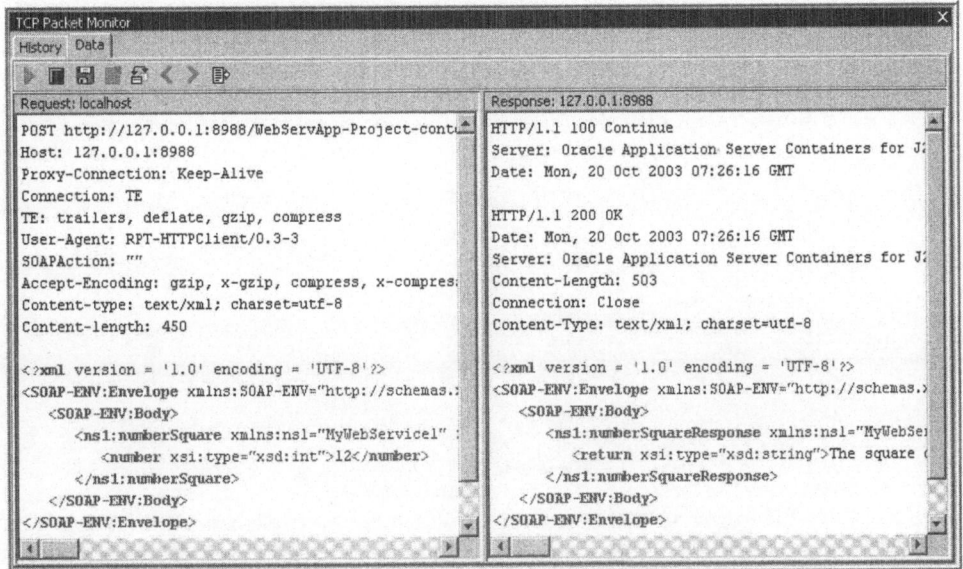

Figure 9-26. TCP Packet Monitor: Data tab

To modify the request and then resend it, change the value in the tag `<number xsi:type="xsd:int">12</number>` from 12 to 10 and then click the Resend Request button. A new entry will appear in the History tab, and after double-clicking it, you can view the response that was received for the modified request. You can also use the Next Request/Response Pair button from right within the Data tab to view the new request/response details. You can thus use the TCP Packet Monitor to try various values and test a Web Service. You can use the Save button to store the request and response to a file.

Summary

In this chapter, you looked at the various tools offered by JDeveloper that are useful for Java development. These tools play a major part in making JDeveloper a comprehensive offering. They help you monitor TCP packets, optimize application performance, improve code quality, and check memory usage.

It is important for anybody using JDeveloper to be familiar with these tools so as to be able to use JDeveloper to its true potential.

CHAPTER 10

Tools and Extensions

IN THE PREVIOUS nine chapters, you have seen how you can use JDeveloper to develop various kinds of Java applications. In this chapter, you will look at how you can make JDeveloper go even further. Java thrives on community backing, and the open-source tools available for Java development. So it is important that you can leverage the power of third-party tools from within JDeveloper. In this chapter, you will look at JDeveloper's integration with popular open-source tools, like the Concurrent Versions System (CVS) and Ant.

This chapter also covers JDeveloper extensions. As the name suggests, extensions are meant to extend the functionality of JDeveloper by providing new capabilities. You will look at existing extensions provided by various providers, as well as how you can develop your own extensions. I will begin with tools coverage and move to extensions later in the chapter.

Apache Ant

Ant has revolutionized the way programmers look at building Java and J2EE applications. The simplicity and portability that Ant has introduced has led to its rapid acceptance across the Java world. Ant is a build utility that takes instructions stated in an XML file and accordingly handles various tasks that need to be performed in the Java build process. Compiling code, creating directories, moving directories, packaging, executing code, generating Javadocs, checking out files from CVS, and uploading files with FTP are just some of the more common tasks that Ant is capable of performing. Ant itself does not have the capability to perform all these tasks. Ant's job is restricted to executing the program that is capable of performing the task. So to compile java code, Ant will use the javac command, whereas to pack files, it will use the jar command.

One question that might come up is "Why use Ant when JDeveloper has good compile, execute, and packing capabilities?" Think of these scenarios and the answer will come to you.

- You are developing an application on JDeveloper, but the environment where it will be deployed and maintained does not have JDeveloper installed.

- You want a build process independent of any IDE and easily portable across platforms.

- You are using JDeveloper to maintain a J2EE project that relies heavily on Ant build scripts for all tasks involved.

- You are using a tool that provides good integration with Ant but not with JDeveloper. This is true of a large number of open-source tools, such as XDoclet (a code generation tool), Cactus (a unit testing framework), and more. If a tool is useful and popular, in all probability it will provide integration with Ant.

- You have a large team working on the project, and you want to standardize and ensure that everyone is following the same structure and procedure.

In all these cases, the solution lies in using Ant and exploiting its various capabilities. I will not delve too deep into Ant; for a detailed coverage of Ant, check out the Ant documentation or one of the many books on the subject. JDeveloper 10g preview is integrated with Ant version 1.5.1. Ant comes as a part of the JDeveloper installation file, so you do not need to download or install Ant separately. The official Apache Ant site is http://ant.apache.org.

I'll revisit some examples from earlier chapters and show you how Ant can change things. In the first example you developed in Chapter 3, you created a class named *AditionClass* that took two numbers as input and printed their addition. Although you used JDeveloper's inbuilt compile and execution capabilities earlier, you will now use Ant.

Open the New Gallery for the project SimpleApp1 in the workspace MyJavaApps. The General ➤ Ant section lists the various Ant-related file creation options that JDeveloper provides.

- The option Empty Buildfile creates a new file containing some basic tags. This option isn't particularly useful, however.

- The option Buildfile from Existing XML File is used to import existing Ant build files into the chosen project.

- The option Buildfile Generated from Active Project Profile is the one you will use in this case. With this option, JDeveloper looks at the Project properties and generates a build file that will be useful and capable of handling the tasks associated with the project. Select the option and click OK. You will see to the screen shown in Figure 10-1.

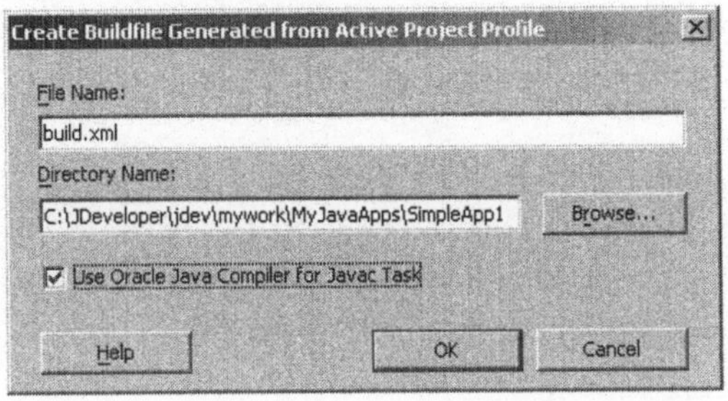

Figure 10-1. Buildfile using Active Project Profile

Select the check box for using the Oracle Java Compiler because, as you saw in Chapter 9, some JDeveloper tools only work with Java code that is compiled using the Oracle Java Compiler. Naming Ant build files as *build.xml* is a convention and not a rule. Stick with build.xml in this case. Click OK, and a build file similar to Listing 10-1 will be generated. Next, take a look at its various component tags of the file and the role that these tags play.

Listing 10-1. Project SimpleApp1 Build File

```xml
<?xml version = '1.0' encoding = 'windows-1252'?>
<!--Ant buildfile generated by Oracle9i JDeveloper-->
<!--Generated Oct 28, 2003 3:55:11 PM-->
<project name="SimpleApp1" default="make" basedir=".">

    <!--Set the JDeveloper home directory-->
    <property name="jdev.home" value="C:\JDeveloper"/>
    <!--Set the output directories-->
    <property name="compile.outdir" value="classes"/>
    <property name="javadoc.outdir" value="javadoc"/>

    <!--Set the classpath-->
    <path id="classpath">
        <pathelement location="${jdev.home}/jdk/jre/lib/rt.jar"/>
        <pathelement location="${jdev.home}/jdk/jre/lib/i18n.jar"/>
        <pathelement location="${jdev.home}/jdk/jre/lib/sunrsasign.jar"/>
        <pathelement location="${jdev.home}/jdk/jre/lib/jsse.jar"/>
        <pathelement location="${jdev.home}/jdk/jre/lib/jce.jar"/>
        <pathelement location="${jdev.home}/jdk/jre/lib/charsets.jar"/>
        <pathelement location="${jdev.home}/jdk/jre/classes"/>
        <pathelement location="${compile.outdir}"/>
        <pathelement location="${jdev.home}/jdev/lib/jdev-rt.jar"/>
    </path>
```

```xml
    <!--Set the source path-->
    <property name="src.dir" value="src"/>
    <path id="srcpath">
        <pathelement location="${src.dir}"/>
    </path>

    <!--Configure Oracle Java Compiler-->
    <property name="build.compiler"
        value="oracle.jdeveloper.compiler.ant.taskdefs.OjcAdapter"/>
    <property name="ojc.update.imports" value="none"/>

    <target name="init">
        <tstamp/>
    </target>

    <target name="compile" depends="init">
        <mkdir dir="${compile.outdir}"/>
        <!--Compile Java source files-->
        <javac destdir="${compile.outdir}" debug="on" encoding="Cp1252">
            <classpath refid="classpath"/>
            <src refid="srcpath"/>
            <include name="pack1/AdditionClass.java"/>
        </javac>
    </target>

    <target name="doc" depends="init">
        <mkdir dir="${javadoc.outdir}"/>
        <!--Create Javadoc-->
        <javadoc sourcepathref="srcpath" classpathref="classpath"
            destdir="${javadoc.outdir}" version="false" author="false"
                encoding="Cp1252" additionalparam="-J-Xmx32m">
            <package name="pack1"/>
        </javadoc>
    </target>

    <target name="clean">
        <!--Delete output directories-->
        <delete dir="${compile.outdir}"/>
        <delete dir="${javadoc.outdir}"/>
    </target>

    <target name="make" depends="compile"/>
    <target name="rebuild" depends="clean,compile"/>
    <target name="all" depends="compile,doc"/>
</project>
```

The *project* tag is where you assign the name *SimpleApp1* to the project. More important, the default target for the project is *make*. Next, you define a few properties that are used in script and you want to be easily configurable. If you wish to compile to a directory named *newclasses* instead of the *classes* directory stated in the script, all you have to change is the value of the property *compile.outdir*.

TIP *The best way to decipher how an Ant script works is to use the Find Text feature and find all usages of a certain word. For example, do a find on* compile.outdir, *and you will see exactly how and where that property is being used.*

The classpath is always a very important part of any build process. The *path* tag is used to define the directories and libraries that you want in the classpath. This reference is used later in the script while compiling the code and generating the javadoc. Next come the targets. The first target is named *init*, and uses the *tstamp* tag. The *tstamp* tag is used to set timestamp properties.

NOTE *Target names like init, compile, and doc are used only to make the script easy to understand. The names used are not important, and you can very well have a target named* america *that will compile the java code.*

Within the various targets are tags such as *javac, mkdir, javadoc,* and *delete*. These tags are special, and are referred to as *tasks*. All the tasks in this example are part of the core tasks that come as part of Ant. Ant is easily extensible, however, and so whenever a tool wants to provide integration with Ant, the tool creators just create their own new tasks.

The important tasks used in this example are:

- **javac:** This task compiles Java code, generating output in the destination directory specified as the value of the destdir attribute.

- **mkdir:** Makes a new directory, if that directory does not exist already.

- **javadoc:** Uses the javadoc tool to generate Javadocs (API specifications) for the source code specified.

- **delete:** Deletes the files and directories specified.

The targets *rebuild* and *all* are quite interesting, because they just trigger other targets in a specific order. The *rebuild* target first cleans the existing compiled classes and javadoc, and then compiles the code.

To invoke the targets that are defined in the build file, right-click the build file listed in the Applications Navigator. The Build Target option will display all the targets, and you can pick the target to invoke. The Default Build Target option will invoke the *make* target because that is the one you defined as the default target in the build file. When you choose this option, you should get a display similar to Listing 10-2 in the Messages Log.

Listing 10-2. On Executing Default Build Target

```
Buildfile: C:\JDeveloper\jdev\mywork\MyJavaApps\SimpleApp1\build.xml
init:
compile:
    [mkdir] Created dir: C:\JDeveloper\jdev\mywork\MyJavaApps\SimpleApp1\classes
    [javac] Compiling 1 source file to
                C:\JDeveloper\jdev\mywork\MyJavaApps\SimpleApp1\classes
make:

BUILD SUCCESSFUL
Total time: 2 seconds
```

With Ant configured for the project SimpleApp1, you now have two build mechanisms in place. One is provided by JDeveloper, and the other is the Ant mechanism. You can also use Ant as the default build mechanism so that even if you fire the Make or Rebuild option from the Project menu, the Ant build mechanism will be used. Move to the Project Properties for SimpleApp1 and select Common ➤ Ant. As shown in Figure 10-2, use the build.xml file you created earlier as the Project Buildfile. The -verbose Ant argument gets you a verbose and more detailed log than otherwise. Click OK. Ant is now the default build mechanism.

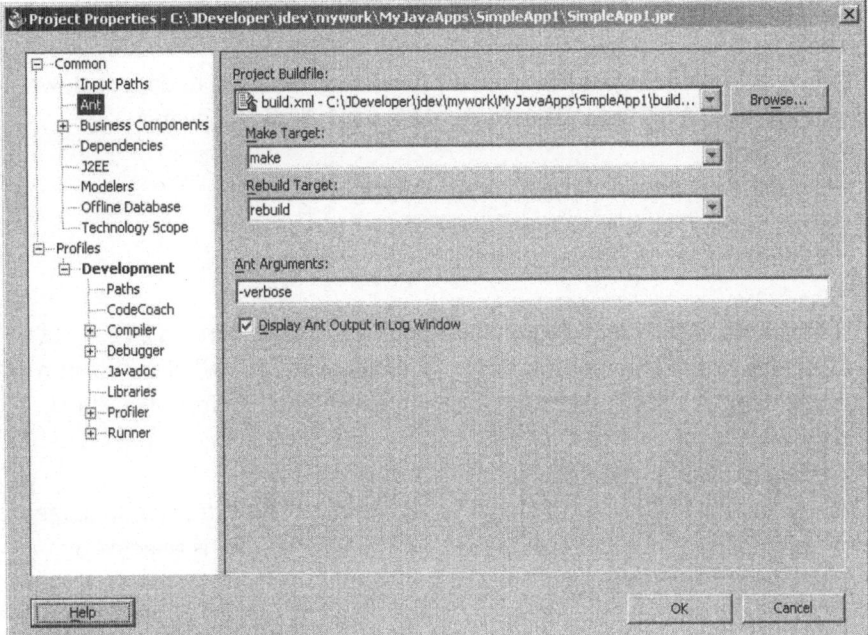

Figure 10-2. Project Properties: Ant

Now that you have looked at JDeveloper's Ant capabilities, have a look at another important feature, integration with source control tools such as Oracle Software Configuration Manager (SCM), Rational ClearCase, and Concurrent Versions System (CVS).

Source Control

Source-control tools make it possible to manage and maintain versions of code easily. These tools are especially important if your code keeps changing constantly, or if you have more than one person working on the same piece of code.

Because source-control tools are such an integral part of the software development process, most of the popular IDEs provide integration with one or more source-control tools. JDeveloper can be integrated with Oracle Software Configuration Manager (SCM), Rational ClearCase, and Concurrent Versions System (CVS). Integration of the IDE eliminates the need for a separate client software for the source-control tool. This also makes all code-related tasks possible from within the IDE, something that most IDEs aim at.

This section discusses how you can integrate with CVS, arguably the most popular of the source control tools in the Java world. Apache (http://apache.org) uses CVS, and so does SourceForge (http://sf.net), which hosts a large number of

Java projects. There are a number of CVS clients available for various platforms available.

To integrate JDeveloper with CVS, the first thing you need to do is to download and install a CVS Client. JDeveloper recommends the following:

- CVSNT for Windows: http://www.cvsnt.org

- cvshome's CVS, for other platforms

Although the JDeveloper documentation recommends version 1.11.1.3 of CVSNT, things worked fine even when I downloaded and installed the version 2.0.11 on a Windows 2000 machine. Once you have the client installed, check whether the folder where the CVS executable is present is stated in the value of the PATH environment variable.

Next select the option Versioning ➤ Select System. The Extension manager section will pop up in the Preferences dialog. The Oracle SCM is selected by default. Change the selection to CVS. Click OK.

Based on the version control tool selected in the Extension Manager, a preference section for that particular version control tool appears in the Preferences dialog. Again select the option Versioning ➤ Select System, and you will find that the CVS option as shown in Figure 10-3 is provided.

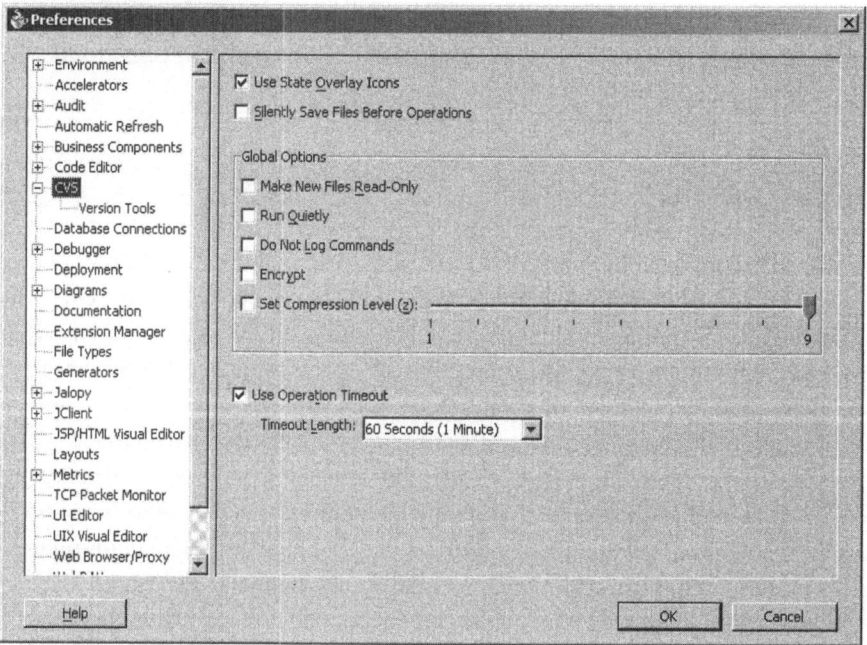

Figure 10-3. Preferences: CVS

Once you have the CVS client installed, and you have chosen CVS as the versioning tool to use, open the Connection Navigator, and you will find that a new option CVS Server appears in the Connections list. Right-click CVS Server and select the option New Connection.

NOTE *If the options available on right-clicking CVS server are grayed out, check your CVS client installation and whether the CVS executable folder is stated in the value of the PATH environment variable.*

Click Next on the Welcome screen. You will create a new CVS connection to the Apache Jakarta (http://jakarta.apache.org) CVS. On the Step 1 screen, name the Connection as *Jakarta,* and click Next. Step 2 is where you fill in details about the access method, host, and repository. These configurations are specific to the server you are trying to access.

For anonymous access to the Apache CVS server, enter the values shown in Figure 10-4, and click Next. These values might have changed by the time you read this, so check out http://jakarta.apache.org/site/cvsindex.html to confirm them. Step 3 displays the value of the CVSROOT. This value is determined based on our input in Step 2. In this case, the CVSROOT value should be :pserver:anoncvs@cvs.apache.org:/home/cvspublic. Click Next. The last screen is where you can test the connection, using the Test Connection button. You need to connect to the Internet for the Apache Jakarta CVS server connection to work. Click Next, and a summary screen displaying details of the connection is displayed. Click Finish.

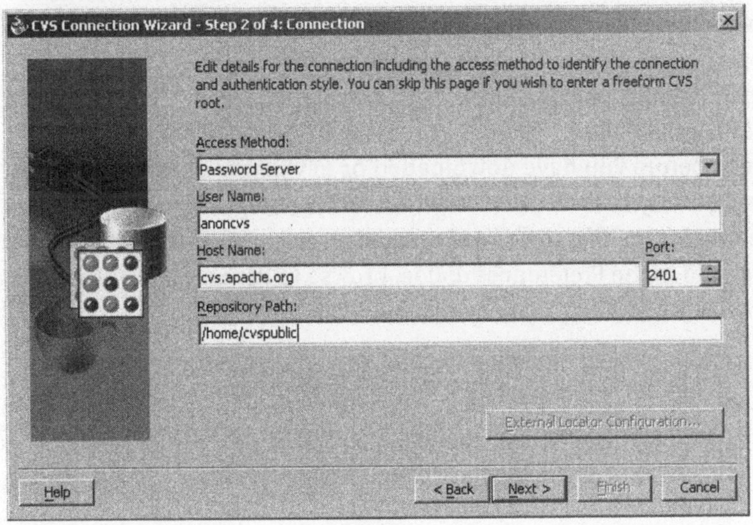

Figure 10-4. CVS Connection Wizard

Once the CVS Connection is in place, the Versioning Menu will provide options to Import, Check Out, or export a Module. To import a module to a specific project, you can also right-click the project and select the Versioning ➤ Import Module. This option requires write access, and will not work in the case of your Apache example. The best option is to use the Check out Module option, and specify the module to check out as well as the project in which the files are to be checked out.

Once you have checked out the code from the CVS into the source folder for a project, enable the option Scan Source Paths To Determine Project Contents in the project properties ➤ Common ➤ Input Paths for the project. Once the code is listed for that project in the Applications Navigator, things are fairly simple. When you select any file that is listed in the Applications Navigator, you can use the Versioning menu available by right-clicking as well as using the Versioning menu in the Menu bar. Because you do not have the right to commit or add to the Apache CVS, some options will stay grayed out. These menus provide all the options that you would expect from a CVS client, such as Compare versions, View History, View Status, Tag, Download revisions, and more.

Extensions

JDeveloper extensions are a systematic way to make JDeveloper go further. A critical requirement for any IDE today is that it should be flexible and easily extensible. All the top IDEs have this capability. Although Sun Java Studio benefits from improvements to the underlying NetBeans platform, WebSphere Studio Application Developer benefits from improvement in the Eclipse platform.

Being based on an open source platform means that any extension written for the NetBeans platform will work on Sun Java Studio and any extension of Eclipse will work on WSAD. JDeveloper isn't based on an open source-platform like NetBeans or Eclipse, and so has provided its own Extension Software Development Kit (ESDK).

JDeveloper is made up of two parts, the Core IDE framework and the extensions. Even before you have downloaded or developed an extension, you already are using many JDeveloper extensions while using JDeveloper. To get an idea of the extensions that are already installed, select Tools ➤ Preferences from the menu, and in the Preferences dialog, browse to the Extension Manager, as shown in Figure 10-5.

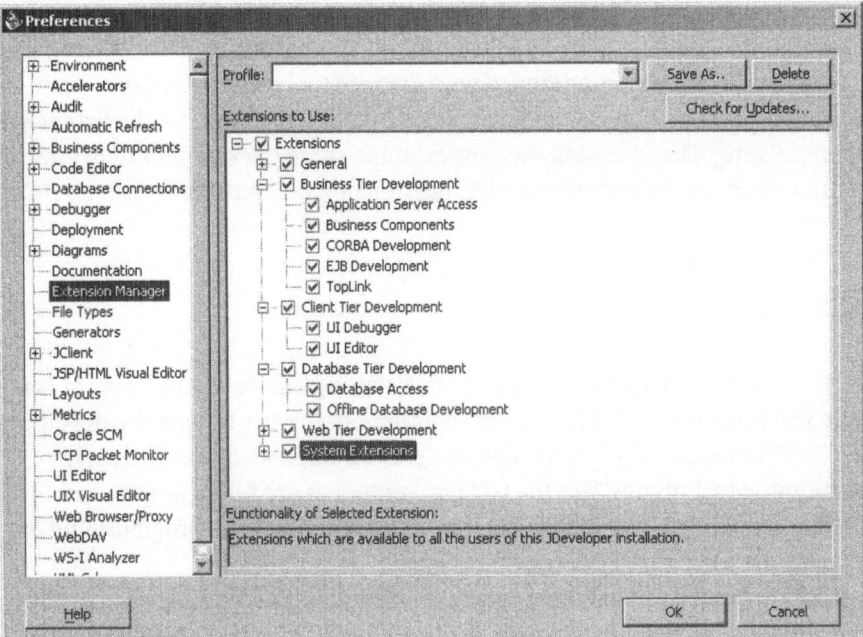

Figure 10-5. Preferences: Extension Manager

TIP *Use the profiles provided in the Extension Manager, or create new profiles to include only those extensions that are relevant to the kind of development you're undertaking. Only these extensions will be loaded when JDeveloper starts up, resulting in a reduced startup time.*

At the time of this writing, version 10*g* is still in preview release and so hardly any extensions built specifically for version 10*g* are available. Most extensions that worked with version 9*i* work well with 10g as well.

NOTE *The Help ➤ Check for Updates option in the menu should also get you a list of possible updates and extensions for JDeveloper. At the time of this writing for version 10g preview, this feature did not work.*

The place to look for extensions to JDeveloper is the Extensions Exchange on OTN: http://otn.oracle.com/products/jdev/htdocs/partners/addins/index.html.

Although you will find all extensions developed by Oracle on the Extensions Exchange, there are third-party extensions that are missing from the Extensions Exchange list. If you are wondering if your favorite tool has a JDeveloper extension, check out the tool developer's site instead of solely relying on the Extensions Exchange listing. The following sections examine some JDeveloper extensions that can be very useful and offer additional functionality for JDeveloper.

JUnit

JUnit is a unit-testing framework that makes writing and executing tests in Java simple and systematic. JUnit is the key component for any test-driven development (TDD) exercise. TDD and JUnit also play an important part in extreme programming techniques. Yes, the last two sentences are full of jargon, and I recommend that you get your hands on a good book on extreme programming or TDD to understand these concepts.

JUnit tests need to be written in a certain format, as recommended by the framework, so the basic structure of all tests you write for JUnit is quite similar. The JUnit extension for JUnit is meant to automatically generate the repetitive code for you.

Download the JUnit extension for JDeveloper 10*g* from http://otn.oracle.com/ software/products/jdev/index.html. From the zip file downloaded, place the two JAR files junit_addin.jar and bc4j_junit_addin.jar into the directory jdev/lib/ext. Start JDeveloper.

The New Gallery for any project should now have a new section in General ➤ Unit Tests (JUnit). The four creation options provided are: Custom Test Fixture, JDBC Test Fixture, Test Case, and Test Suite.

Jalopy

Jalopy is an open-source tool that can check and format Java source code based on a certain set of rules. You can download Jalopy from http://jalopy.sf.net. Download the Jalopy version integrated with JDeveloper.

Check out my article "Three tools that make Java code review painless and effective" at http://builder.com.com/5100-6370-5031836.html. There I touch upon Jalopy, PMD, and CheckStyle as three tools that make reviewing and formatting code a fast and simple exercise. The reason why you should integrate a tool like Jalopy with JDeveloper is that Jalopy provides functionality that as yet is not present in JDeveloper. A number of the top IDEs provide this functionality, but surprisingly, JDeveloper hasn't as yet introduced a code-formatting feature.

To integrate Jalopy with JDeveloper, download the file jalopy-jdeveloper-1.1.1.zip from the Jalopy site. Next, extract the contents of the zip file, and as per the instructions stated in the documentation, place all the jars in the extracted lib directory into the directory jdev/lib/ext.

Now start JDeveloper, and you will find a new Format <filename> option when you right-click the file listing in the Applications Navigator, as well as when you right-click in the code editor. You will also find that a Jalopy option has been introduced in the Preferences dialog, providing many Jalopy tweaking possibilities.

Wireless Extension

JDeveloper Wireless Extension (JWE) is a nice new JDeveloper extension for developing wireless applications. The user guide states that you can develop the following types of applications using this extension:

- Multi-channel applications, which can be accessed through multiple delivery methods such as voice, messaging, or WAP.

- Java 2 Micro Edition (J2ME) applications, including regular J2ME MIDlet applications and MIDlet applications that can communicate with web services.

JWE is available for download on the JDeveloper Extension Exchange. The installation procedure is the same as that for the other extensions. Just find the file jwe.jar that is provided in the download, and place it in the directory jdev/lib/ext. Start JDeveloper.

JWE provides good J2ME features, and you can even test applications with various emulators that can be integrated with the tool. The JWE also has features to help wireless enable existing J2EE applications.

Now that you have seen some useful extensions to JDeveloper, see how you can create your own extensions for JDeveloper.

Extension Software Development Kit (ESDK)

All JDeveloper extension development is based on the ESDK, so the first step to creating new extensions is to get hold of the ESDK. The ESDK is available as a separate download on OTN at http://otn.oracle.com/products/jdev/htdocs/partners/addins.

The installation procedure for ESDK is rather simple. Just extract the contents of the zip file into the directory where you have JDeveloper installed while maintaining the directory structure in the zip file. Start JDeveloper.

Two new extensions are introduced, and if you open up the Extension Manager section in the Preferences dialog, you will find that Extensions SDK

Samples and Extension SDK Tools have been added to the list of System Extensions. If these options aren't already checked, do that and restart JDeveloper.

You will look at the steps involved in creating and deploying a simple extension. The actual extensions you might have to create can differ a lot, but the steps involved are quite similar. You will now develop a new extension that will be listed in the Tools Menu and display the current date and time as well as the value of the *java.home* system property.

First create a new Application Workspace named *ExtensionsSpace*, using the Application Template Custom Application. State the package prefix as *com.jdevbook.chap10*. In the New Gallery for the project within the application workspace, select the option General ➤ Extension SDK Tools ➤ Extension Wizard, and click OK. This will start up the Extension Wizard. Click Next on the Welcome Screen. In Step 1, define the values as shown in Figure 10-6, and click Next.

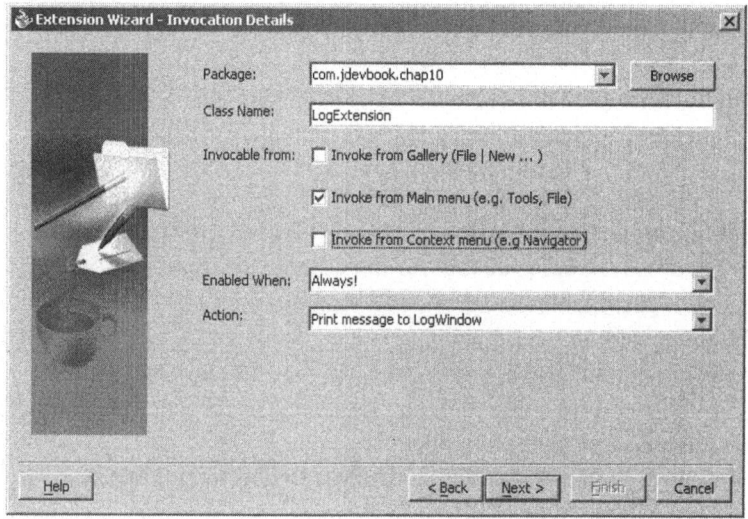

Figure 10-6. Extension Wizard

The wizard will now ask for details of what is to be displayed in the menu. Here choose the Tools menu, set the Menu Label to &LogExtension, and click Next. Click Finish on the final screen and LogExtension.java will be displayed for editing. Many methods have already been generated, and each of these has a part in the working of the extension. You only need to edit the method executeCommand as follows:

```
private boolean executeCommand()
{
  LogPage logPage = Ide.getLogManager().getMsgPage();
  logPage.log("Date & Time: "+ new java.util.Date());
  logPage.log("java.home = "+System.getProperty("java.home"));
  return true;
}
```

Make the LogExtension.java file, and then select the Project.deploy file that would have been automatically created for the project. Right-click and select the option Deploy to JAR file. JDeveloper will cleverly generate the JAR file in the extensions directory at jdev/lib/ext. Restart JDeveloper. LogExtension should now appear in the Tools menu, and when you click it, the date and time and the value of the *java.home* system property will be printed to the log window.

There's a lot more to using extensions than what you have seen in this simple example. Pay particular attention to the interfaces and methods that you need to implement. The examples that come part of the SDK download can also help as even the code for these examples is provided as part of the download.

Summary

In this chapter you had a look at JDeveloper's integration with popular tools, such as Apache Ant and CVS. You also had a look at some popular JDeveloper extensions and how you can create your own extensions. How easily new functionality can be built onto an IDE is critical in the competitive IDE market. JDeveloper has good extension capabilities that need to be exploited properly by developers and tool vendors to make JDeveloper do more.

CHAPTER 11

Tips and Tricks

IN THIS CHAPTER, you will look at tips and tricks that can be useful while using JDeveloper. These are solutions to some problems you might encounter as well as tricks to make you even more efficient at using JDeveloper. This chapter also presents some keyboard shortcuts.

The Tips

The following are tips to help you use JDeveloper more effectively.

Configuring the Web Browser and Proxy Server

The Web Browser/Proxy section in the Preferences dialog box (Tools ➤ Preferences) is where you can define the browser and proxy server that JDeveloper will use while executing Web applications. If you have access to the Internet only through a proxy server, you will need to configure the proxy server to use features such as Check for Updates or other Web Services features.

Speeding Up JDeveloper Startup: Extension Profiles

The minimum hardware requirements for running JDeveloper are quite high, and not everyone has the luxury of running high-end machines with loads of random access memory (RAM). So is there a way to speed up JDeveloper on startup?

The easiest way to speed up the JDeveloper startup on a sluggish machine involves making good use of the Extension Manager section in the Preferences dialog box (Tools ➤ Preferences). If you are developing a Java User Interface (UI) using Abstract Window Toolkit (AWT) and Swing, uncheck all extension categories and then select the Client Tier Development category. JDeveloper will automatically select the bare-minimum tools from the General category. Click the Save As button to save this profile for later use. Click OK, and restart JDeveloper. This will significantly speed up the startup time.

Furthermore, in the Applications Navigator, only load applications that you are actually using. The fewer the applications that need to load, the quicker the startup time.

Using Technology Scopes

Technology scope is a way of telling JDeveloper, "I am working with X, Y, and Z technologies. Only show me tools and features related to these technologies, and do not bother me with anything else." You can configure the technology scope for a project through the Common ➤Technology Scope section in Project properties. You can set the technology scope at the time of creating an application workspace by clicking the Edit Template button provided in the New Application Workspace window.

Refer to Chapter 3 for a discussion about technology scopes and application templates.

Refactoring Your Code

Refactoring is when you make changes to the code and improve its internal structure without changing how it works. However, even simple things such as renaming or moving a class can get quite tedious if done manually, because of the implications it might have for many other classes in the application. JDeveloper provides excellent refactoring capabilities so you can easily rename a class, move a class, and extract new methods by selecting that bit of code. These features are provided when you select the Tools ➤ Refactor command.

Installing ADF Runtimes

In Chapter 7, you developed applications using the Oracle Application Development Framework (ADF) and executed them on the embedded Oracle Application Server Containers for Java (OC4J) server. ADF applications can very well be deployed on any other server, such as Tomcat and WebLogic; however, for this you first need to install the ADF runtime on these servers. After selecting the Tools ➤ ADF Runtime Installer command, specify the location where Tomcat, WebLogic, or JBoss is installed. The wizard will then install the ADF Runtime Installer onto those servers.

Changing the JDeveloper Look and Feel

The JDeveloper look and feel is highly configurable. You can specify the look and feel for JDeveloper as a whole, and you can even specify the color to be used for something as specific as an arrow in a diagram.

To change the look and feel of JDeveloper, select one of the four choices provided in the Look and Feel drop-down list in the Environment section of the Preferences dialog box. You will need to restart JDeveloper for the new look and feel to be visible. All the figures in this book use the Windows look and feel.

Generating Project Javadoc with Diagrams

You can change the Javadoc configuration for a project from the Project Properties ➤ Development ➤ Javadoc screen. Apart from the normal Javadoc configuration, you can also specify if you want to document diagrams used in the project. So if you have a Web Service diagram, that diagram can be converted into PNG, JPG, and other formats and saved right into the Javadocs for the project.

This is a really useful feature because now all your project documentation can be maintained in the Javadocs, and you do not need to maintain separate project diagrams.

Editing Default Project Properties

Every time a new project is created, it inherits project properties from the default project properties. So if there is some property that you keep changing in every project created, you might as well change that in the default project properties. Once a change is made in the default project properties, every new project created afterward will have those properties. You can view and change the default project properties by choosing Project ➤ Default Project Properties from the menu bar.

Using Local/Hosted Documentation

If you rarely use the JDeveloper documentation or cannot spare the more than 70 megabytes that the documentation takes up, you have the option to not maintain local documentation but instead to use the documentation hosted on the Oracle Technology Network (OTN). The Documentation section in the Preferences dialog box provides this configuration.

Highlighting All Occurrences in Find

While using the Find tool to search for words in code or text, I more often than not use the Highlight All Occurrences option. So instead of checking that box every time I use Find, I just changed the Initial Find options in the Code Editor ➤ Find Options section in the Preferences dialog box to make the Highlight All Occurrences option checked by default.

Using Regular Expressions Find

The Find tool has a nice capability to use *regular expressions*. So if you want to search for the words *java* and *html* in a piece of text, just specify *java|html* as the text to search for and check the Regular Expressions check box. JDeveloper will now find all occurrences of both words.

Configuring External Tools

Although JDeveloper provides almost everything you require for Java development, you might have situations where you need to launch an external tool to get a task done. JDeveloper provides the capability to configure external tools that you can execute right from within JDeveloper. For example, if you want to edit all *.php files using your favorite PHP editor, you can configure that editor as an external tool using Tools ➤ External Tools. Not only can you define when and where the tool will be displayed, but you can even pass some arguments to the external tool.

Splitting the Code Editor

If you have two code files being displayed in two separate tabs in the Code Editor, you might have to constantly switch between these tabs. You could instead split the Code Editor in such a way that both files are displayed simultaneously. Simply click the tab for a file, and drag it to the left or right to split the editor window vertically. If you drag it to the bottom of the screen, the window will split horizontally.

Checking for Updates

You can easily install updates and extensions to JDeveloper from within JDeveloper. Select Help ➤ Check for Updates to start the Check for Updates Wizard. You will need an OTN account to use this feature. You can register at the OTN at http://otn.oracle.com/membership.

Changing Properties and the Default Package

You can use the Property Inspector to change some of the properties for a project. Select the project listed in the Applications Navigator, and you will notice that the Property Inspector now lists project properties—such as defaultPackage, userAuthor, userCompany, and so on—that can be modified easily.

Generating Accessors (Getter/Setter)

A common requirement is to generate getter and setter methods for any new fields you introduce. Instead of having to manually write those methods, you can select Code ➤ Generate Accessors, or you can right-click anywhere in the code and select Generate Accessors. In the window that pops up, select the fields for which you want the getter and setter methods to be generated.

Overriding Methods

You may often have a requirement where you need to change the method implementation provided in a superclass. To override a method in the super class it is important to get the method signature exactly the same as that stated in the superclass. Use the Tools ➤ Override Methods option, and you will get a window listing all the methods inherited from the superclass. Just select the method to be overridden, and the method code will be generated for you.

Organizing Imports

During development if you often tend to use the asterisk (*) character to import entire packages instead of importing specific classes, you can use the JDeveloper Organize Imports tool to automatically edit the code and import only classes that you actually use in the code. You can access the Organize Imports tool by using the Code menu or by right-clicking in the Code Editor. You have the following options: Sort Imports, Widen Imports, Narrow Imports, and Remove Unused Imports.

Managing Libraries

JDeveloper uses libraries to easily manage related Java archive (JAR) files and classes. So if you have a set of JAR files that you use often, it makes sense to create a new library containing these JAR files and then associate that library with various projects. For example, if you are developing an application using a framework, there might be three or four JAR files provided by the framework, all of which need to be used at the same time. In such a case you could create a new library holding all of the framework-related JARs and then associate this library with various projects.

Use Tools ➤ Manage Libraries to manage libraries, Java 2 Standard Edition (J2SE) definitions, and Java Server Page (JSP) tag libraries.

Toggling Line Numbers

Displaying line numbers for your code can make working with the code a little easier. To enable line numbers, right-click in the line gutter on the left of the Code Editor and select the option Toggle Line Numbers.

Surrounding With

JDeveloper provides a *Surround With* tool with which you can just select a block of code and insert a for loop, while loop, try-catch-finally, and so on around it. Select a piece of code, and then either select Code ➤ Surround With or select the Surround With option from the right-click menu.

Editing Component Palettes

The Component Palette is useful for easily inserting components into JSP pages, UIX pages, Swing UI, and so on. It is just as easy to insert new components into the palette as it is to edit existing components. Either select Tools ➤ Configure Palette or right-click in the Component Palette and select Properties to get the Configure Component Palette. Here you can easily add new components or edit existing ones.

Scanning Source Path to Determine Project Contents

The Project Properties dialog box provides a Scan Source Path to Determine Project Contents option. This feature is not enabled by default; however, I recommend enabling the feature because all files for a project are generally maintained in a separate directory, and if you have many people working on the project, these files might also keep changing constantly. It is easier to have JDeveloper scan and pick up new files rather than doing it manually.

Comparing Files for Differences

JDeveloper provides a Compare Files tool that can be useful if you are not using a source-control tool and yet have more than one person working on the same file. Select Tools ➤ Compare Files, and provide the two files you want to compare. JDeveloper will compare the two files and highlight all differences between them.

Using Code Templates

You looked at code templates in Chapter 3. However, I cannot emphasize using and creating code templates enough. Because a lot of Java coding is repetitive in nature, code templates can save you a lot of time. You can check out the code templates that come predefined as well as define new templates in the Code Editor ➤ Code Templates section in the Preferences window. Also use the Imports tab in this dialog box to import the classes that you are using as part of the template.

JDeveloper Help

JDeveloper's help has four sections:

- **Table of Contents**: This displays a list of all the help books that are provided. You can expand each book listing to view the subsections of the book.

- **Index Search**: The Index Search section is where only the index is searched and not the contents of all the books.

- **Full Text Search**: The entire text is searched.

- **Glossary Search**: This search is useful if you are looking for definitions of words such as *instantiate*, *relational database*, and so on.

Using Run Manager

You can view the Run Manager by selecting View ➤ Run Manager. This window helps you know which processes are running and terminate processes if they hang or misbehave.

Navigating Code Using Bookmarks

Bookmarks mark locations in the code to which you can easily navigate. If you have 1,000 lines of code in one file, it makes sense to have bookmarks in place that will help you quickly move to specific code with which you need to work. To set a bookmark, either right-click in the line gutter and select the Toggle Bookmark option or move the cursor to the line to be bookmarked and press Ctrl+K. Once you have set the bookmarks, you can use the Search ➤ Bookmarks menu command to easily move through the bookmarks.

You will now look at keyboard shortcuts that will make working with JDeveloper easier.

Keyboard Shortcuts

How comfortable developers are with a tool certainly depends on how easily the developer can get things done using just the keyboard and not having to touch the mouse. As interactive and useful as a mouse can get, it certainly cannot match the speed that keyboard shortcuts can give you.

For keyboard usage, JDeveloper gives you the option of using seven different key mappings. In the Accelerators section in the Preferences dialog box, click the Load Preset button to see a list of the key mapping alternatives.

Table 11-1 lists useful shortcuts for the default key mapping.

Table 11-1. Default Keyboard Shortcuts

Description	Keys
Go to matching brace	Alt+] and Alt+[
Completion insight	Ctrl+spacebar
Parameter insight	Ctrl+Shift+spacebar
Delete next word start	Ctrl+T
Delete previous	Shift+Backspace
Delete until end of line	Ctrl+Shift+Y
Run project	F11
Debug project	Shift+F9
Make project	Ctrl+F9
Rebuild project	Alt+F9
Make selected class	Ctrl+M
Find in Navigator	Alt+Home
File list	Alt+0
Tab size 2	Ctrl+2
Tab size 4	Ctrl+4
Tab size 8	Ctrl+8

Table 11-1. Default Keyboard Shortcuts (continued)

Description	Keys
Close window	Ctrl+W and Ctrl+F4
Find	Ctrl+F
Replace	Ctrl+R
Go to line	Ctrl+G
Find in files	Ctrl+Shift+F
Go to Java class	Ctrl+Minus
Toggle bookmark	Ctrl+K
Go to bookmark	Ctrl+Shift+K
Go to next bookmark	Ctrl+Q
Go to previous bookmark	Ctrl+Shift+Q
Expand template	Ctrl+Enter
Toggle line comments	Ctrl+/
Next editor frame	Ctrl+Tab
Frame on right	Alt+Right
Frame on left	Alt+Left
Step over	F8
Step into	F7
Step out	Shift+F7
Resume	F9

Index

forums.apress.com

JOIN THE APRESS FORUMS AND BE PART OF OUR COMMUNITY. You'll find discussions that cover topics of interest to IT professionals, programmers, and enthusiasts just like you. If you post a query to one of our forums, you can expect that some of the best minds in the business—especially Apress authors, who all write with *The Expert's Voice*™—will chime in to help you. Why not aim to become one of our most valuable participants (MVPs) and win cool stuff? Here's a sampling of what you'll find:

DATABASES
Data drives everything.

Share information, exchange ideas, and discuss any database programming or administration issues.

PROGRAMMING/BUSINESS
Unfortunately, it is.

Talk about the Apress line of books that cover software methodology, best practices, and how programmers interact with the "suits."

INTERNET TECHNOLOGIES AND NETWORKING
Try living without plumbing (and eventually IPv6).

Talk about networking topics including protocols, design, administration, wireless, wired, storage, backup, certifications, trends, and new technologies.

WEB DEVELOPMENT/DESIGN
Ugly doesn't cut it anymore, and CGI is absurd.

Help is in sight for your site. Find design solutions for your projects and get ideas for building an interactive Web site.

JAVA
We've come a long way from the old Oak tree.

Hang out and discuss Java in whatever flavor you choose: J2SE, J2EE, J2ME, Jakarta, and so on.

SECURITY
Lots of bad guys out there—the good guys need help.

Discuss computer and network security issues here. Just don't let anyone else know the answers!

MAC OS X
All about the Zen of OS X.

OS X is both the present and the future for Mac apps. Make suggestions, offer up ideas, or boast about your new hardware.

TECHNOLOGY IN ACTION
Cool things. Fun things.

It's after hours. It's time to play. Whether you're into LEGO® MINDSTORMS™ or turning an old PC into a DVR, this is where technology turns into fun.

OPEN SOURCE
Source code is good; understanding (open) source is better.

Discuss open source technologies and related topics such as PHP, MySQL, Linux, Perl, Apache, Python, and more.

WINDOWS
No defenestration here.

Ask questions about all aspects of Windows programming, get help on Microsoft technologies covered in Apress books, or provide feedback on any Apress Windows book.

HOW TO PARTICIPATE:
Go to the Apress Forums site at **http://forums.apress.com/**.
Click the New User link.